# THE $7 A MEAL HEALTHY COOKBOOK

**FEED A FAMILY FOR $7 OR LESS**

## 301 NUTRITIOUS, DELICIOUS RECIPES THAT THE WHOLE FAMILY WILL LOVE

Chef Susan Irby

Avon, Massachusetts

*The Living Cookbook* and CalorieKing.com were used for nutrition and costing analysis.

Contains material adapted and abridged from *The Everything® College Cookbook* by Rhonda Lauret Par-
kinson, copyright © 2005 by F+W Media, Inc., ISBN 10: 1-59337-303-1, ISBN 13: 978-1-59337-303-0; *The
Everything® Flat Belly Cookbook* by Fitz Koehler, MSESS and Mabelissa Acevedo, LDN, copyright © 2009
by F+W Media, Inc., ISBN 10: 1-60550-676-1, ISBN 13: 978-1-60550-676-0; *The Everything® Gluten-Free
Cookbook* by Nancy T. Maar and Rick Marx, copyright © 2005 by F+W Media, Inc., ISBN 10: 1-59337-394-5,
ISBN 13: 978-1-59337-394-8; *The Everything® Healthy Meals in Minutes* by Patricia M. Butkus, copyright
© 2005 by F+W Media, Inc., ISBN 10: 1-59337-302-3, ISBN 13: 978-1-59337-302-3; *The Everything® Italian
Cookbook* by Dawn Altomari, BPS, copyright © 2005 by F+W Media, Inc., ISBN 10: 1-59337-420-8, ISBN
13: 978-1-59337-420-4; *The Everything® Mediterranean Cookbook* by Dawn Altomari-Rathjen and Jennifer
Bendelius, copyright © 2003 by F+W Media, Inc., ISBN 10: 1-58062-869-9, ISBN 13: 978-1-58062-869-3;
*The Everything® No Trans Fat Cookbook* by Linda Larsen, copyright © 2007 by F+W Media, Inc., ISBN 10:
1-59869-533-9, ISBN 13: 978-1-59869-533-5; *The Everything® One-Pot Cookbook, 2nd Edition* by Pamela
Rice Hahn, copyright © 2009 by F+W Media, Inc., ISBN 10: 1-59869-836-2, ISBN 13: 978-1-59869-836-7; *The
Everything® Quick and Easy 30-Minute, 5-Ingredient Cookbook* by Linda Larsen, copyright © 2006 by F+W
Media, Inc., ISBN 10: 1-59337-692-8, ISBN 13: 978-1-59337-692-5; *The Everything® Quick Meals Cookbook,
2nd Edition* by Rhonda Lauret Parkinson, copyright © 2008 by F+W Media, Inc., ISBN 10: 1-59869-605-X,
ISBN 13: 978-1-59869-605-9; and *The Everything® Vegetarian Cookbook* by Jay Weinstein, copyright © 2002
by F+W Media, Inc., ISBN 10: 1-58062-640-8, ISBN 13: 978-1-58062-640-8.

Published by
Adams Media, a division of F+W Media, Inc.
57 Littlefield Street, Avon, MA 02322. U.S.A.
*www.adamsmedia.com*

ISBN 10: 1-4405-0338-9
ISBN 13: 978-1-4405-0338-2

Printed in the United States of America.
J  I  H  G  F  E  D  C  B  A

**Library of Congress Cataloging-in-Publication
Data** is available from the publisher.

This publication is designed to provide accurate
and authoritative information with regard to the
subject matter covered. It is sold with the under-
standing that the publisher is not engaged in
rendering legal, accounting, or other professional
advice. If legal advice or other expert assistance
is required, the services of a competent professional person should be sought.
—From a *Declaration of Principles* jointly adopted
by a Committee of the American Bar Association
and a Committee of Publishers and Associations

Many of the designations used by manufactur-
ers and sellers to distinguish their product are
claimed as trademarks. Where those designations appear in this book and Adams Media was
aware of a trademark claim, the designations
have been printed with initial capital letters.

*This book is available at quantity discounts for
bulk purchases. For information, please call
1-800-289-0963.*

# CONTENTS

# INTRODUCTION

When I became a chef, I learned that most people really want to learn how to enjoy healthy foods. It wasn't as if my cooking students set out every day to eat foods that were full of fat and laden with calories; most of them truly did not know what healthy eating meant.

My mother always taught me a "colorful plate is a healthy plate." She cooked nutritious, delicious, well-balanced meals for my family literally every day. Looking back, I cannot imagine how she did it, but I do my best to do the same for my family and for others. Once I became a professional chef, I jetted off to Italy to work at Beccofino Ristorante and Wine Bar in Florence, Italy, with Executive Chef Francesco Berardinelli. There, Chef Francesco introduced me to the world of fresh herbs, citrus, and infusing flavors. His innovative menus and simplistic style helped mold me into the chef I am today—The Bikini Chef. My cooking specialty focuses on figure-flattering flavors—great-tasting gourmet food that is pleasing to your palate and helps you look and feel great in a bikini or anything else you're wearing.

Eating healthy often carries the misconception of being more expensive, but that is not necessarily true anymore. This book features a whopping 301 recipes that will help you enjoy a more balanced diet and stay within your budget.

When cooking on a budget, a few essential guidelines apply. First, preplan your meals. Select a few recipes, then make a shopping list of the ingredients you need. Always check your pantry first to be sure you know what you already have. Shopping with a list helps you stay on target and avoid overspending, plus it saves time, and time is money. Another good general rule to follow is to never shop hungry. You tend to overspend and buy unnecessary items.

When you are ready to go to the store, make sure to check your local papers and your coupons for any items on special. If you find chicken or beef on sale, for example, try to stock up and keep extra portions in the freezer for future meals. Freeze them in individual or family-size servings for ease in defrosting.

When shopping on a specific budget, always send the most experienced shopper to the store. An inexperienced person will not know how to compare prices, and may also not realize the price differences between specific brands. Plus, inexperienced shoppers often do not adhere to the shopping list resulting in either the wrong items, or needless items, and a blown budget.

The cost for each recipe was computed combining personal research at local markets and CobornsDelivers (*www.cobornsdelivers.com*). The cost you see is for the entire recipe, not per serving. Nutritional values (given per serving) were based upon both *The Living Cookbook* and CalorieKing (*www.calorieking.com*). I highly recommend CalorieKing.com, as they have information on virtually every meal, brand, restaurant, and food item imaginable. As you go throughout the book, you may notice some recipes seem a little higher in calories, fat, or carbohydrates than you might imagine. Keep in mind that the key to a healthy lifestyle is everything in moderation. So pair those higher-fat or higher-calorie foods with other lower-fat, lower-calorie foods and enjoy in moderation.

In the first two chapters, you'll find information about the fundamental principles of good nutrition, along with some simple tips on living a healthy lifestyle. These are designed to help answer basic questions and to give you some ideas on how to make changes toward living a healthier lifestyle. Buon appetito!

The $7 a Meal Healthy Cookbook

# CHAPTER 1

# BASIC ELEMENTS OF GOOD NUTRITION

Think of your body as an engine that needs fuel. If you drove a nice car that required unleaded fuel, would you put diesel fuel in it every day? No, of course not! Naturally, it is foolish to think we are going to fuel our bodies every single day with the perfect balance of nutrients, calories, foods, and beverages to optimize our overall health. And, as silly as that even sounds, it is true! There are too many foods that look and taste so good they become irresistible to us. It is human nature to want to indulge in life's culinary pleasures. Therefore, it is important to understand a few basics of good nutrition and a healthy lifestyle in order to find a balance between eating healthy and enjoying some of life's not-so-healthy culinary temptations.

## A COLORFUL PLATE IS A NUTRITIOUS PLATE

Generally speaking, colorful foods such as beets, broccoli, and blueberries have more nutrients and flavor than white or beige foods, such as baked potatoes, white rice, and white bread. If your plate is filled with beige, earthy colors, your calories and carbohydrates are generally going to be higher and your tastebuds more flat and less satisfied, often causing you to eat more. This is not to say that white or beige foods are not good for you, but only that they need to be properly incorporated into your diet with other nutritious foods.

A nutritious plate is filled, for example, with green spinach, red peppers, yellow corn, and golden chicken. This meal is stocked full of nutrients, most likely fewer calories, and will result in a more satisfied palate because of the variety of flavors and textures.

## PAY ATTENTION TO PORTION CONTROL

One of the biggest factors in eating healthy is portion control. Plain and simple, the more calories you consume than you expend on a regular basis, the more weight you will gain. One essential way to enjoy healthy meals and live a healthy lifestyle is to pay attention to how much and how large your portions of food are. As a general rule, the size of your balled-up fist equates to about 4 to 5 ounces of food, which is the optimum amount of any one food for any one meal (for example, one "fist" of chicken, one "fist" of rice, one "fist" of spinach). Stick within those portion sizes and then pass on second helpings!

## LAY OFF SOFT DRINKS, WINE, BEER, AND COCKTAILS

Most of these beverages are filled with sugar and tend to make you feel more hungry when you drink them. Plus, generally speaking, they are high in calories and carbohydrates. Diet sodas may be low in calories but contain chemically made sweeteners, which are often difficult for your body to break down. Consume these beverages in moderation, as you should everything.

## EAT THREE SMALLER MEALS PER DAY

Don't pack the bulk of your calorie intake into one meal, especially if it is the dinner meal. Eating smaller meals throughout the day helps prevent overeating and will help your body fuel itself throughout the day.

## SNACK ON HEALTHY SNACKS

Even when you are eating smaller meals throughout the day, you still may feel hungry at times. During those times, choose healthy snacks such as fruit and fresh vegetables instead of going for the chips and dip. In this book, you will find some great recipes you and your family will love for snacking!

## EVERYTHING IN MODERATION

This principle is so important. Eating healthy foods does not mean you, or your family members, are on a diet. How many times have you ordered a fruit plate for lunch at a restaurant and the person you are dining with asks you if you are on a diet?! Why does everyone think that just because a person wants to eat something healthy, it means they are on a diet? When you enjoy everything in moderation, you fuel your body with the nutrients it needs but also allow yourself to "splurge" with some not-so-healthy foods you love. Have a plate of nachos, have dessert, enjoy some potato chips—just don't make those foods the key elements of your daily eating habits or those of your family. If you are the primary cook in your household, it is up to you to serve healthy meals to your family. Doing so tells them that good nutrition is important and that you care about their health and well-being. You set a good example by incorporating healthy vegetables and proteins into your daily diet so the not-so-healthy items are fewer and farther between.

## EATING HEALTHY DOESN'T HAVE TO BE BORING OR TASTE BAD

Since when did good nutrition get such a bad rap? I'm not sure, but I do know that eating healthy is far from boring and you can enjoy some unbelievably delicious foods while also fueling your body properly. This book will provide you with 301 recipes packed with essential nutrients, all designed to satisfy the taste buds of your whole family.

# CHAPTER 2

# A HEALTHY LIFESTYLE

A healthy lifestyle incorporates the basic elements of good nutrition laid out in Chapter 1, plus another element: exercise. When I mention the word *exercise* in some of my cooking classes, I get a lot of rolled eyes and "ugh"s. The fact is, however, optimum health involves exercise. The problem is a lot of people think exercise means they have to join a gym and work out every day and that exercise is a huge commitment. But it doesn't have to be that big of a deal. Still, with spouses, kids, dogs, cats, work, and so on, who can think about going to the gym? Sleep sounds like a better alternative. Unless you are already a dedicated gymgoer, exercise may not sound like so much fun. So, you have to make it fun! Once you start exercising, you will find you feel more invigorated, have more energy, and you will most likely sleep better.

Here are some suggestions for incorporating exercise into your lifestyle without feeling like you have to have sweat pouring off of your body to be healthy.

## WALK THE DOG

Get your family together and take the dogs for a walk. Dogs never get tired of a walk around the block, or two! Dogs are the best reason (or excuse) to exercise in the world. If you don't have a dog, offer to walk the neighbor's dog or try another suggestion.

## PLAY A TEAM SPORT

Get your family together and shoot some hoops! Or play a pickup game of soccer, a tennis tournament, or a few innings of softball. Who cares if you are not that great at it—the point is you are doing something together, with your family, and you are exercising, burning off some of those calories, and moving your muscles. The point is, get outside and throw something other than throwing the trash in the trash can.

## HULA HOOP

When you stop laughing at this suggestion, get out there and try it! It is a great form of exercise, and it's fun! Not only does Hula Hoop-ing help improve your coordination, it tightens your stomach muscles and your fanny, and it gets your heart rate up! Believe it or not, Hula Hooping is even great entertainment for casual parties. What better place to work off some of those calories and have a blast in the meantime?

## JUMP ROPE

Jumping rope with the kids is a great form of exercise. When I had a personal fitness trainer, one of the key things he would make me do was jump rope. With the personal trainer it was hard, but with my daughter and her friends, it is easy! The kids have fun games they play while jumping rope so it helps take your mind off the fact you are exercising.

## ROLLERBLADE OR BICYCLE

If you are like me and can't stand up on Rollerblades, use the "old school" roller skates or bicycles. Either way, these activities are great for your legs, fanny, and your psyche! Take the family around the neighborhood—it's fun, you are burning calories, and you are enjoying the outdoors.

## WALK WITH FRIENDS

The thing I like most about walking with friends is that you chat the whole time you are walking, so you never feel like you are really exercising. The second thing I like is that you make a date to do it. If you have other people you are committed to walking with, you are more likely to do it than you are if you choose to walk alone. When you are walking, carry a set of 2-pound weights in your hands for the extra calorie burn, and tone your arms!

## GO SWIMMING

Swimming is one of the best exercises you can do because it works nearly every muscle in your body. You stay refreshed from the water, you can swim for hours, and it's fun. Get one of those balls that soaks up water, and throw it to your family and friends while in the pool. You will be surprised how many muscles you work while playing a silly game and how long you spend playing.

## BUY A PILATES BALL

If you still can't muster up the energy to exercise outside, or if it is just too plain cold outside, invest in a Pilates ball. They are not that expensive and come with several exercise instructions. Get up early, before the kids, and exercise, or if you are not a morning person, exercise immediately after they go to school, or immediately when you come home from work. Put a little workout schedule for yourself on the family calendar. This way, you make your own commitment to exercising and your family can see the times each week you have set aside to take care of yourself. Chances are when they see you exercising, they will want to, too.

# CHAPTER 3

# BREAKFASTS

# Bruschetta of Eggs, Tomatoes, and Peppers

**Serves 4**

Prep time: 6 minutes
Cook time: 5 minutes
Total cost: $3.56
Calories: 375
Fat: 11g
Carbohydrates: 34g
Protein: 9g
Cholesterol: 44mg
Sodium: 381mg

½ loaf Italian or French bread

½ cup extra-virgin olive oil

¼ cup pesto (in the refrigerated pasta section of the grocery store)

2 eggs

1 red bell pepper, seeded and chopped

¼ cup mozzarella cheese, shredded

1 medium tomato, seeded and diced

Traditionally, bruschetta is an Italian appetizer of toasted bread rubbed with fresh garlic and topped with extra-virgin olive oil. This version is a combination of Italian- and American-style bruschetta.

1. Slice the bread into 4¾-inch lengthwise slices. Brush 1 side of each with a bit of the oil; toast on grill or grill pan. When that side is toasted, brush oil on the other side, flip, and toast that side.
2. Place the toasted bread on a baking sheet, and spread with pesto. Mix eggs with bell pepper. Heat the remaining oil in sauté pan to medium temperature; add the egg mixture and cook omelet style. Cut the omelet and place on the bread; top with cheese and tomatoes.

**Cooking Omelets**
If you have never cooked an omelet, review the instructions for the Easy Omelet (page 11).

# Oven-Baked Frittata

Serves 8

Prep time: 10 minutes
Cook time: 1 hour
Total cost: $6.72
Calories: 208
Fat: 8g
Carbohydrates: 12g
Protein: 9g
Cholesterol: 11mg
Sodium: 134mg

2 baking potatoes, peeled and sliced into ¼-inch slices

1 each yellow and red bell peppers, seeded and chopped

1 large red onion, roughly chopped

2 teaspoons olive oil

Sea salt and black pepper to taste

5 whole eggs

1 cup plain nonfat yogurt

1 cup skim milk

3 ounces fontina cheese, grated

Frittatas are open-faced omelets that are usually cooked on the stovetop and then finished in the oven. Here, everything is cooked in the oven making it much simpler!

1.  Preheat oven to 375°F. Toss potatoes, peppers, and onion in oil. Season with salt and pepper. Place vegetables on parchment-lined baking sheet and roast in oven for about 20 minutes. While vegetables are baking, whisk together eggs, yogurt, milk, and cheese in a mixing bowl and set aside.
2.  Remove vegetables from oven and transfer to baking dish. Layer vegetables in dish and pour yogurt mixture over vegetables. Place baking dish in oven and bake until egg mixture is completely set, about 30 to 40 minutes.

**Lowering Fat in Recipes**
Cooking with nonfat yogurt and low-fat or nonfat milk helps to cut down on your fat intake, and therefore calories, but most often does not sacrifice flavor.

Breakfasts

# Breakfast Bread Pudding

**Serves 8**

Prep time: 5 minutes
Cook time: 50 minutes
Total cost: $6.76
Calories: 373
Fat: 11g
Carbohydrates: 24g
Protein: 15g
Cholesterol: 46mg
Sodium: 398mg

½ teaspoon extra-virgin olive oil

5 eggs

¼ cup low-fat milk

¼ cup plain yogurt

2 ounces blue cheese

3 slices seedless rye bread, torn into large pieces

3 slices pumpernickel bread, torn into large pieces

Ground black pepper

Substitute sourdough or wheat bread if you prefer.

Preheat oven to 375°F. Grease 2-quart casserole dish with oil. In mixing bowl, beat the eggs. Add the milk, yogurt, and cheese. Place bread pieces in prepared casserole dish, then pour egg mixture over. Bake for 40 to 50 minutes, until mixture is set and the top is golden brown. To serve, cut into squares and season with pepper.

# Easy Omelet

Serves 1

Prep time: 4 minutes
Cook time: 8 minutes
Total cost: $1.47
Calories: 194
Fat: 15g
Carbohydrates: 6g
Protein: 12g
Cholesterol: 306mg
Sodium: 89mg

2 eggs per omelet

1 tablespoon low-fat milk

Cooking spray if using non-stick skillet or omelet pan

2 teaspoons butter if using uncoated skillet or omelet pan

The idea of making an omelet often intimidates people but don't let it scare you. The key to an omelet is in the folding. If you don't fold it perfectly every time, don't worry—you can always have scrambled eggs or a frittata, an open-faced omelet.

1. Beat the eggs and milk in a bowl until combined; do not allow them to become frothy. Spray the nonstick skillet and heat slightly over medium heat, or if using an uncoated skillet, melt the butter over medium heat, tilting the skillet to coat the bottom.
2. Pour in the eggs; stir gently with a fork while they thicken to distribute the eggs from top to bottom. Stop stirring when the eggs begin to set. As the eggs thicken, lift the edges of the omelet and allow the uncooked eggs to flow underneath. Allow to cook until the bottom is golden and the top is set but shiny. With a long, flat spatula, gently loosen the edge of the omelet and fold the omelet in half toward you. With the help of the spatula, slide the omelet out of the pan and onto a plate. If making multiple omelets, cover them with foil to keep warm.

# Omelet with Spinach and Red Peppers

Serves 1

Prep time: 8 minutes

Cook time: 10 minutes

Total cost: $1.52

Calories: 305

Fat: 24g

Carbohydrates: 10g

Protein: 24g

Cholesterol: 424mg

Sodium: 154mg

2 eggs

Sea salt and black pepper to taste

¼ cup cooked spinach, drained (frozen is okay)

2 tablespoons grated Parmesan cheese

2 tablespoons fresh red peppers, chopped

Add your favorite ingredients to any omelet, just be sure to adhere to the quantities of the ingredients so as not to "overstuff" your omelet.

1. In small mixing bowl, beat eggs until well combined using wire whisk or fork. Coat a nonstick skillet with nonstick spray (see Easy Omelet, page 11, for uncoated skillets) and heat slightly over medium heat.
2. Add eggs to skillet and salt and pepper to taste. Cook on medium until eggs are just setting. Add spinach, cheese, and red peppers to center of eggs. Fold omelet over and cook for 1 to 2 minutes.
3. Flip omelet and cook for an additional 1 minute or until eggs are cooked.

### Cooking Tip

Be sure to use a spatula to lift the edges of the omelet and tilt the skillet to drain off excess egg in the center of the omelet. This helps prevent burning your omelet while waiting for the center to finish cooking.

The $7 a Meal Healthy Cookbook

# Vegetarian Omelet

Serves 1

Prep time: 10 minutes
Cook time: 10 minutes
Total cost: $1.68
Calories: 298
Fat: 24g
Carbohydrates: 5g
Protein: 20g
Cholesterol: 424g
Sodium: 332mg

2 eggs

Sea salt and black pepper to taste

1 Roma tomato, chopped

2 tablespoons cremini mushrooms, chopped

1 tablespoon green onion, chopped

Since this recipe serves one person, have each person in your family add their favorite vegetables and perhaps even some cheese to customize their omelet.

1. In small mixing bowl, beat eggs until well combined using wire whisk or fork. Coat a nonstick skillet with nonstick spray (see Easy Omelet, page 11, for uncoated skillet instructions) and heat slightly over medium heat.
2. Add eggs to skillet and salt and pepper to taste. Cook on medium until eggs are just setting. Add tomatoes, mushrooms, and onions to center of eggs. Fold omelet over and cook for 2 minutes.
3. Flip omelet and cook for an additional 2 minutes or until done.

# French Toast with Fresh Fruit

Serves 2

Prep time: 15 minutes
Cook time: 15 minutes
Total cost: $4.54
Calories: 325
Fat: 10g
Carbohydrates: 24g
Protein: 13g
Cholesterol: 74mg
Sodium: 380mg

½ teaspoon olive oil

3 small loaves challah bread, sliced into 2½- to 3-inch-thick slices

1 cup seasonal fresh fruit, such as strawberries, diced

4 eggs

¼ cup skim milk

1 cup orange juice

¼ cup nonfat plain yogurt

1 tablespoon confectioners (powdered) sugar

Challah bread can be found in your grocery store pastry department.

1. Preheat oven to 375°F. Line baking sheet with parchment paper. Prepare bread slices by cutting a slit into the bottom of the crust, forming a pocket. Fill pockets with diced fruit.
2. In large mixing bowl, beat eggs and milk. Dip bread into egg mixture, letting it fully absorb the mixture then removing quickly. Place bread on baking sheet. Bake for 10 minutes on 1 side, flip and bake 10 minutes more.
3. While bread is baking, pour the orange juice in small saucepan. Boil until reduced by half and mixture becomes syrupy. Remove bread (or French toast) from oven, cut in half diagonally. Serve each with a dollop of yogurt, drizzle of juice, and sprinkling of sugar.

**Presentation Tip**
To sprinkle sugar, use a small strainer so the sugar dusts over the plate and food. Dust right before serving as the sugar will dissolve in the juice.

The $7 a Meal Healthy Cookbook

# Italian Frittata with Pecorino Cheese

 Serves 4

Prep time: 15 minutes
Cook time: 10 minutes
Total cost: $3.97
Calories: 126
Fat: 5g
Carbohydrates: 1g
Protein: 7g
Cholesterol: 165mg
Sodium: 249mg

6 eggs

1 tablespoon white or yellow onion, chopped

1 tablespoon red bell peppers, chopped

¼ cup cooked ham, diced,

2 tablespoons grated pecorino cheese

This open-faced omelet originated in Italy. If you don't have an ovenproof skillet, cover the frittata with a lid to cook the center if it is still a little runny.

1. In medium mixing bowl, beat eggs using wire whisk or fork until combined.
2. Coat a small to medium-size ovenproof, nonstick skillet with nonstick spray (see Easy Omelet, page 11, for uncoated skillet instructions). On medium-high heat, add onions, peppers, and ham to skillet. Sauté for 2 minutes.
3. Add eggs to skillet and cook for 2 to 3 minutes. Place cheese on top of frittata, then place skillet in oven under the broiler and broil for 2 to 3 minutes or until cheese melts and eggs are set. Remove from pan and serve.

# No-Oat Oatmeal

- Prep time: 2 minutes
- Cook time: 45 to 60 minutes
- Total cost: $2.28
- Calories: 85
- Fat: 1g
- Carbohydrates: 15g
- Protein: 4g
- Cholesterol: 0mg
- Sodium: 30mg

1½ cups soy milk

1½ cups water

1 cup brown rice

1 tablespoon honey

¼ teaspoon nutmeg

8 tablespoons fresh fruit
  (optional)

This recipe is perfect for the person who is looking for a healthy, tasty alternative to oatmeal.

Place all ingredients except fresh fruit in a medium-size saucepan. Bring the mixture to a slow simmer and cover with a tight-fitting lid. Simmer for 45 to 60 minutes, until the rice is tender and done. Serve in bowls, topped with your favorite fresh fruit.

# Fresh Fruit with Yogurt and Mint

Serves 6

Prep time: 10 minutes

Cook time:

Total cost: $4.05

Calories: 184

Fat: 2g

Carbohydrates: 19g

Protein: 21g

Cholesterol: 10mg

Sodium: 189mg

6 cups plain nonfat yogurt

¼ fresh cantaloupe, peeled and thinly sliced

¼ fresh honeydew melon, peeled and thinly sliced

2 fresh kiwi fruit, peeled and sliced

1 fresh peach, thinly sliced

1 fresh plum, thinly sliced

½ pint fresh raspberries

6 mint sprigs, leaves chopped

Add crunchy granola, if you like, for extra protein, energy, and flavor.

Spoon yogurt into serving bowls and arrange the fruit around the rim, sprinkling raspberries on top. Garnish with freshly chopped mint.

# Smoked Trout with Leeks and Eggs

Serves 6

Prep time: 12 minutes
Cook time: 25 minutes
Total cost: $6.64
Calories: 156
Fat: 10g
Carbohydrates: 5g
Protein: 5g
Cholesterol: 122mg
Sodium: 131mg

3 tablespoons butter

⅓ cup chopped fresh leeks

½ cup nonfat milk

½ cup nonfat sour cream

5 ounces smoked trout, finely flaked

4 eggs

Sea salt and black pepper to taste

1 tablespoon chopped chives

Leeks are related to the onion and garlic family. They have a mild onion-like taste and are used in many ways in cooking. The edible portion of leeks are the white base and the light green stalk.

1.  Preheat oven to 325°F. Melt the butter in a medium nonstick skillet and add the leeks; cover and cook until soft but not brown, about 3 minutes. Remove from heat.
2.  Brush 4 small ovenproof ramekins or soufflé dishes with a little melted butter from the pan. In small bowl, mix together milk and sour cream. Add the trout and a third of the milk mixture to the pan with the leeks and stir to combine. Spoon equal amounts of the leek mixture into the 4 ramekins.
3.  Make a well in the center of the leek mixture in each dish. Break an egg into the center of each well and top with 1 tablespoon of milk mixture, salt and pepper, and ½ teaspoon of the chives. Place the ramekins in a baking dish or roasting pan and pour in enough water to come halfway up the sides of the ramekins. Bake for 20 to 25 minutes, or until the whites are set and the yolks are cooked but still tremble when lightly shaken. Remove the water bath and place on serving plates.

# Fruit Smoothie of Strawberries, Cantaloupe, and Blueberries

 Serves 4

→ Prep time: 12 minutes
→ Blend time: 2 minutes
→ Total cost: $3.75
→ Calories: 64
→ Fat: 1g
→ Carbohydrates: 4g
→ Protein: 3g
→ Cholesterol: 1mg
→ Sodium: 47mg

1½ cups cubed cantaloupe

1 cup frozen strawberries

½ cup strawberry nonfat
   yogurt

¼ cup blueberries

4 tiny mint sprigs

Serve these for a ladies' brunch!

Combine the cantaloupe and strawberries in a blender and process until smooth. With the blender running, add the yogurt through the feed tube and process until smooth. Equally divide into 4 portions in chilled glasses. Add several blueberries in the center of each glass and place mint sprigs between the berries for garnish. Serve immediately.

# Prosciutto-Wrapped Figs with Honey

Serves 4

Prep time: 15 minutes
Cook time: none
Total cost: $6.89
Calories: 159
Fat: 9g
Carbohydrates: 7g
Protein: 8g
Cholesterol: 28mg
Sodium: 640mg

4 ounces prosciutto, thinly sliced

4 fresh figs, quartered

1 teaspoon honey

2 tablespoons fresh-squeezed lemon juice

2 tablespoons extra-virgin olive oil

Sea salt and black pepper as needed

Toothpicks for serving

Fresh figs are ideal for this recipe but you can also enjoy dried figs when fresh figs are out of season. Prepare the dried figs in the same way as this recipe and if your budget allows, add goat or blue cheese for extra delicious flavor!

Trim excess fat from prosciutto strips and cut prosciutto in half, lengthwise. Wrap each fig piece with a strip of prosciutto. Combine remaining ingredients in a small bowl and whisk well. Spoon over figs and serve with toothpicks.

**Buying Prosciutto**
Purchase prosciutto freshly sliced from the meat department at most grocery stores or purchase presliced and packaged near the specialty deli meat counter.

The $7 a Meal Healthy Cookbook

# Oven-Baked Eggs with Ham and Fresh Herbs

Serves 4

Prep time: 5 minutes
Cook time: 20 to 25 minutes
Total cost: $3.24
Calories: 88
Fat: 14g
Carbohydrates: 2g
Protein: 17g
Cholesterol: 80mg
Sodium: 582mg

2 tablespoons butter, unsalted

3 ounces ham, thinly sliced

3 large eggs

1 teaspoon Dijon mustard

¼ cup nonfat plain yogurt

¾ cup Cheddar cheese, shredded

2 teaspoons fresh chives, chopped

2 teaspoons fresh Italian parsley, chopped

Italian flat leaf parsley has a milder, more crisp flavor than curly parsley. It's more attractive than curly parsley, and therefore more popular today among chefs than curly parsley.

Preheat oven to 375°F. Lightly grease 4 6-ounce ramekins with the butter. Line the ramekins with the ham. Combine eggs, Dijon, and yogurt, and mix well. Stir ¼ cup cheese into egg mixture. Add half the chives and parsley to mixture, and stir well. Spoon mixture into the prepared ramekins. Sprinkle with the remaining cheese and herbs. Bake for 20 to 25 minutes, until golden and set. Garnish with remaining herbs.

**Healthy Tip**
Fresh herbs are a great way to add flavor and color without adding fat and calories. As the Bikini Chef, I use fresh herbs in almost every recipe I make.

# Easy Scrambled Eggs

Serves 3

- Prep time: 10 minutes
- Cook time: 8 minutes
- Total cost: $2.40
- Calories: 221
- Fat: 15g
- Carbohydrates: 2g
- Protein: 11g
- Cholesterol: 123mg
- Sodium: 134mg

6 eggs

⅓ cup low-fat milk

Sea salt and black pepper to taste

2 tablespoons butter

Scrambled eggs are easy, tasty, and nutritious. Use them as a base and add your favorite things such as cheese, or spice up with a salsa for added flavor with few calories.

Beat the eggs, milk, and seasonings together lightly (with white and yellow streaks still visible) or well (until a uniform color) as preferred, using a fork or whisk. Heat the butter in a skillet and pour the egg mixture in. After the eggs begin to thicken, stir gently with a wooden spoon until eggs are thick but still moist.

**Tip for Fluffy Eggs**
Add a splash of club soda for extra-fluffy eggs, or for added protein add 2 tablespoons cottage cheese.

The $7 a Meal Healthy Cookbook

# Eggs with Red Bell Peppers and Mushrooms

 Serves 6

Prep time: 12 minutes

Cook time: 10 minutes

Total cost: $4.75

Calories: 241

Fat: 16g

Carbohydrates: 4g

Protein: 13g

Cholesterol: 123mg

Sodium: 136mg

2 tablespoons butter, unsalted

1 yellow onion, chopped

2 cloves garlic, minced

½ pound mushrooms, sliced

1 red bell pepper, chopped

6 eggs

Sea salt and black pepper to taste

Whenever I cook for a brunch, I am sure to bring vegetables to blend in with the eggs. Vegetables are a great way to include extra flavor and nutrients without adding fat!

1. In a large skillet, heat the butter over medium heat. Add the onions, garlic, mushrooms, and bell pepper. Sauté, stirring occasionally, until the vegetables are tender, about 5 minutes.
2. Meanwhile, beat the eggs lightly in a bowl. Add the eggs to the vegetables, season with salt and pepper, and scramble until thoroughly cooked. Serve at once.

# Fresh Fruit Skewers with Honey-Yogurt Sauce

Serves 4

Prep time: 15 minutes

Cook time: none

Total cost: $5.08

Calories: 192

Fat: 7g

Carbohydrates: 3g

Protein: 3g

Cholesterol: 14mg

Sodium: 55mg

4 wooden skewers

1 cup cantaloupe, cut into 1- to 2-inch cubes

1 cup fresh pineapple, cut into 1- to 2-inch cubes

1 cup fresh strawberries, large ones halved, small ones whole

1 cup fresh blueberries

¾ cup vanilla nonfat yogurt

¼ cup mascarpone cheese or ¼ cup sour cream

1 tablespoon powdered sugar

1 tablespoon honey

1 teaspoon vanilla extract

Fruit skewers make a beautiful presentation for a breakfast buffet or even an afternoon pool party. Prepare the day before to save time.

1. On each skewer thread cantaloupe, pineapple, strawberry, and blueberries.
2. Whisk together the yogurt, mascarpone, sugar, honey, and vanilla extract. Pour into serving dishes. Serve fruit skewers with dipping sauce on side.

**Healthy Tip**
Honey is a healthy way to sweeten foods. Use it almost anywhere in place of sugar, except when baking pastry items.

# Muesli with Honey and Oats

 Serves 6

Prep time: 15 minutes
Refrigerate: 8 hours
Total cost: $3.06
Calories: 269
Fat: 4g
Carbohydrates: 34g
Protein: 5g
Cholesterol: 1mg
Sodium: 13mg

2 cups quick-cooking rolled oats

½ cup orange juice

¾ cup chopped prunes, raisins, or currants

⅓ cup chopped nuts or wheat germ

¼ teaspoon sea salt

¼ cup honey

1¼ cups nonfat milk

Those who are big fans of the low-carb diet may not be a big fan of muesli. However, muesli is typically lower in fat, sodium, and cholesterol and higher in protein than other breakfast foods and is a healthy choice for the active individual or family.

Place the oats in a bowl and pour the juice over them; toss until juice is evenly absorbed. Stir in the fruit, nuts, and salt. Pour the honey over the mixture and toss until evenly combined. Stir in the milk. Cover and refrigerate at least 8 hours. Do not cook; serve cold with brown sugar and additional milk if desired.

# Scrambled Eggs with Lox

**Serves 4**

Prep time: 15 minutes
Cook time: 10 minutes
Total cost: $3.98
Calories: 184
Fat: 8g
Carbohydrates: 5g
Protein: 14g
Cholesterol: 264mg
Sodium: 703mg

6 eggs

½ cup low-fat milk

1 3-ounce package cream cheese, softened

1 teaspoon fresh dill, chopped

Salt and pepper to taste

3 ounces lox or smoked salmon

1 tablespoon butter, unsalted

Salmon has a high content of omega-3 fatty acids, which are great for your heart and skin.

Using a wire whisk, beat eggs and milk together. Add cream cheese and combine thoroughly. Stir in dill, salt, pepper, and lox. Melt butter in 10-inch skillet over medium heat. Pour in egg mixture and scramble egg mixture until thickened but still moist.

**Extra Nutrients**

Fresh spinach is a natural and healthy addition to this recipe. If you have some on hand, add about ½ cup fresh spinach leaves to the skillet with the dill and other ingredients for a recipe that is packed full of flavor and nutrients without adding unwanted fat and calories.

The $7 a Meal Healthy Cookbook

# Quick Waffles

**Makes 6 waffles**

Prep time: 10 minutes
Cook time: 5 minutes
Total cost: $2.46
Calories: 350
Fat: 20g
Carbohydrates: 38g
Protein: 6g
Cholesterol: 68mg
Sodium: 22mg

2 cups plain flour

4 teaspoons baking powder

¼ teaspoon sea salt

2 eggs

1¾ cups low-fat or nonfat milk

½ cup canola oil

A waffle iron is essential for making waffles. You can find them in any kitchen store or a department store's home section.

1.  Preheat waffle iron following manufacturer's instructions. Stir together the flour, baking powder, and salt, and make a well in the middle of the mixture. Beat the eggs lightly, then beat in the milk and oil until well combined. Add all at once to the dry ingredients and combine until just moistened. Batter will have a few lumps.
2.  Use the manufacturer's directions to determine how much batter to use per waffle; use about 1 cup for a standard 7-inch circular waffle. Do not open the iron while the waffle is cooking! Remove with a fork to avoid burning your fingers.

# Waffles with Fresh Fruit Syrup

Makes 6 waffles

Prep time: 10 minutes
Cook time: 15 minutes
Total cost: $4.46
Calories: 379
Fat: 22g
Carbohydrates: 42g
Protein: 8g
Cholesterol: 68mg
Sodium: 48mg

½ cup orange juice

½ cup apple juice

½ cup sugar

2 tablespoons honey

Juice of 1 lemon

1½ cups fresh berries such as raspberries, blueberries, or strawberries

2 cups plain flour

4 teaspoons baking powder

¼ teaspoon sea salt

2 eggs

1¾ cups low-fat or nonfat milk

½ cup canola oil

Citrus syrups are delicious served over bowls of fresh fruit or used as a glaze for chicken.

1. Make syrup by heating orange juice, apple juice, sugar, honey, and lemon juice over medium heat in small-quart boiler. Bring to a boil and reduce liquid by half. Add berries and simmer for 1 minute. Remove from heat and set aside to cool.
2. Preheat waffle iron following manufacturer's instructions. Stir together the flour, baking powder, and salt, and make a well in the middle of the mixture. Beat the eggs lightly, then beat in the milk and oil until well combined. Add all at once to the dry ingredients and combine until just moistened. Batter will have a few lumps.
3. Use the manufacturer's directions to determine how much batter to use per waffle; use about 1 cup for a standard 7-inch circular waffle. Do not open the iron while the waffle is cooking! Remove with a fork to avoid burning your fingers. Serve waffles with syrup.

# Simple Corn Crepes

Serves 6

Prep time: 6 minutes
Cook time: 12 minutes
Total cost: $1.02
Calories: 80
Fat: 3g
Carbohydrates: 8g
Protein: 3g
Cholesterol: 53mg
Sodium: 237mg

2 eggs

1 cup milk or buttermilk

Pinch sea salt

1 cup corn flour

2 teaspoons sugar (optional)

2 tablespoons butter, melted

Canola oil for frying

Traditionally associated with French cuisine, crepes are a light pancake that are perfect for brunches or even dessert.

1. Place eggs, milk, and salt in a food processor and blend until smooth. With the motor on low, slowly add flour and sugar. Scrape down sides of bowl, turn back to low speed, and add butter.
2. Heat nonstick skillet over medium heat and add 2 teaspoons of oil. Pour in batter to make crepes. Tilt pan to spread batter evenly. Place crepes on parchment paper dusted with a little corn flour to prevent sticking. To store, place in Ziploc bag in refrigerator or freezer. Serve them with fresh fruit or cheese.

# Corn Crepes with Eggs and Parmesan Cheese

**Serves 6**

Prep time: 15 minutes
Cook time: 20 minutes
Total cost: $7.00
Calories: 302
Fat: 17g
Carbohydrates: 8g
Protein: 20g
Cholesterol: 392mg
Sodium: 531mg

2 eggs, whole (for crepe batter)

1 cup milk or buttermilk

Pinch sea salt

1 cup corn flour

2 teaspoons sugar (optional)

2 tablespoons butter, unsalted

Canola oil for frying

12 ½-ounce slices jack or pepper jack cheese

12 eggs, poached or fried sunny-side up

12 teaspoons salsa

12 teaspoons grated Parmesan cheese

Crepes can sound intimidating but they don't have to be. Just follow these simple instructions and you can make crepes. If you don't feel comfortable cooking poached eggs, don't worry about it; just scramble the eggs.

1. Place 2 whole eggs, milk, and salt in a food processor and blend until smooth. With the motor on low, slowly add flour and sugar (sugar is optional). Scrape down sides of bowl, turn back to low speed and add butter.
2. Heat nonstick skillet over medium heat and add 2 teaspoons of oil. Pour in batter to make crepes. Tilt pan to spread batter evenly. Place crepes on parchment paper dusted with a little corn flour to prevent sticking. To store, place in Ziploc bag in refrigerator or freezer.
3. Preheat broiler to high heat. Place crepes on baking sheet lined with parchment paper. Place slice of jack cheese on each crepe. Place one egg on each piece of cheese. Spoon 1 teaspoon salsa on top of each egg. Sprinkle crepes with Parmesan cheese and broil until cheese is hot and beginning to melt, about 2 minutes.

# CHAPTER 4

# APPETIZERS

# Skewers of Grilled Vegetables

Serves 8

Prep time: 18 minutes
Cook time: 10 minutes
Total cost: $5.85
Calories: 36
Fat: 0g
Carbohydrates: 2g
Protein: 2g
Cholesterol: 0mg
Sodium: 10mg

1 large yellow onion, cut into eighths

1 red bell pepper, cut into 2-inch squares

1 green bell pepper, cut into 2-inch squares

1 yellow bell pepper, cut into 2-inch squares

8 cremini or button mushrooms, stems removed and halved

2 tablespoons olive oil

Sea salt and black pepper to taste

8 wooden skewers about 5 to 6 inches long

Presoak wooden skewers for about 45 minutes. If 5- to 6-inch skewers are not available, purchase the long ones and cut them to the desired length.

1. Preheat grill or broiler. Place all vegetables in bowl. Pour in olive oil, then add sea salt and pepper to taste. Toss vegetables to coat.
2. Skewer vegetables in random order, such as red bell pepper square, onion slice, mushroom half, green bell pepper square, onion slice, mushroom half, and yellow bell pepper square.
3. Place the skewers on the grill or under the broiler, paying close attention while they cook as they can easily burn. Try to turn the vegetables only once or twice, as the vegetables become tender while cooking and can fall off the skewer. Cook until the vegetables are fork-tender.

**Time-Saving Tip**
This is definitely a recipe you want to make ahead of time. Do all the preparation the day before up until the point of cooking. When you are ready to grill, just heat up the grill and throw them on!

The $7 a Meal Healthy Cookbook

# Smoked Salmon on Sliced Cucumber

 Serves 8

Prep time: 15 minutes

Cook time: none

Total cost: $6.99

Calories: 99

Fat: 3g

Carbohydrates: 1g

Protein: 15g

Cholesterol: 19mg

Sodium: 1,695mg

6 ounces smoked salmon, flaked and diced

2 tablespoons red onion, finely diced

1 tablespoon capers, chopped

1 teaspoon fresh chives or dill, chopped

1 tablespoon olive oil

Sea salt and black pepper to taste

1 cucumber, sliced

As the Bikini Chef, foods that are figure flattering are my specialty. I try to use cucumbers whenever I can as a low-cal, refreshing, and delicious alternative to crackers or bread.

In medium mixing bowl, combine all ingredients except for cucumber slices. Mix gently with a fork until the olive oil is evenly distributed. Arrange cucumber slices on a serving platter. Use a small teaspoon to mound ¾ teaspoon of salmon mixture onto center of each cucumber slice.

**Presentation Tip**
When slicing cucumber, make green stripes by leaving alternating strips of green peel when peeling the cucumber. Then slice the cucumber.

# Cucumber Cups of Goat Cheese, Black Olives, and Herbs

Serves 4

Prep time: 10 minutes
Cook time: none
Total cost: $6.25
Calories: 106
Fat: 8g
Carbohydrates: 1g
Protein: 5g
Cholesterol: 20mg
Sodium: 155g

2 cucumbers, peeled and cut into 1- to 1¼-inch-thick sections

4 ounces goat cheese, plain or herbed, crumbled

4 ounces canned, pitted black olives, chopped

2 tablespoons fresh Italian flat-leaf parsley, leaves chopped

2 tablespoons fresh basil, julienned

Black pepper to taste

If you don't have a melon baller, use a small teaspoon or even a measuring teaspoon to scoop out the cucumber. The key is to leave a ¼- to a ½-inch layer of cucumber to support the filling.

1. Prepare cucumber cups by scooping ¾ of the center of the cucumber using a melon baller. Place cups upside down in a single layer on paper towels for about 10 minutes before using to drain.
2. In mixing bowl, combine goat cheese, olives, parsley, basil, and pepper. Toss with fork to combine. Arrange cucumber cups on serving platter. Using a teaspoon, fill each cup with goat cheese mixture until nicely mounded on top. Garnish with chopped parsley before serving.

**Serving Tip**
Depending upon the type of appetizer party you are having, sometimes you need appetizers that are more like a meal or hearty side dish. Cucumber is delicious but is not that filling. Place goat cheese mixture on crostini (toasted baguette slices) for a more filling appetizer.

# Cucumber Cups of Baked Chicken with Spicy Salsa and Cilantro

 Serves 6

Prep time: 10 minutes
Cook time: none
Total cost: $3.75
Calories: 92
Fat: 3g
Carbohydrates: 5g
Protein: 7g
Cholesterol: 4mg
Sodium: 314mg

2 cucumbers, peeled and cut into 1- to 1¼-inch sections

½ cup hot salsa

½ cup romaine lettuce, finely chopped

⅓ cup red onion, finely diced

¼ teaspoon garlic salt

⅔ cup baked chicken, diced

⅓ cup pepper jack or other Mexican-style cheese, shredded

2 tablespoons fresh cilantro, leaves chopped

Pinch black pepper, to taste

Cucumbers are relatively neutral in flavor so filling them with foods that are highly flavorful creates a perfect balance. Plus, they are extremely low in calories making them great for snacking any time of day.

1. Prepare cucumber cups by scooping ¾ of the center of the cucumber using a melon baller. Place cups upside down in a single layer on paper towels for about 10 minutes before using to drain.
2. In medium mixing bowl, combine all ingredients except cucumber. Toss with fork to combine. Arrange cucumber cups on serving platter. Using a teaspoon, fill each cup with chicken mixture until nicely mounded on top. Top with any additional cilantro.

# Roma Tomatoes with Fresh Thyme

Serves 4

Prep time: 8 minutes
Cook time: 11 minutes
Total cost: $2.52
Calories: 23
Fat: 2g
Carbohydrates: 2g
Protein: 4g
Cholesterol: 0mg
Sodium: 4mg

4 Roma or plum tomatoes

3 cloves garlic

¼ cup fresh thyme, leaves removed from stems

Sea salt and black pepper to taste

Extra-virgin olive oil for drizzling after baked

At the restaurant where I worked in Florence, Italy, we baked hundreds of Roma tomatoes each day using them for a similar appetizer on our regular menu.

1. Preheat oven to 385°F. Cut the tomatoes into quarters and remove seeds. Lay out each slice in a single layer on a parchment-lined baking sheet. Mince the garlic, and chop the thyme slightly to open up the flavors. Sprinkle the tomatoes with the garlic, thyme, salt, and black pepper.
2. Bake in the oven for approximately 10 to 12 minutes, then remove and serve on top of crackers or Melba rounds and drizzle with olive oil. Or skip the carbs and calories and enjoy the Italian way with olive oil!

### Roma Tomatoes

Roma tomatoes are also called plum tomatoes in many supermarkets. They are the smaller, more oval shaped tomatoes that are widely used in Italy. Enjoy as you would any other ripe tomato.

The $7 a Meal Healthy Cookbook

# Roasted Cayenne Peanuts

 Serves 12

Prep time: 5 minutes
Cook time: 20 minutes
Total cost: $5.48
Calories: 211
Fat: 17g
Carbohydrates: 6g
Protein: 9g
Cholesterol: 0mg
Sodium: 7mg

1 egg white

2 tablespoons curry powder

¼ teaspoon cayenne pepper

Pinch of sea salt

1 teaspoon sugar

3 cups unsalted peanuts, shelled

Walnuts or almonds are also delicious with this recipe. If you like, use 1 cup of each!

1. Preheat oven to 300°F. Line 2 baking sheets with parchment paper. In medium mixing bowl, whip egg white until frothy. Add curry powder, cayenne, salt, and sugar. Whisk until well blended. Add peanuts and stir until evenly coated.
2. Spread nuts in single layer on the baking sheets. Roast, uncovered, for about 20 minutes, until the nuts are dry and toasted. Stir and turn the nuts at least 2 times during the roasting process. Remove nuts from oven and transfer to separate parchment sheet to cool.

**Baking Tip**
When roasting any kind of nut in an oven or on the stovetop, watch them carefully as they may seem slow to roast, but once they begin, they can burn quickly and easily.

# Crostini with Roasted Garlic and Herbs

Serves 6

Prep time: 3 minutes
Cook time: 30 minutes
Total cost: $4.99
Calories: 110
Fat: 1g
Carbohydrates: 21g
Protein: 4g
Cholesterol: 3mg
Sodium: 220mg

2 heads garlic

¼ cup extra-virgin olive oil

1 sourdough baguette, sliced into ½-inch slices and toasted

1 bunch fresh Italian parsley, chopped

Roasted garlic makes for an easy appetizer for any party. Spread on baguette slices, as here, or serve with roasted peppers and goat cheese.

1. Preheat oven to 400°F. Slice tops off each garlic head (or bulb) revealing the sliced cloves inside. Place both bulbs on aluminum foil and pour olive oil over each. Wrap foil around garlic and place on center rack of oven and bake for 30 minutes.
2. Remove garlic from oven, place in center of serving platter, and arrange baguette slices around garlic; top garlic with fresh parsley and serve.

The $7 a Meal Healthy Cookbook

# Parmesan Crisps with Apricots and Thyme

**Serves 8**

Prep time: 5 minutes
Cook time: 30 minutes
Total cost: $6.92
Calories: 101
Fat: 3g
Carbohydrates: 14g
Protein: 2g
Cholesterol: 6mg
Sodium: 95mg

½ cup apricot preserves

¼ cup dried apricots, finely chopped

2 tablespoons water

1 tablespoon honey

½ teaspoon fresh thyme, leaves chopped

1½ cups Parmigiano-Reggiano cheese, grated

Parmigiano-Reggiano cheese is an authentic Italian cheese that is very dense and actually lower in fat content than other cheeses.

1. Preheat oven to 350°F. Line baking sheet with parchment paper. In heavy saucepan, combine preserves, apricots, water, honey, and thyme leaves. Bring to a simmer. Simmer for 5 to 8 minutes, stirring frequently, until dried apricots are softened and mixture is thickened. Remove from heat and let cool slightly.
2. Meanwhile, using a tablespoon, place mounds of cheese 4 inches apart on prepared baking sheet. Gently pat to form 2-inch rounds. Bake for 4 to 6 minutes or until cheese is melted and turns light golden brown. Let crisps cool for 5 minutes on baking sheet, then transfer to paper towels. Serve with apricot mixture.

# Cream Cheese Dip
# with Fresh Dill

Serves 8

Prep time: 10 minutes

Chill: 20 mins. to 2 hrs.

Total cost: $4.14

Calories: 85

Fat: 12g

Carbohydrates: 4g

Protein: 4g

Cholesterol: 28mg

Sodium: 184mg

1 8-ounce package cream
cheese, softened

½ cup low-fat mayonnaise

½ cup plain nonfat yogurt

1 tablespoon fresh dill, chopped

2 fresh garlic cloves, chopped

Pinch sea salt

This tasty and simple dip is perfect served with cucumber slices, carrot sticks, and celery for a truly low-fat treat.

In medium bowl, beat cream cheese until soft and fluffy. Add mayonnaise and yogurt and mix well. Stir in dill, garlic, and salt until combined. Serve immediately, or cover and refrigerate for 20 minutes to 2 hours before serving.

# Avocado and Cantaloupe with Raspberry Vinaigrette

● Serves 8

Prep time: 10 minutes
Cook time: none
Total cost: $6.99
Calories: 63
Fat: 7g
Carbohydrates: 5g
Protein: 1g
Cholesterol: 0mg
Sodium: 11mg

¼ cup olive oil

3 tablespoons raspberry vinegar

1 tablespoon honey

¼ teaspoon ground ginger or ½ teaspoon fresh ginger

Pinch sea salt

2 avocados, peeled

½ cantaloupe, seeds removed

Avocados are fairly high in calories and fat, but they contain the good fat that your body needs for energy. They also have no cholesterol and are naturally low in sodium!

1.  In medium bowl, combine olive oil, 2 tablespoons vinegar, honey, ginger, and salt. Mix well using wire whisk. Cut avocados into chunks, or make balls using a melon baller. Sprinkle remaining tablespoon vinegar over prepared avocado.
2.  Use a melon baller to scoop cantaloupe into small balls. Place cantaloupe and avocado in serving bowl and drizzle raspberry vinaigrette over all. Serve in martini glasses or sherbet glasses for an elegant predinner appetizer presentation.

# Easy Guacamole

Serves 8

Prep time: 15 minutes
Cook time: none
Total cost: $5.09
Calories: 88
Fat: 11g
Carbohydrates: 5g
Protein: 1g
Cholesterol: 5mg
Sodium: 104mg

3 tablespoons lemon juice

Pinch sea salt

2 ripe avocados

¼ cup red onion, finely chopped

1 tomato, seeded and chopped

¼ cup low-fat sour cream

Pinch black pepper

Avocados turn brown, or oxidize, rapidly when the flesh is exposed to air. To prevent this, drizzle lemon juice or lime juice over the avocados as soon as you cut them open.

1. In medium bowl, combine lemon juice and salt. Mix well. Cut avocados in half, remove pit, scoop out avocado, and mix with lemon-juice mixture. Toss to coat, mashing avocados with a fork; make mixture as smooth or chunky as you like.
2. Stir in red onion, tomato, sour cream, and pepper and mix well. Serve immediately or place in refrigerator, wrapped in plastic wrap.

The $7 a Meal Healthy Cookbook

# Oven-Broiled Pears with Citrus Glaze and Gorgonzola

Serves 10

Prep time: 10 minutes
Cook time: 5 minutes
Total cost: $6.99
Calories: 58
Fat: 1g
Carbohydrates: 11g
Protein: .5g
Cholesterol: 1mg
Sodium: 25mg

2½ teaspoons olive oil

2 oranges, zested and juiced

5 Anjou or Bartlett pears, quartered but not peeled

¼ cup Gorgonzola cheese, crumbled

1 teaspoon honey

Pinch black pepper

At the restaurant I worked at in Italy, we cooked with a variety of fruits, including fresh cherries and wild berries of all kinds. One of my favorite recipes was similar to this one, where we poached the pears and topped them with mascarpone cheese.

1. Preheat broiler. Lightly grease baking sheet with 1 teaspoon of oil. Toss pears with remaining oil and orange juice and place skin side down on the baking sheet. Sprinkle cheese over the pears and drizzle with honey. Sprinkle with zest and a little pepper.
2. Place under broiler and cook until browned. Serve warm.

# Meatballs with Chili Pepper Glaze

Serves 8

Prep time: 8 minutes
Cook time: 20 minutes
Total cost: $6.38
Calories: 230
Fat: 13g
Carbohydrates: 5g
Protein: 2g
Cholesterol: 27mg
Sodium: 500mg

1 16-ounce package frozen mini-meatballs

1 tablespoon olive oil

1 yellow onion, chopped

Sea salt and black pepper to taste

¾ cup chili sauce

½ cup peach jam

¼ cup water

You can make your own meatballs if you prefer, but there are so many delicious, affordable premade meatballs available that it makes sense to save yourself the time of rolling them.

Bake meatballs as directed on package. Meanwhile, heat olive oil in heavy saucepan and add onion, salt, and pepper. Cook and stir until onion is starting to turn brown and caramelize. Add chili sauce, peach jam, and water; stir, and bring to a boil. Add the cooked meatballs and stir to coat. Serve hot.

**Spicy and Sweet Flavors**
Chili peppers and peaches may not sound like they go together; however, any time you have a spicy ingredient, the sweetness of fruit helps balance out the spice to make for a perfect blend of flavors.

The $7 a Meal Healthy Cookbook

# Spinach Puffs with Parmesan Cheese

Serves 10

Prep time: 15 minutes
Cook time: 20 minutes
Total cost: $6.93
Calories: 215
Fat: 11g
Carbohydrates: 15g
Protein: 4g
Cholesterol: 123mg
Sodium: 182mg

2 packages frozen spinach, thawed and well drained

2 cups dry herb-seasoned bread stuffing mix

6 eggs

1 cup yellow onion, finely chopped

½ cup butter, melted

¾ cup Parmesan cheese, grated

¾ cup fresh Italian parsley, chopped

1½ teaspoons garlic powder

½ teaspoon dried thyme

½ teaspoon black pepper

½ teaspoon sea salt

This dish is traditional to Tuscany, Italy; however, they use ricotta cheese instead of the Parmesan cheese used here.

Preheat oven to 375°F. In a large bowl, combine all ingredients and mix well. Form into 1- to 1¼-inch balls (puffs) and place on a parchment-lined baking sheet. Bake for 15 to 20 minutes. Serve warm.

**Make-Ahead Tip**
Puffs may be frozen and stored until needed. When cooking straight from the freezer, do not thaw them first. Place them directly on a baking sheet and bake for 20 to 25 minutes.

# Reuben Dip with Swiss Cheese

Serves 10

Prep time: 8 minutes
Cook time: 30 to 35 mins.
Total cost: $6.99
Calories: 111
Fat: 17g
Carbohydrates: 5g
Protein: 7g
Cholesterol: 40mg
Sodium: 413mg

1 8-ounce package cream cheese, softened

½ cup Thousand Island dressing

1 cup Swiss cheese, shredded

¼ pound sliced corned beef, chopped

1 cup sauerkraut, drained

This recipe is made in honor of the classic Reuben sandwich, which contains all the ingredients listed here except for cream cheese.

1. Preheat oven to 375°F. In medium bowl, beat cream cheese until fluffy. Stir in ¼ cup Thousand Island dressing and ½ cup Swiss cheese. Mix well to combine. Spread in bottom of 9" oven-safe pie plate. Top cream cheese mixture with corned beef and sauerkraut, spreading evenly to cover. Drizzle with remaining ¼ cup Thousand Island dressing and top with remaining cheese. Cover with foil.
2. Bake in oven for 30 minutes until cheese melts and mixture is hot.

**Serving Tip**
This dip is great served hot with pretzels, celery, or whole-grain crackers.

The $7 a Meal Healthy Cookbook

# Spiced Cream Cheese–Stuffed Mushrooms

 Serves 12

Prep time: 8 minutes
Cook time: 12 minutes
Total cost: $4.58
Calories: 25
Fat: 2g
Carbohydrates: 1g
Protein: .5g
Cholesterol: 7mg
Sodium: 20mg

1 tablespoon prepared horseradish

4 ounces cream cheese, softened

2 teaspoons lemon juice

Pinch five spice powder

24 large button or cremini mushrooms, wiped clean, stems removed

Cream cheese is a great foundation for many appetizer recipes as it blends well with other flavors and is easy to spread. Substitute lighter Neufchâtel cheese if you desire.

Preheat oven to 350°F. In small bowl, mix prepared horseradish with half of the cream cheese. In a separate bowl, combine lemon juice, five-spice powder, and remaining cream cheese. Spoon approximately 1 level teaspoon cream cheese/horseradish mixture into half the mushroom caps. Spoon the cream cheese/lemon mixture into the other half of the mushroom caps. Place all mushrooms on a parchment-lined baking sheet. Bake for 10 to 12 minutes until cream cheese is heated through.

**Five-Spice Powder**

Five-spice powder is native to China and features 5 main spices with additional secondary spices. A very strong, flavorful powder, use it sparingly on chicken, beef, pork, and other meats.

# Feta-Stuffed Grape Leaves

Serves 6

Prep time: 15 minutes
Cook time: 20 minutes
Total cost: $6.87
Calories: 54
Fat: 1g
Carbohydrates: 9g
Protein: 1g
Cholesterol: 4mg
Sodium: 574mg

1 teaspoon olive oil

1 leek, rinsed, finely chopped

1 cup white rice

2 cups vegetable broth

2 ounces feta cheese, crumbled

Pinch black pepper

1 small jar grape leaves, drained, rinsed, and separated

¼ bunch fresh oregano, leaves chopped

Stuffed grape leaves are commonly associated with Mediterranean dishes. Add golden currants and chopped hazelnuts for a variation on this delicious recipe.

1. Heat oil over medium heat in medium-size saucepan. Add leeks and oregano. Toss them in oil; add rice and toss again. Pour stock in with rice mixture and stir. Cover and cook approximately 15 to 20 minutes, until rice is thoroughly cooked. Cool rice in a medium-size mixing bowl, then add feta and pepper.
2. Lay out grape leaf. Place spoonful of rice mixture on center of leaf, then fold each end over the other and seal tightly. Repeat until all grape leaves and rice mixture are used.

# Roasted Roma Tomatoes with Fresh Basil and Provolone

Serves 10

Prep time: 8 minutes
Cook time: 8 minutes
Total cost: $7.00
Calories: 184
Fat: 6g
Carbohydrates: 5g
Protein: 7g
Cholesterol: 20mg
Sodium: 50mg

20 Roma tomatoes, halved

1 tablespoon fresh basil leaves

3 thick slices Italian bread,
¼" cubed

½ cup provolone cheese,
shredded

Black pepper to taste

1 tablespoon olive oil

Sea salt to taste

Roma tomatoes are also known as plum tomatoes. They are smaller and more oval in shape compared to beefsteak tomatoes and have firmer flesh than other tomatoes. They are traditionally used in Italian cooking.

1. Preheat oven to 400°F. Scoop out tomatoes, reserving insides. Mix together tomato insides with basil, bread, cheese, and pepper in a medium mixing bowl.
2. Stuff each tomato half with basil mixture. Place on parchment-lined baking sheet, drizzle with oil, and sprinkle with sea salt. Roast for 8 minutes and serve.

# Ricotta-Gorgonzola Torta with Lemon

Serves 6

Prep time: 10 minutes
Cook time: 30 minutes
Total cost: $6.97
Calories: 202
Fat: 14g
Carbohydrates: 6g
Protein: 12g
Cholesterol: 21mg
Sodium: 137mg

12-ounces fresh whole-milk ricotta cheese

4 ounces or ½ cup Gorgonzola cheese, crumbled

1 teaspoon fresh oregano, leaves chopped

1 teaspoon fresh lemon zest

1 teaspoon fresh lemon juice

Sea salt and black pepper to taste

3 egg whites, beaten stiff with hand mixer or standing mixer

½ cup hazelnuts, chopped and toasted

Springform pans have a latch on the side allowing the pan to expand and contract, making it easy to remove after baking. If you don't have one, use a cake ring instead.

Preheat oven to 350°F. In food processor, mix together cheeses, oregano, lemon zest, lemon juice, salt, and pepper until smooth. Place in a bowl and fold in beaten egg whites until combined. Transfer cheese mixture into a 9" springform pan lined with parchment paper or sprayed with nonstick spray. Bake for 30 minutes or until slightly golden. Remove from oven, sprinkle with hazelnuts, cool slightly, and serve.

**Lemon Zest**
Lemon zest is the yellow skin of the lemon, also known as the rind or peel. The zest has a crisp, lemony flavor that is great for adding flavor to foods without the juice and calories. When removing the zest, be sure to skim the top of the yellow and do not go any deeper to the white pith part as the pith is bitter tasting.

The $7 a Meal Healthy Cookbook

# Rolled Eggplant with Ricotta

 Serves 6

Prep time: 15 minutes
Cook time: 12 minutes
Total cost: $5.75
Calories: 110
Fat: 5g
Carbohydrates: 12g
Protein: 5g
Cholesterol: 8mg
Sodium: 114mg

1 medium eggplant (about 1 pound), sliced very thinly, ⅛-inch thick

½ cup rice flour

Sea salt and black pepper to taste

½ cup olive oil

1 cup ricotta cheese

¼ cup black olives, chopped

¼ cup Parmesan cheese, grated

Add a little lemon zest to the ricotta cheese for extra flavor but not extra calories!

1. Preheat oven to 350°F. Salt eggplant slices and stack them on a plate. Let sit under a weight (another plate weighted down) for about ½ hour to let brown juices out. Pat eggplant slices with paper towels to dry. In mixing bowl, place flour and season with salt and pepper. Heat oil to hot but not smoking. Dip slices in flour and fry until almost crisp, about 2 minutes per side.
2. Drain fried slices on paper towels. Place spoonful of ricotta cheese and a little chopped olive on the end of each slice. Roll and secure with a toothpick. Sprinkle rolls with Parmesan cheese and bake for 8 minutes. Serve warm.

# Antipasto Platter

Serves 8

Prep time: 15 minutes

Cook time: none

Total cost: $6.80

Calories: 356

Fat: 11g

Carbohydrates: 6g

Protein: 5g

Cholesterol: 52mg

Sodium: 764mg

2 4-ounce jars mushrooms, undrained

1 8-ounce package frozen artichoke hearts, thawed and drained

¾ cup Italian salad dressing

1 bunch asparagus spears, stalks trimmed

1 jar roasted red bell peppers, drained

8 ounces Cheddar cheese, cubed or sliced

8 ounces Swiss or provolone cheese, cubed or sliced

½ pound thinly sliced salami

Antipasto platters are the perfect appetizer for a last minute party or for surprise guests as it requires no cooking and tastes delicious! There is no hard-and-fast rule about how to serve your antipasto platter, so serve with or without bread and crackers and feel free to use your favorite combinations of cheeses and vegetables. Marinated olives are also a nice touch.

In a bowl, combine mushrooms, artichoke hearts, and salad dressing. Toss well. On a serving platter, arrange asparagus, red peppers, cheeses, and salami. Place artichoke hearts and mushrooms in a decorative bowl for serving and place on the platter. Serve chilled or room temperature using toothpicks.

# Sweet Potato Crisps

Serves 8

Prep time: 10 minutes
Cook time: 6 minutes
Total cost: $4.68
Calories: 186
Fat: 8g
Carbohydrates: 19g
Protein: 4g
Cholesterol: 0mg
Sodium: 320mg

2 large sweet potatoes,
   peeled and thinly sliced

3 cups canola oil

Sea salt and black pepper to
   taste

Sweet potatoes are high in vitamin A, which is great for your skin and is also known to help prevent cancer.

Heat oil in a deep fryer to 375°F. Fry sweet potato slices for about 3 to 4 minutes, depending upon thickness of chips. When the chips are very crisp, remove from the oil and drain. Add salt and pepper. Serve with dip or eat as is.

# Roasted Spiced Walnuts and Pecans

● Serves 8

Prep time: 8 minutes
Cook time: 25 minutes
Total cost: $6.48
Calories: 315
Fat: 28g
Carbohydrates: 9g
Protein: 8g
Cholesterol: 11mg
Sodium: 15mg

2 cups walnuts, whole or halved

2 cups pecan halves

3 tablespoons butter

¼ cup honey

⅓ cup brown sugar

1 teaspoon cinnamon

1 teaspoon ground ginger

½ teaspoon cardamom

⅛ teaspoon cayenne pepper

Spices add flavor to foods without adding fat and calories. Cardamom is actually known to enhance your mood. You can't go wrong with that!

1. Preheat oven to 375°F. Spread walnuts and pecans on parchment-lined baking sheet and toast for 8 minutes or until you can smell the fragrance of the nut. Remove from oven and set aside. Reduce oven temperature to 325°F.

2. Meanwhile, in small saucepan, combine butter, honey, and remaining ingredients over medium heat. Stir frequently so the sugars don't burn, just until mixture comes to a boil. Drizzle mixture over nuts and toss to coat. Return nuts to oven and bake for 15 to 20 minutes, stirring every 5 minutes. Remove from oven and cool completely. Store in airtight container.

**Spiced Nuts**
Spiced nuts are great to have in your pantry for a quick and easy snack, appetizer for surprise guests, or for a tasty addition to recipes such as grilled fish, pork, or chicken. Just keep them stored in an airtight container for freshness.

# Buffalo Mozzarella with Tomatoes and Basil

Serves 8

Prep time: 10 minutes
Cook time: none
Total cost: $7.00
Calories: 98
Fat: 9g
Carbohydrates: 0g
Protein: 4g
Cholesterol: 20mg
Sodium: 85mg

8 ounces buffalo mozzarella

1 bunch fresh basil leaves, stems removed

6 Roma tomatoes, sliced

Extra-virgin olive oil

Sea salt and black pepper

Extra-virgin olive oil is the best oil to use when drizzling foods for flavor. When cooking, however, use olive oil, as it has a higher burning temperature.

Slice mozzarella into 2-inch slices. Arrange on platter by placing tomato slice first, then basil leaf, then cheese. When finished, drizzle with olive oil and sprinkle with just a pinch of salt and pepper. Enjoy!

**Insalata Caprese**
Insalata caprese is the Italian name of this simple yet delicious salad that was made famous by the Italian island of Capri for which this salad is named.

# CHAPTER 5

# SALADS

# Caesar Salad

 Serves 6

Prep time: 15 minutes
Cook time: none
Total cost: $2.94
Calories: 96
Fat: 7g
Carbohydrates: 1g
Protein: 1g
Cholesterol: 5mg
Sodium: 108mg

2 tablespoons low-fat mayonnaise

Juice of ½ lemon

1 teaspoon Worcestershire sauce

1 teaspoon Dijon mustard (Grey Poupon recommended)

Black pepper to taste

3 tablespoons extra-virgin olive oil

¼ cup Parmesan cheese, grated

1 head romaine lettuce, washed, dried, and cut into bite-sized pieces

1 cup croutons (optional)

Croutons add fat and calories that aren't needed. If you can resist, skip the croutons and add a healthy protein such as diced, baked chicken or grilled salmon.

In medium mixing bowl, combine mayonnaise, lemon juice, Worcestershire sauce, mustard, and pepper. Whisk well until blended. Whisk in olive oil. Add cheese and lettuce and toss to coat. Top with croutons, if desired.

**Chopping Lettuce**
Tearing lettuce can bruise the lettuce, making the tender leaves turn brown. An easy way to slice romaine is to cut off the end, slice the head lengthwise into planks, then turn the sliced planks sideways and slice into 1-inch slices.

# Black Bean Salad with Romaine

Serves 8

Prep time: 15 minutes
Cook time: none
Total cost: $6.93
Calories: 92
Fat: 2g
Carbohydrates: 14g
Protein: 3g
Cholesterol: 1mg
Sodium: 530mg

1 15-ounce can black beans, rinsed and drained

1 12-ounce can yellow corn kernels, drained

½ cup red onion, chopped

½ cup green bell pepper, chopped

2 cloves garlic, chopped

¾ cup low-fat Italian dressing

½ teaspoon Tabasco sauce

½ teaspoon chili powder

Sea salt and black pepper to taste

1 head romaine lettuce, washed, dried, and chopped into 2-inch pieces

**Chill**
**15 to 20 minutes**

Beans are a natural source of protein; however, if you need extra protein, this is a great recipe to which you can add chicken or turkey.

In large mixing bowl, combine all ingredients except lettuce. Toss well. Chill for 15 to 20 minutes. Remove from refrigerator, add lettuce, and toss well. Serve immediately.

The $7 a Meal Healthy Cookbook

# Pasta Salad with Breast of Chicken

Serves 6

→ Prep time: 10 minutes
→ Cook time: 5 minutes
→ Total cost: $6.74
→ Calories: 227
→ Fat: 4g
→ Carbohydrates: 13g
→ Protein: 24g
→ Cholesterol: 61mg
→ Sodium: 462mg

**Chill**
**1 hour**

Pinch sea salt (for pasta water)

1 head fresh broccoli, chopped

3 cups cooked chicken breast, chopped

½ pound pasta shells, cooked and drained

2 large tomatoes, chopped

½ red onion, chopped

Black pepper to taste

1 cup Italian dressing

Pasta salad recipes are very fun to make because you are not limited to just these ingredients. Feel free to use your favorite type of pasta, perhaps bow-tie or corkscrew, and add shredded carrots, black olives, or red bell peppers for a variation on this already simply delicious dish.

1. In large pot filled ¾ with water, bring water to a boil. Add pinch of salt, then add broccoli and allow to boil for 20 seconds. Remove broccoli from boiling water and transfer to colander to drain.
2. In large mixing bowl, combine broccoli, chicken, pasta, tomatoes, onion, and pepper. Pour dressing over and toss well to coat. Cover and chill before serving.

# Napa Cabbage with Mustard Ginger Dressing

**Serves 6**

Prep time: 20 minutes
Cook time: none
Total cost: $5.86
Calories: 79
Fat: 1g
Carbohydrates: 18g
Protein: 1g
Cholesterol: 3mg
Sodium: 26mg

4 cups napa (Chinese) cabbage, shredded

1 8¼-ounce can crushed pineapple, drained

1 8-ounce can sliced water chestnuts, drained

¼ cup scallions, chopped

¼ cup low-fat mayonnaise

1 tablespoon mustard

1 teaspoon peeled and grated fresh gingerroot

**Chill**
**1 hour**

Chinese cabbage is a light, crispy cabbage more like a lettuce than traditional green or red cabbage. As with any salad green, toss with dressing just before serving to avoid soggy cabbage.

In medium mixing bowl, combine cabbage, pineapple, water chestnuts, and scallions. Toss to combine. Cover and chill. In small mixing bowl, whisk together mayonnaise, mustard, and ginger. Cover and chill. When ready to serve, pour mayonnaise mixture over cabbage mixture and toss well to coat.

# Mixed Greens with Dijon Vinaigrette

Serves 4

Prep time: 10 minutes
Cook time: none
Total cost: $3.81
Calories: 116
Fat: 14g
Carbohydrates: 0g
Protein: 2g
Cholesterol: 5mg
Sodium: 95mg

¼ cup apple cider vinegar

2 tablespoons lemon juice

2 cloves garlic, minced

1 tablespoon Dijon mustard

Sea salt and black pepper to taste

¼ cup extra-virgin olive oil

10 to 12 ounces mixed greens, washed and dried

¼ cup Parmesan cheese, grated

Try using mustard vinaigrettes for cooking chicken, fish, and vegetables. The mustard gives foods a flavor lift without adding fat and calories, plus it's inexpensive!

In large mixing bowl, combine vinegar, lemon juice, garlic, and mustard. Whisk well to combine. Add salt and pepper as desired (about 1 pinch each). Drizzle in olive oil and whisk again to combine. Add mixed greens and cheese. Toss well to coat. Serve immediately.

**Making Your Own Dressing**
When making an olive oil–based dressing, use extra-virgin olive oil and whisk in the olive oil last to get an even, thick consistency as well as bring out the delicious olive oil flavor.

# Wild Rice Salad with Fresh Tomatoes and Basil

Serves 4

- Prep time: 15 minutes
- Cook time: none
- Total cost: $6.67
- Calories: 197
- Fat: 7g
- Carbohydrates: 26g
- Protein: 2g
- Cholesterol: 0mg
- Sodium: 0mg

**Rest**
20 minutes

2 cups cooked wild rice

3 large vine-ripe tomatoes, seeded and chopped

3 green onions, chopped

3 tablespoons fresh basil, chopped

1 clove garlic, chopped

Sea salt and black pepper as desired

2 tablespoons extra-virgin olive oil

Wild rice is a positive alternative to white rice. It is flavorful, has more nutrients, and has different layers of textures for a true palate pleaser.

In large mixing bowl, place rice, tomatoes, onion, basil, and garlic. Season with salt and pepper as desired. Drizzle oil over rice mixture and toss to combine. Let stand at room temperature about 20 minutes before serving to allow flavors to combine.

# Chicken Salad with Cucumber and Melon

 Serves 4

Prep time: 15 minutes
Cook time: none
Total cost: $6.47
Calories: 356
Fat: 13g
Carbohydrates: 7g
Protein: 29g
Cholesterol: 89mg
Sodium: 301mg

2½ cups cooked chicken breast, chopped

1½ cups honeydew melon or cantaloupe, peeled, seeded, and cut into 2-inch cubes

1½ cups cucumber, peeled and diced

1½ cups seedless green grapes

½ cup low-fat mayonnaise

2 tablespoons plain nonfat yogurt

1½ teaspoons cider vinegar

Pinch sea salt and black pepper

⅓ cup fresh cilantro, leaves chopped

2 tablespoons fresh lime juice (about 1 large lime)

**Chill**
**1 hour**

This is a great recipe to serve for brunch or a ladies luncheon. Serve them in papaya boats for a beautiful, unique presentation that is also delicious!

In a large mixing bowl, combine chicken, melon, cucumber, and grapes. Separately, in small mixing bowl, whisk together remaining ingredients. Pour over chicken mixture and toss to combine. Cover and chill for at least 1 hour before serving.

**Money-Saving Tip**
This great recipe works well with leftover chicken breasts. You can also substitute turkey breasts or canned tuna, if you prefer.

# Romaine Lettuce with Pears and Goat Cheese

**Serves 4**

Prep time: 10 minutes
Cook time: none
Total cost: $5.12
Calories: 201
Fat: 18g
Carbohydrates: 7g
Protein: 3g
Cholesterol: 10mg
Sodium: 23mg

¼ cup extra-virgin olive oil

¼ cup champagne or apple cider vinegar

6 cups romaine lettuce

1 Bartlett pear, seeded and diced

2 tomatoes, diced

2 tablespoons toasted walnuts

¼ cup goat cheese, crumbled

Goat cheese and pears are one of my favorite combinations, but you can substitute apples and Gorgonzola for another tasty variation.

In large mixing bowl, whisk together oil and vinegar until well combined. Add all other ingredients and toss well.

# Mediterranean Salad with Feta and Kalamata Olives

Serves 4

Prep time: 15 minutes
Cook time: none
Total cost: $5.97
Calories: 181
Fat: 18g
Carbohydrates: 5g
Protein: 1g
Cholesterol: 5mg
Sodium: 704mg

¼ cup extra-virgin olive oil

¼ cup balsamic vinegar

6 cups romaine lettuce

2 tomatoes, diced

1 cucumber, diced

½ cup kalamata olives, pitted, chopped

2 pepperoncini, diced

¼ cup red onions, diced

½ cup feta cheese, crumbled

The Mediterranean diet consists mainly of fresh fruits, fresh vegetables, and olive oil, which is said to lower cholesterol, blood pressure, and monounsaturated fat.

In large mixing bowl, whisk together oil and vinegar. Whisk until well combined. Add remaining ingredients and toss well to coat.

**Health-Conscious Vinaigrettes**

Making your own vinaigrettes is easy and is usually healthier than bottled dressings, which tend to be higher in sodium and preservatives and contain more chemically processed ingredients.

# Mixed Greens with Radicchio and Oranges in Honeyed Vinaigrette

Serves 6

Prep time: 15 minutes
Cook time: none
Total cost: $6.08
Calories: 130
Fat: 10g
Carbohydrates: 8g
Protein: 1g
Cholesterol: 0mg
Sodium: 0mg

¼ cup apple cider vinegar

1 tablespoon honey

Sea salt and black pepper to taste

¼ cup extra-virgin olive oil

6 cups mixed greens, washed and dried

3 oranges, peeled, membranes removed

2 heads radicchio, chopped

Radicchio is a leafy vegetable that has a slightly bitter taste. This honey vinaigrette helps to balance the bitterness of the leaves. Radicchio is also delicious grilled, which mellows the bitter flavor.

1. In a large mixing bowl, combine vinegar, honey, salt, and pepper. Whisk well to combine. Add olive oil while whisking. Mix thoroughly.
2. Separately, combine mixed greens, oranges, and radicchio and toss to combine. Add into vinaigrette and toss to coat.

**Supreming Fruit**
To supreme fruit means to remove the peel and pith from the fruit. To do this, take a chef's knife and slice off each end of the fruit. Use your knife to cut away peel or rind. Then, place a small bowl underneath the fruit to catch the juices as you cut. Using a small knife or paring knife, carefully cut the fruit out from the pith or membrane by sliding your knife between the pith and the fruit, on both sides of the pith, thereby releasing the fruit. You should be left with the fruit only, tossing aside any seeds.

The $7 a Meal Healthy Cookbook

# Chinese Chicken Salad

 Serves 6

Prep time: 15 minutes
Cook time: 10 minutes
Total cost: $6.89
Calories: 535
Fat: 40g
Carbohydrates: 23g
Protein: 21g
Cholesterol: 26mg
Sodium: 69mg

¼ cup sugar

Pinch sea salt and black pepper

½ cup plus 2 tablespoons peanut oil

6 tablespoons rice vinegar

¼ cup sliced almonds

¼ cup sesame seeds

8 green onions, chopped

1 head cabbage, grated or minced

2 cups cooked chicken breast, chopped

2 packages ramen noodles, broken

Chinese chicken salad is always a hit. Add mandarin oranges for extra flavor, color, and, of course, vitamin C.

1. In a small mixing bowl, combine sugar, salt, pepper, ½ cup peanut oil, and vinegar. Set aside.
2. Heat remaining 2 tablespoons oil in large skillet over medium heat. Add almonds and sesame seeds. Sauté until lightly browned, about 2 minutes. Add the onions and cabbage. Sauté for 5 minutes, or until tender. Add the chicken, sauté for 1 minute. Add the noodles and stir to combine. Add vinegar mixture, tossing well to coat. Serve.

# Curried Chicken Salad with Mango Chutney

Serves 6

Prep time: 15 minutes
Cook time: none
Total cost: $6.76
Calories: 138
Fat: 8g
Carbohydrates: 8g
Protein: 15g
Cholesterol: 46mg
Sodium: 272mg

**Chill**
**1 hour**

½ cup low-fat mayonnaise

2 tablespoons mango or other chutney

Fine zest of 1 lemon

1 tablespoon lemon juice

1 teaspoon sea salt

1 teaspoon curry powder

2 cups cooked chicken breasts, diced

1 cup celery, chopped

¼ cup red onion, chopped

½ pint fresh strawberries, sliced in half

6 lettuce leaves

Chutneys are great for cooking, as they are very versatile and are available in many flavor combinations. Use them for topping pork, turkey, or even fish, or mix with cream cheese for a delicious and easy spread.

In large mixing bowl, stir together mayonnaise, chutney, lemon juice, lemon zest, salt, and curry powder. Mix well. Add the chicken, celery, and onion. Toss well and cover. Chill for up to 1 hour. Just before serving, add strawberries and toss gently. Place lettuce leaves on serving platter. Place chicken mixture on lettuce leaf.

# Mixed Greens with Balsamic Vinaigrette and Dried Cranberries

 Serves 4

Prep time: 10 minutes
Cook time: none
Total cost: $4.84
Calories: 143
Fat: 10g
Carbohydrates: 12g
Protein: 1g
Cholesterol: 0mg
Sodium: 2mg

¼ cup balsamic vinegar

¼ cup extra-virgin olive oil

Sea salt and pepper to taste

6 cups mixed greens

1 red bell pepper, seeded and diced

1 medium red onion, diced

1 large tomato, diced

1 cucumber, diced

2 tablespoons dried cranberries

Balsamic vinaigrette is simply balsamic vinegar whisked together with extra-virgin olive oil. Create your own variation by adding a pinch of sugar, a squeeze of lemon and orange juice, and some fresh herbs (such as thyme).

In large mixing bowl, whisk together vinegar, oil, salt, and pepper. Add remaining ingredients and toss well to coat.

**Mixed Greens**
Mixed greens can usually be purchased two ways at the grocery store: in bulk or in prepackaged bags. Buy them in bulk, when possible, as the greens taste more fresh and you control the quantity you need.

# Red Leaf Lettuce with Feta Cheese

🥄 Serves 4

Prep time: 15 minutes
Cook time: none
Total cost: $6.04
Calories: 175
Fat: 19g
Carbohydrates: 1g
Protein: 2g
Cholesterol: 5mg
Sodium: 103mg

6 cups red leaf lettuce

1 large tomato, sliced into wedges

1 large red onion, thinly sliced

4 ounces feta cheese, crumbled

2 tablespoons balsamic vinegar

2 cloves garlic, minced

5 tablespoons extra-virgin olive oil

Sea salt and black pepper to taste

If you don't have feta cheese, try goat cheese, Brie, or even white Cheddar for a tasty twist.

In mixing bowl, place lettuce, tomato, onion, and feta cheese. Toss well. Separately, in small mixing bowl, whisk together vinegar, garlic, oil, salt, and pepper. Mix well. Pour vinaigrette over greens mixture and toss to coat.

# Grilled Vegetable Salad

 Serves 4

- Prep time: 10 minutes
- Cook time: 10 minutes
- Total cost: $6.52
- Calories: 175
- Fat: 18g
- Carbohydrates: 7g
- Protein: 1g
- Cholesterol: 0mg
- Sodium: 3mg

¼ cup plus 2 tablespoons olive oil

1 red bell pepper, seeded and chopped

1 shallot, peeled and diced

1 cup broccoli florets

4 asparagus spears, chopped

1 fresh ear of corn, kernels cut off cob

Salt and pepper to taste

¼ cup balsamic vinegar

6 cups romaine lettuce, chopped

This is a great salad for a BBQ! For outdoor grilling, grill corn whole and cut the kernels off the cob after grilling.

1. Heat 2 tablespoons oil over medium to medium-high heat on a grill pan or in sauté skillet. Add red bell pepper, shallot, broccoli, asparagus, and corn and sprinkle with pinch of salt and pepper. Cook until vegetables are tender, about 5 minutes.
2. In mixing bowl, whisk together remaining oil and vinegar. Add lettuce and other vegetables. Toss well and serve.

# Three-Bean Salad

Serves 8

Prep time: 10 minutes
Cook time: none
Total cost: $4.56
Calories: 118
Fat: 7g
Carbohydrates: 6g
Protein: 2g
Cholesterol: 0
Sodium: 95mg

**Chill**
**4 hours or**
**overnight**

½ cup sugar

⅓ cup canola oil

⅔ cup apple cider vinegar

Sea salt and pepper to taste

1 16-ounce can French-cut green beans, drained

1 16-ounce can yellow beans, drained

1 16-ounce can red kidney beans, drained

1 yellow onion, chopped

An easy salad that takes no time to throw together, three-bean salad is healthy, delicious, and fits with any budget! Go easy on the sugar to avoid unwanted calories.

In large mixing bowl, whisk together sugar, vinegar, oil, salt, and pepper. Whisk well. Add in beans and onions. Mix well. Chill at least 4 hours or overnight, stirring occasionally, if desired.

# Romaine Lettuce with BBQ Chicken

 Serves 4

Prep time: 10 minutes
Cook time: 20 minutes
Total cost: $6.36
Calories: 256
Fat: 13g
Carbohydrates: 10g
Protein: 22g
Cholesterol: 62mg
Sodium: 1,176mg

1 pound boneless chicken breast, skin removed

2 tablespoons olive oil

1 cup BBQ sauce

¼ cup Italian or ranch dressing

1 large head romaine lettuce, chopped

1 large tomato, diced

1 cucumber, diced

½ medium red onion, diced

This is a great salad to serve as a meal. Kids even like it because of the sweet BBQ sauce, but they usually want you to leave out the onions.

1. Chop chicken into 1- to 2-inch cubes. In mixing bowl, coat chicken with olive oil. Preheat skillet to medium heat. Add chicken and ⅓ cup water. This helps prevent burning. Cover with lid and let chicken cook, about 8 to 10 minutes, adding water if needed. When cooked, remove from heat and toss with BBQ sauce. Set aside.
2. In separate mixing bowl, pour in dressing. Add remaining ingredients and toss to coat. Add chicken and serve.

**Healthy Tip**
Although BBQ chicken is great on this salad, substitute turkey or even salmon for a delicious variation that is equally healthy.

# Salad of Orzo, Red Bell Pepper, and Fresh Herbs

Serves 4

Prep time: 15 minutes
Cook time: none
Total cost: $6.48
Calories: 188
Fat: 10g
Carbohydrates: 20g
Protein: 3g
Cholesterol: 0mg
Sodium: 0mg

¼ cup extra-virgin olive oil

2 cups fresh basil leaves, finely chopped

4 cloves garlic, finely chopped

½ cup fresh Italian flat-leaf parsley, finely chopped

Sea salt to taste

1 pound orzo pasta, cooked al dente and drained thoroughly

1 red bell pepper, seeded and diced

½ red onion, finely chopped

Sometimes called Italian rice, orzo is made from wheat semolina flour. In the United States, orzo is considered to be a rice-shaped pasta slightly smaller than a pine nut.

In mixing bowl, whisk together oil, basil, parsley, garlic, and salt. Add the orzo, red pepper, and red onion. Toss well to combine.

# Spinach Salad with Grilled Salmon

 Serves 2

Prep time: 15 minutes
Cook time: none
Total cost: $6.43
Calories: 405
Fat: 24g
Carbohydrates: 12g
Protein: 19g
Cholesterol: 47mg
Sodium: 121mg

¼ cup extra-virgin olive oil

¼ cup balsamic vinegar

Sea salt and black pepper to taste

5 ounces salmon fillet, grilled, skin off, broken into pieces

2 cups fresh spinach leaves, washed and dried

½ cup red grapes, sliced in half

1 tablespoon dried cranberries

Both salmon and spinach are very healthy foods. Salmon is high in omega-3 fatty acids, which are great for your skin, and spinach is high in beta carotene, which helps fight against cancer.

In a large mixing bowl, whisk together olive oil, balsamic vinegar, salt, and pepper. Whisk together well. Add salmon, spinach, grapes, and cranberries. Toss to combine and serve.

**Cooking Tip**
The easiest way to grill salmon is to coat it with a little olive oil, sea salt, and pepper, place it on a piece of aluminum foil, and broil it in the oven. It only takes about 5 minutes and it's easy on cleanup!

# Fresh Spinach Salad with Roasted Turkey

Serves 2

Prep time: 15 minutes
Cook time: none
Total cost: $5.88
Calories: 306
Fat: 22g
Carbohydrates: 5g
Protein: 19g
Cholesterol: 48mg
Sodium: 32mg

¼ cup balsamic vinegar

1 squeeze fresh lemon

Sea salt and black pepper to taste

¼ cup extra-virgin olive oil

2 cups fresh spinach leaves, washed and drained

4 ounces honey-roasted turkey breast, chopped

1 tomato, chopped

1 Gala or Fuji apple, chopped

Turkey is less often thought of for everyday recipes but it is lower in fat than chicken and is a tasty, healthy substitution for chicken, beef, and pork recipes.

In large mixing bowl, combine vinegar, lemon, salt, and pepper and whisk together. Drizzle in olive oil while whisking. Add spinach, turkey, tomato, and apple. Toss well to coat.

**Tip for Tossing Salads**
The easiest way to make sure all your greens are coated with the vinaigrette is to place your vinaigrette or dressing in the bottom of the salad bowl first, before you add the greens and any other ingredients. Then, toss from the bottom up until all greens are coated.

# Cucumber Salad with Sesame Vinaigrette

Serves 2

Prep time: 10 minutes
Cook time: none
Total cost: $4.48
Calories: 63
Fat: 16g
Carbohydrates: 1g
Protein: 0g
Cholesterol: 0mg
Sodium: 2mg

1 teaspoon sugar

3 tablespoons rice wine vinegar

Sea salt and black pepper, as needed

3 tablespoons sesame oil

2 large cucumbers, partially peeled and diced

1 teaspoon jalapeño pepper, chopped

Sesame oil is the natural oil extracted from sesame seeds. It provides a distinctive flavor different than that of olive or canola oil and is widely used in Asian cooking.

In mixing bowl, combine sugar, vinegar, salt, and pepper. While whisking, drizzle in the sesame oil. Add cucumber and jalapeño and toss to combine.

**Sesame Oil Substitution**
If you don't cook a lot, you may not have sesame oil in your pantry. If you don't, don't stress; substitute olive oil or canola oil.

# Smoked Turkey Salad with Grapes

Serves 4

Prep time: 12 minutes
Cook time: none
Total cost: $6.92
Calories: 301
Fat: 11g
Carbohydrates: 25g
Protein: 26g
Cholesterol: 84mg
Sodium: 275mg

3 cups smoked turkey breast, chopped

1 cup celery, chopped

½ cup green seedless grapes, halved

½ cup red seedless grapes, halved

½ cup low-fat mayonnaise

¼ cup plain yogurt, regular or nonfat

1 tablespoon honey

Juice of 1 lemon

Sea salt and black pepper to taste

Serve this delicious salad on wheat bread or a toasted bagel as a sandwich—or for a fun presentation, serve in a martini glass on a small bed of mixed greens.

1. In a large mixing bowl, combine turkey, celery, and grapes. Set aside.
2. In separate mixing bowl, combine remaining ingredients. Add the yogurt mixture to the turkey and lightly toss to coat.

**Smoked Foods**

Smoking foods is an excellent way to add tons of flavor without adding fat and calories. If you really like smoked foods, invest in a stovetop smoker. You can smoke fish, chicken, turkey—practically anything—right in your kitchen with little smoke in your house and easy cleanup.

# Arugula Greens with Balsamic Vinaigrette and Goat Cheese

Serves 6

Prep time: 12 minutes
Cook time: none
Total cost: $6.18
Calories: 126
Fat: 12g
Carbohydrates: 1g
Protein: 4g
Cholesterol: 16mg
Sodium: 39mg

¼ cup extra-virgin olive oil

¼ cup balsamic vinegar

2 tablespoons lemon juice

1 tablespoon shallots, minced

Sea salt and black pepper to taste

5 cups loosely packed arugula greens

1 tablespoon fresh basil leaves, finely chopped

5 ounces goat cheese, crumbled

Shallots are part of the onion family. Their flavors are more condensed so you don't need as many shallots as onions when cooking.

Combine the oil, vinegar, lemon juice, shallots, salt, and pepper in a large mixing bowl and whisk together. Add remaining ingredients and toss to coat.

**Salad Serving Tip**

Tossing salad too early will cause greens to become limp and soggy. To ensure crisp greens, toss salad with vinaigrette just before serving, or, for buffet style service, serve vinaigrette on the side.

# SOUPS

# Italian Minestrone

Serves 8

Prep time: 10 minutes
Cook time: 35 minutes
Total cost: $6.71
Calories: 156
Fat: 2g
Carbohydrates: 24g
Protein: 3g
Cholesterol: 3mg
Sodium: 343mg

1 tablespoon olive oil

2 yellow onions, chopped

2 carrots, peeled and chopped

2 stalks celery, chopped

2 cloves garlic, chopped

1 16-ounce can chopped tomatoes, undrained

½ cup fresh green beans, trimmed and chopped

½ tablespoon fresh oregano, leaves chopped

8 cups water or chicken broth

2 cups cooked pasta, such as shells or rotini

⅓ cup Parmesan cheese, grated

Minestrone is a traditional Italian soup that can be made from whatever vegetables you have on hand. It is a very filling soup that is not expensive to make.

Heat oil in large stockpot (boiler) over medium heat. Add onion, carrots, celery, and garlic and sauté for 5 minutes. Stir in tomatoes, beans, oregano, and water and simmer for 25 minutes, uncovered. Add pasta and simmer for 5 minutes, until heated through. Sprinkle with cheese and serve.

**Recipe Suggestion**
If your budget allows, add a package of frozen meatballs to this already delicious pasta soup. Add them with the tomatoes and simmer for 25 minutes.

# Tomato-Basil Soup

Serves 6

Prep time: 10 minutes
Cook time: 1 hour, 10 mins.
Total cost: $6.99
Calories: 126
Fat: 2g
Carbohydrates: 13g
Protein: 4g
Cholesterol: 1mg
Sodium: 110mg

2 tablespoons olive oil

1 yellow onion, chopped

6 cloves garlic, chopped

8 Roma tomatoes, chopped, or 1 large can diced tomatoes with juice

8 cups water or vegetable broth

¼ bunch fresh basil, leaves chopped

¼ bunch fresh Italian flat-leaf parsley, leaves chopped

¼ cup Parmesan cheese, grated

2 tablespoons capers, drained

Black pepper to taste

As the Bikini Chef, I always try to include fresh herbs in my recipes—even desserts—as a way to bring out the flavors of the foods without adding unwanted fat and calories.

Heat the oil in a large stockpot on medium for about 3 minutes. Add the onions and sauté for about 2 minutes. Add the garlic and sauté for about 2 minutes. Add the tomatoes. Reduce heat to low and add the vegetable broth. Simmer for 45 minutes, uncovered. Add the herbs and simmer for 20 minutes, uncovered. Sprinkle each serving with the Parmesan, capers, and pepper.

**Preparation Tip**

Puréed soups make for a nice presentation and are sort of in fashion. Puréeing is easily done in a blender. Just be sure to purée in batches so as not to overfill the blender. Overfilling can result in a soup explosion, burning your arm! Reserve the cheese, capers, and pepper for garnish when serving.

The $7 a Meal Healthy Cookbook

# Cannellini Beans with Italian Sausage

● Serves 4

Prep time: 8 minutes
Cook time: 65 minutes
Total cost: $6.76
Calories: 548
Fat: 29g
Carbohydrates: 67g
Protein: 33g
Cholesterol: 32mg
Sodium: 1435mg

1 tablespoon olive oil

½ yellow onion, chopped

2 garlic cloves, chopped

½ pound hot or mild Italian sausage, removed from casing

6 cups beef or chicken broth

2 large cans cannellini or white beans, with juice

1 tablespoon fresh thyme, leaves chopped

Sea salt and black pepper to taste

For a leaner version of this soup, skip the sausage or add cooked chicken or turkey!

In large-quart boiler over medium heat, heat oil and add onion and garlic. Sauté for 5 minutes. Add sausage and brown about 5 minutes. Add broth, beans, and thyme and simmer for about 45 minutes. Season with salt and pepper as desired.

### Dried Versus Canned Beans

Dried beans are great for cooking if you have lots of time to cook as they need soaking overnight or up to 2 or 3 hours before cooking. Using canned saves on time, but be sure to compare sodium content as canned products can be super-high in sodium and can vary drastically by brand.

# Fresh Vegetable Soup with Chicken

Serves 4

Prep time: 10 minutes
Cook time: 42 minutes
Total cost: $6.56
Calories: 135
Fat: 2g
Carbohydrates: 5g
Protein: 23g
Cholesterol: 59mg
Sodium: 591mg

3 tablespoons olive oil

1 yellow onion, chopped

½ head broccoli, chopped

2 carrots, peeled and chopped

1 red bell pepper, seeded and chopped

Salt and black pepper to taste

4 cups chicken broth

2 cups cooked chicken, diced

2 tablespoons Italian parsley, chopped

For an even more filling soup, add diced potatoes when you add the broccoli and carrots!

Heat oil in a large quart boiler over medium heat. Add the onions and cook until soft, about 5 minutes. Add broccoli, carrots, and peppers. Cook about 4 minutes. Add salt, pepper, and broth and bring to a simmer. Cook until vegetables are tender, about 25 minutes. Add the chicken and parsley, return to a simmer, and simmer for 8 minutes.

**Cooking with Chicken**
Chicken is a great item to have on hand either frozen in individual servings or cooked leftover chicken from another meal. Throw into soups such as this one for a quick, easy, and affordable meal.

# Pasta and Bean Soup

Serves 8

Prep time: 8 minutes
Cook time: 25 minutes
Total cost: $5.28
Calories: 169
Fat: 3g
Carbohydrates: 28g
Protein: 9g
Cholesterol: 4mg
Sodium: 392mg

3 tablespoons olive oil

1 medium onion, chopped

3 cloves garlic, chopped

1 teaspoon fresh oregano, leaves chopped

1 large can (16-ounce) tomato sauce

Sea salt and black pepper to taste

1 tablespoon Worcestershire sauce

2 large cans red beans, undrained

1 small bunch Italian parsley, chopped

6 cups vegetable broth or chicken broth

2 cups cooked pasta such as fusilli

In Italy, pasta fagiole is a very popular dish during the winter months. Substitute any canned beans you like.

1. In a large pot, heat olive oil over medium heat; add onions and garlic and sauté for 5 minutes or until onions are tender. Add oregano, tomato sauce, salt, pepper, and Worcestershire sauce. Bring to a simmer then add beans, parsley, and broth.
2. Bring to a boil. Add cooked pasta and bring back to boil for 1 minute.

# Purée of Broccoli Soup

Serves 5

Prep time: 15 minutes
Cook time: 20 minutes
Total cost: $5.94
Calories: 126
Fat: 3g
Carbohydrates: 24g
Protein: 4g
Cholesterol: 6mg
Sodium: 315mg

1 head broccoli, stems and florets chopped

1 medium onion, chopped

2 large baking potatoes, peeled and diced

2 cloves garlic, chopped

1½ cups vegetable broth

2 teaspoons fresh thyme, leaves chopped

Black pepper to taste

Pinch nutmeg

1½ cups low-fat milk

Sea salt to taste

The potatoes help make this puréed soup thick and creamy, but you can leave them out if you are concerned about your carb intake. Add a dollop of low-fat or nonfat sour cream when serving to add extra flavor with minimal fat and calories.

1. In a large-quart boiler, combine broccoli stems and florets, onion, potatoes, garlic, broth, thyme, pepper, and nutmeg. Bring to a boil. Reduce the heat, cover, and simmer for 15 minutes or until potatoes are tender.
2. In a blender or food processor, purée the soup, in batches if necessary, until smooth. Return to the saucepan. Add the milk. Heat through on medium heat without boiling, about 5 minutes. Season with salt to taste.

# Spicy Gazpacho

**Serves 6**

Prep time: 15 minutes
Chill time: 1 hour
Total cost: $5.36
Calories: 112
Fat: 4g
Carbohydrates: 5g
Protein: 2g
Cholesterol: 0mg
Sodium: 350mg

8 tomatoes, seeded and finely diced

2 cucumbers, peeled and finely diced

2 green bell peppers, seeded and finely diced

1 clove garlic, finely diced

2 tablespoons extra-virgin olive oil

1½ teaspoons red wine vinegar

2 teaspoons Worcestershire sauce

1 teaspoon sea salt

2 cups tomato juice

Dash hot sauce or more as desired

For dinner parties, serve this as an appetizer in little espresso cups. It tastes great, it's flavorful, and serving in cups makes it easy to enjoy! Make ahead of time as this recipe gets better with age.

Combine all ingredients and mix well, adding additional hot sauce as your tastes allow. Cover and refrigerate for 1 hour.

# Tuscan Bean Soup

Serves 8

Prep time: 5 minutes
Cook time: 35 minutes
Total cost: $5.76
Calories: 276
Fat: 5g
Carbohydrates: 45g
Protein: 14g
Cholesterol: 16mg
Sodium: 717mg

4 tablespoons extra-virgin olive oil

1 bunch green onion, chopped

3 cloves garlic, finely chopped

1 tablespoon fresh rosemary, stems removed, finely chopped

4 cups chicken broth

2 32-ounce cans great Northern beans with juice

½ cup ham or 1 ham bone

Sea salt and black pepper to taste

For my clients who love Italian gourmet food, this is one of my pocket faves. Drizzle a little extra-virgin olive oil on top when serving—you can't go wrong!

In large-quart boiler over medium heat, heat 1 tablespoon olive oil until fragrant, about 1 minute. Add onion and garlic and cook for 8 minutes. Add rosemary, broth, beans, and ham (or ham bone). Bring to a boil. Stir, cover, and reduce heat to simmer. Simmer 25 minutes. Season with salt and pepper as desired. Serve and drizzle remaining olive oil over individual servings for extra flavor.

The $7 a Meal Healthy Cookbook

# Miso Soup

Serves 4

Prep time: 15 minutes
Cook time: 10 minutes
Total cost: $4.56
Calories: 61
Fat: 2g
Carbohydrates: 8g
Protein: 3g
Cholesterol: 0mg
Sodium: 750mg

¼ cup miso paste

3½ cups chicken broth

8 ounces medium to firm tofu, cubed

4 sprigs Italian parsley, chopped

4 cremini or button mushrooms, brushed and sliced

2 shiitake mushrooms, sliced

Sea salt and black pepper to taste

The mystery of miso is that it is hard to make but this simple recipe will solve that for you!

In large-quart boiler, whisk the miso into 2 tablespoons of slightly warmed broth and blend well. Gradually add the miso liquid into the remaining broth. Bring the soup to a simmer. Add the tofu cubes, parsley, and mushrooms. Maintain a simmer until the mushrooms and tofu are heated. Do not boil or the soup will become bitter and cloudy. Serve soup in bowls and serve immediately. Season with salt and pepper as desired.

**Miso**

Miso is a fermented soybean paste that can be found in most well-stocked supermarkets. It lasts for a year or more if stored properly, and can be used to make aioli or as a substitute for peanut butter in some recipes.

# Mexican Posole

Serves 6

Prep time: 15 minutes
Cook time: 24 minutes
Total cost: $6.97
Calories: 378
Fat: 4g
Carbohydrates: 43g
Protein: 30g
Cholesterol: 52mg
Sodium: 663mg

1 16-ounce package pork roast, chopped

1 4-ounce can chopped green chilies, undrained

2 14-ounce cans chicken broth

1 tablespoon chili powder

1 teaspoon ground cumin

1 teaspoon fresh oregano, leaves chopped

1 15-ounce can hominy, drained

2 cups (16 ounces) frozen corn

3 tablespoons plain flour

¼ cup water

Sea salt and black pepper to taste

Posole is a Mexican stew made with hominy, green chilies, and cubes of tender pork.

1. In large saucepan over medium heat, combine pork (with any juices), chilies, broth, chili powder, cumin, oregano, hominy, and corn. Bring to a boil over high heat, then reduce heat to low, cover, and simmer for 12 to 15 minutes until pork is hot and tender.
2. In small bowl, combine flour and water. Mix well until smooth. Stir into stew and raise to medium heat. Cook and stir until stew thickens, about 5 to 8 minutes. Season with salt and pepper as desired.

**Hominy**
Hominy is made by removing the bran and germ from the kernels of corn. It can be made by soaking the corn kernels in a weak solution of lye and water, or by physically crushing the corn. Yellow hominy is generally sweeter than the white. You can substitute barley for it in any recipe, if you prefer.

The $7 a Meal Healthy Cookbook

# Sausage Gumbo

Serves 4

Prep time: 15 minutes
Cook time: 30 minutes
Total cost: $6.91
Calories: 388
Fat: 6g
Carbohydrates: 37g
Protein: 34g
Cholesterol: 52mg
Sodium: 1225mg

8 ounces hot or mild Italian sausage, removed from casing

1 14½-ounce can beef broth

1 14½-ounce can Italian stewed tomatoes, undrained

2 cups water

2 baking potatoes, peeled and cut into 1- to 2-inch cubes

1 10-ounce package frozen mixed vegetables

1 teaspoon dried Italian seasoning

Sea salt and black pepper to taste

Other alternatives for this recipe include substituting chopped chicken or leaving out the potatoes and serving over white rice.

In large-quart boiler, sauté sausage until browned, breaking up pieces. Add beef broth, tomatoes, and water. Bring to a boil. Stir in potatoes, mixed vegetables, Italian seasoning, and salt and pepper. Return to boiling. Reduce heat and simmer, covered, 20 to 25 minutes, or until potatoes are tender.

**Gumbo**

True gumbo usually has fresh okra in it; however, fresh okra can be extremely hard to find. Use fresh green beans instead or just use frozen mixed vegetables as suggested here.

# Creamy Tomato Bisque

Serves 4

Prep time: 15 minutes
Cook time: 12 minutes
Total cost: $6.04
Calories: 261
Fat: 18g
Carbohydrates: 22g
Protein: 8g
Cholesterol: 44mg
Sodium: 490mg

1 tablespoon olive oil

1 yellow onion, finely chopped

1 10-ounce container refrigerated Alfredo sauce

1½ cups chicken broth

1½ cups low-fat milk

2 14-ounce cans diced tomatoes, undrained

½ teaspoon dried basil leaves

¼ teaspoon dried marjoram leaves

Sea salt and black pepper to taste

Bisque is any kind of thick, creamy soup of puréed fish or vegetables and is usually made with cream. If your budget allows, add cooked shrimp or lobster for a delicious seafood bisque.

1. In a heavy saucepan, heat olive oil over medium heat and add onion. Cook and stir until onion is tender, about 4 minutes. Add Alfredo sauce and chicken broth; cook and stir with wire whisk until mixture is smooth. Add milk and stir; cook over medium heat for 2 to 3 minutes.
2. Meanwhile, purée tomatoes in food processor or blender until smooth. Add to saucepan along with seasonings and stir well. Heat soup over medium heat, stirring frequently, until mixture just comes to a simmer. Serve immediately.

### Alfredo Sauce

Alfredo sauce is a creamy white sauce that you can make from scratch or use the premade sauce found in the refrigerated dairy and cheese section of your grocery store. Cream sauces can add extra unwanted calories and fat, so enjoy in small portions to keep a lean and healthy figure.

The $7 a Meal Healthy Cookbook

# Easy Beef Stew

**Serves 6**

Prep time: 10 minutes
Cook time: 25 minutes
Total cost: $6.54
Calories: 162
Fat: 7g
Carbohydrates: 5g
Protein: 17g
Cholesterol: 49mg
Sodium: 365mg

3 tablespoons olive oil

1 onion, chopped

3 garlic cloves, minced

1 16-ounce package cooked roast beef, chopped

1 large can brown gravy

1 16-ounce package frozen mixed vegetables

1 10-ounce can cream of mushroom soup

2 cups water

½ tablespoon fresh thyme leaves, chopped

Sea salt and black pepper as needed

Stews are similar to soups, but stews are made with heartier ingredients such as potatoes and use thickeners such as flour or cornstarch.

1. In heavy large saucepan, heat olive oil over medium heat. Add onion and garlic; cook and stir until tender, 4 to 5 minutes. Add beef, gravy, mixed vegetables, soup, water, and thyme leaves.
2. Cook over medium-high heat until soup comes to a boil, about 8 minutes. Reduce heat to low and simmer for 7 minutes longer, until vegetables and beef are hot and tender. Serve immediately.

# Purée of Asparagus Soup

Serves 6

Prep time: 10 minutes
Cook time: 30 minutes
Total cost: $6.48
Calories: 218
Fat: 14g
Carbohydrates: 9g
Protein: 4g
Cholesterol: 27mg
Sodium: 432mg

2 tablespoons olive oil

1 medium onion, chopped

4 cloves garlic, chopped

1 bunch fresh asparagus, including stalks, chopped

Sea salt to taste

¼ cup white wine or sherry

3 cups vegetable broth

1 10-ounce package frozen peas

2 cups light sour cream

Black pepper to taste

1 teaspoon dried basil

The alcohol in the wine cooks off, but it also extracts flavors from the other ingredients surrounding it to make a very tasty dish.

1. In a large-quart boiler, heat olive oil over medium heat until fragrant, about 1 minute. Add onion, garlic, asparagus, and salt. Cook 8 minutes, until onions are translucent but not browned. Add wine or sherry and cook 1 minute. Add the broth. Simmer for 20 minutes, until asparagus is very tender. Remove from heat and stir in frozen peas.
2. Purée in food processor, in batches, until smooth. Transfer back to pot and heat to a simmer. Add sour cream, season with pepper and basil. Serve hot or cold.

The $7 a Meal Healthy Cookbook

# Vegetable Soup with Brown Rice

Serves 8

Prep time: 15 minutes

Cook time: 30 minutes

Total cost: $6.85

Calories: 141

Fat: 0.5g

Carbohydrates: 28g

Protein: 5g

Cholesterol: 2mg

Sodium: 139mg

1 tablespoon olive oil

½ cup yellow onions, diced

1 clove fresh garlic, minced

1 16-ounce package frozen California-blend vegetables

2 large baking potatoes, peeled and cubed

2 14- to 16-ounce cans vegetable broth

1 celery stalk, chopped

1 teaspoon dried Italian seasoning

1 teaspoon fresh oregano, leaves chopped

¼ cup fresh Italian flat-leaf parsley, leaves chopped

2 cups instant brown rice

2 cups water

Sea salt and black pepper to taste

Brown rice is similar to white rice in calories and carbohydrates, but, brown rice contains higher amounts of other nutrients such as vitamin B and magnesium.

In large boiler over medium heat, heat oil. Add onions and garlic and sauté until fragrant, about 3 minutes. Add vegetables, potatoes, broth, celery, herbs, rice, and water. Bring to a boil, reduce heat and simmer for 25 minutes, or until potatoes are tender. Add more water or broth, if needed. Season with salt and pepper as desired.

# New Orleans–Style Chicken Creole

Serves 6

Prep time: 12 minutes
Cook time: 35 minutes
Total cost: $6.94
Calories: 134
Fat: 2g
Carbohydrates: 12g
Protein: 19g
Cholesterol: 42mg
Sodium: 402mg

1 tablespoon olive oil

½ cup yellow onions, chopped

1 clove fresh garlic, minced

2 boneless, skinless chicken breasts, cut in cubes

1 red bell pepper, seeded and diced

1 green bell pepper, seeded and diced

1 stalk celery, chopped

2 tomatoes, diced

1 cup chicken broth

2 tablespoons fresh Italian flat-leaf parsley, leaves chopped

1 teaspoon fresh thyme, leaves chopped

¼ teaspoon cayenne pepper

1 cup okra, chopped (substitute green beans if you cannot find okra)

Sea salt and black pepper to taste

Creole cooking originated in Louisiana and blends cuisines from all over the world. It's usually served with rice, so feel free to add rice here. And, if your budget allows, throw in some cooked bay shrimp for an added bonus!

In large-quart boiler over medium heat, heat olive oil. Add onion and garlic and sauté for about 5 minutes, until tender. Add chicken and sauté until cooked through, about 6 to 7 minutes. Add remaining ingredients, stir to combine. Cover and simmer about 20 minutes or until flavors combine. Season with salt and pepper as desired.

# Mexican Beef Stew

 Serves 6

Prep time: 10 minutes
Cook time: 25 minutes
Total cost: $6.12
Calories: 162
Fat: 8g
Carbohydrates: 6g
Protein: 17g
Cholesterol: 49mg
Sodium: 365mg

2 tablespoons olive oil

1 yellow onion, chopped

1 pound ground beef

1 package taco seasoning

2 15-ounce cans chili beans, undrained

1 16-ounce package frozen corn

1 14-ounce can tomatoes with green chilies, undrained

2 cups water

1 tablespoon chili powder

½ teaspoon cumin

½ teaspoon cayenne pepper

Cumin is traditional to Indian, Mexican, and Cuban cuisines. A great source of iron, cumin brings out the sweetness of other ingredients in the recipe and helps balance out spicy foods.

In large saucepan over medium heat, heat olive oil. Add onions and sauté until tender, about 5 minutes. Add ground beef and cook until browned, about 5 minutes. Add remaining ingredients, stir, cover, and simmer for about 20 minutes, until flavors are combined.

# French Onion Soup

Serves 6

Prep time: 15 minutes
Cook time: 25 minutes
Total cost: $6.72
Calories: 498
Fat: 10g
Carbohydrates: 74g
Protein: 28g
Cholesterol: 20mg
Sodium: 132mg

2 tablespoons olive oil

2 tablespoons butter plus
  ¼ cup butter softened

2 large yellow onions, chopped

2 tablespoons plain flour

1 quart beef broth

6 slices French bread

1 tablespoon fresh Italian
  flat-leaf parsley

2 garlic cloves, minced

2 cups Gruyère cheese, shredded

French onion soup is traditionally made with Gruyère cheese, but if you prefer, you can substitute mozzarella or provolone for a milder flavor.

1. In large saucepan, combine olive oil and 2 tablespoons butter over medium heat until butter is foamy. Add onions; cook over medium heat for 10 minutes, stirring frequently, until onions brown around edges. Sprinkle flour over onions; cook and stir for 2 to 3 minutes.

2. Stir in broth, bring to a simmer, and cook for 10 minutes. Meanwhile, spread French bread slices with ¼ cup butter, parsley, and garlic. Toast bread until browned and crisp. Sprinkle with 1 cup cheese and toast until cheese melts. When serving soup, divide soup among bowls and top with remaining cheese. Float toasted cheese bread on top.

# Meatball Soup with Vegetables

Serves 6

Prep time: 10 minutes
Cook time: 20 minutes
Total cost: $6.96
Calories: 237
Fat: 4g
Carbohydrates: 23g
Protein: 27g
Cholesterol: 92mg
Sodium: 468mg

1 pound frozen meatballs

2 cups V8 juice or other tomato juice blend

2 cups frozen mixed vegetables

1½ cups beef broth

3 cups water

½ teaspoon dried Italian seasoning

½ teaspoon black pepper

1 cup vermicelli pasta noodles

This hearty soup is perfect for kids, as it contains many of their favorite ingredients, such as meatballs and pasta. Serve this as a quick snack after school instead of less healthy potato chips or fast food.

In large-quart boiler, combine all ingredients except pasta and mix gently. Bring to a boil over high heat, reduce heat, and let simmer for 10 minutes. Add pasta and simmer an additional 10 minutes, until pasta is tender.

# Corn Chowder with Pepper Jack Cheese

Serves 6

Prep time: 10 minutes
Cook time: 15 minutes
Total cost: $4.90
Calories: 370
Fat: 10g
Carbohydrates: 40g
Protein: 6g
Cholesterol: 35mg
Sodium: 671mg

2 tablespoons olive oil

1 yellow onion, chopped

1 package taco seasoning mix

2 cups canned creamed corn

2 10-ounce cans chicken broth

1½ cups water

2 cups shredded pepper jack cheese

2 tablespoons plain flour

Serve this soup with salsa, sour cream, or chopped avocado.

1. In large-quart boiler, heat olive oil over medium heat. Add onion and sauté until crisp-tender, about 4 minutes. Sprinkle taco seasoning mix over the onions and stir. Then add corn, chicken broth, and water. Bring to a simmer and cook for 10 minutes, stirring occasionally.
2. Meanwhile, in medium bowl, toss cheese with flour. Add to soup and lower heat; cook and stir for 2 to 3 minutes, until cheese is melted and soup is thickened. Serve hot.

**Cooking Tip**
Stir melting cheese frequently as it tends to burn if it rests too long over heat.

The $7 a Meal Healthy Cookbook

# Potato Corn Chowder with Red Bell Peppers

 Serves 6

Prep time: 10 minutes
Cook time: 25 minutes
Total cost: $7.00
Calories: 370
Fat: 9g
Carbohydrates: 32g
Protein: 15g
Cholesterol: 31mg
Sodium: 817mg

4 ears sweet corn, shucked, kernels cut, cobs reserved

1 tablespoon olive oil

1 large onion, chopped

1 red bell pepper, seeded and chopped

2 stalks celery, chopped

6 red potatoes, cut into 1-inch chunks

3 sprigs fresh thyme, leaves chopped

1 bay leaf

3 teaspoons sea salt

1 teaspoon chili powder

4 ounces (1 stick) unsalted butter

8 cups vegetable broth or water

4 teaspoons cornstarch mixed in ¼ cup water

8 cups nonfat milk

White pepper to taste

½ bunch fresh chives, chopped

If your budget allows, add fresh seafood such as clams for an easy clam chowder.

1. Cut corn kernels from the cob using a slicing motion, going down the cob, with a large chef's knife. Reserve the cobs and set kernels aside. In a large-quart boiler over medium heat, heat olive oil until fragrant, about 1 minute. Add corn cobs, onion, bell pepper, celery, potatoes, thyme, bay leaf, salt, and chili powder. Cook for 8 minutes. Add butter and cook gently, allowing vegetables to stew in the butter, about 5 minutes.

2. Add the vegetable stock. Increase heat to high heat and bring to a full boil. Allow to boil for 1 minute, then reduce heat to simmer and cook for 10 minutes. Remove the corn cobs, add cornstarch mixture and simmer 5 minutes more. Stir in the milk, and adjust seasoning with salt and white pepper to taste. Serve sprinkled with chives.

# Black Bean Soup

Serves 6

Prep time: 10 minutes
Cook time: 18 minutes
Total cost: $4.83
Calories: 171
Fat: 2g
Carbohydrates: 23g
Protein: 8g
Cholesterol: 3mg
Sodium: 551mg

2 tablespoons olive oil

1 yellow onion, chopped

3 cloves garlic, minced

2 15-ounce cans black beans, drained and rinsed

1 14-ounce can tomatoes, with juice

5 cups chicken broth

1 teaspoon Tabasco sauce

Sea salt and white pepper to taste

White pepper has more heat than black pepper so use more sparingly. Chefs use white pepper often when making cream sauces or other dishes that are white so as not to ruin the color of the dish with black pepper flakes.

In large saucepan over medium heat, heat olive oil. Add onion and garlic. Cook for 2 to 3 minutes, stirring occasionally. Add beans to saucepan along with other ingredients. Bring to a simmer and cook for 12 minutes. Stir to combine and serve.

**Sherry Wine**
When serving this soup, add a bit of low-fat sour cream and a splash of sherry wine for the perfect finish to this traditional Caribbean dish.

The $7 a Meal Healthy Cookbook

# Three-Bean Chili

 Serves 6

Prep time: 10 minutes
Cook time: 18 minutes
Total cost: $6.28
Calories: 362
Fat: 3g
Carbohydrates: 31g
Protein: 11g
Cholesterol: 2mg
Sodium: 849mg

2 tablespoons olive oil

1 yellow onion, chopped

1 package taco seasoning

2 15-ounce cans dark red kidney beans, drained

2 15-ounce cans black beans, drained

2 15-ounce cans white beans, drained

2 14-ounce canned diced tomatoes with green chiles, undrained

1 cup water

For added protein and flavor, add ground beef or ground turkey right after you sauté the onions. Cook for about 5 to 6 minutes until cooked through, then add remaining ingredients and finish cooking as directed.

In heavy saucepan over medium heat, add olive oil and sauté onion until tender, about 4 to 5 minutes. Sprinkle taco seasoning mix over onions; cook and stir for 1 minute. Add drained beans, tomatoes, and water. Bring to a simmer; cook for 10 to 12 minutes, until thickened and blended.

**Taco Seasoning**

Taco seasoning is a blend of spices and herbs. If you don't have any at home, make your own by combining chili powder, onion powder, garlic powder, a little cornstarch, dried oregano, dried red pepper flakes, a little sea salt, and cumin. If you make a bunch, store in a cool, dry place for longer use. Taco seasoning spices up ground beef and soups, and can even be used as a dry marinade for chicken or steak, and to season popcorn.

# Tortellini Soup with Sausage

Serves 6

Prep time: 10 minutes
Cook time: 18 minutes
Total cost: $6.72
Calories: 302
Fat: 28g
Carbohydrates: 56g
Protein: 29g
Cholesterol: 91mg
Sodium: 1,304mg

1 pound sweet Italian bulk sausage

1 8-ounce jar sliced mushrooms

4 cloves garlic, minced

3 14-ounce cans beef broth

1½ cups water

1 teaspoon dried Italian seasoning

½ teaspoon black pepper

1 24-ounce package frozen cheese tortellini

You can also add marinara or cheese sauce to this recipe. Just be aware that if you use cheese sauce, you may need to exercise a few minutes more to burn off those extra calories.

1. In large saucepan over medium heat, brown sausage with mushrooms and garlic, stirring to break up sausage. When sausage is cooked, drain thoroughly. Add broth, water, Italian seasoning, and pepper, and bring to a boil over high heat. Reduce heat to low and simmer for 8 to 10 minutes.
2. Stir in frozen tortellini and cook, stirring frequently, over medium-high heat for 10 minutes or until tortellini are hot and tender. Serve immediately.

# CHAPTER 7

## CHICKEN AND TURKEY ENTRÉES

# Chicken Curry with Basmati Rice

Serves 5

Prep time: 10 minutes
Cook time: 25 minutes
Total cost: $6.85
Calories: 250
Fat: 2g
Carbohydrates: 21g
Protein: 35g
Cholesterol: 4mg
Sodium: 240mg

2 cups basmati rice

4 cups water

Sea salt and red pepper flakes to taste

2 cloves garlic, chopped

1 yellow onion, chopped

Juice of 1 lemon

1 teaspoon cumin

½ cup fresh Italian parsley, chopped

1 cup low-fat yogurt

1 tablespoon curry powder

Tabasco to taste

1 pound boneless chicken breasts, skin removed, cut into 1- to 2-inch cubes

Curry is a blend of many spices, including turmeric and coriander, and is native to India.

1. Place rice and water in quart boiler. Bring to a boil, stir, reduce heat, cover, and simmer about 15 minutes. Add the salt and pepper flakes, garlic, onion, lemon juice, cumin, and parsley. Stir to combine, cover, and simmer an additional 2 to 3 minutes, if needed.
2. Turn broiler to high. In mixing bowl, combine yogurt, curry, and Tabasco. Toss chicken to coat. Place on aluminum foil and place under broiler for 5 minutes. Turn chicken and broil an additional 5 minutes or as needed until cooked through.
3. Mix cooked chicken into the rice and serve.

# Skillet Chicken with Rice

Serves 4

Prep time: 10 minutes
Cook time: 15 minutes
Total cost: $5.68
Calories: 420
Fat: 11g
Carbohydrates: 43g
Protein: 34g
Cholesterol: 6mg
Sodium: 570mg

3 boneless chicken breast halves, skin removed

1 tablespoon olive oil

1 15-ounce jar mild or medium salsa

¾ cup chicken broth

½ cup green bell pepper, seeded and chopped

1 cup quick-cooking rice

Sea salt and lemon pepper to taste

Lemon pepper really does taste lemony and is a nice change from black pepper. It's great with chicken, fish, beef, and even on popcorn!

Cut the chicken into 1-inch cubes. Heat oil in large skillet and sauté chicken until cooked, about 8 minutes. Stir in salsa, chicken broth, and green pepper. Bring to a boil. Stir in the uncooked rice. Let stand, covered, 5 minutes until rice is cooked. Season with salt and lemon pepper.

**Salsa!**
Salsa is packed full of flavor and is low in calories and fat. Use salsa to spice up eggs, grilled fish, and poultry dishes.

# Wild Rice Salad with Chicken and Walnuts

Serves 4

Prep time: 10 minutes
Cook time: 15 minutes
Total cost: $5.84
Calories: 332
Fat: 13g
Carbohydrates: 19g
Protein: 34g
Cholesterol: 93mg
Sodium: 365mg

1 4.3-ounce package wild rice

¼ cup olive oil

3 tablespoons balsamic vinegar

3 cups cooked chicken, cut into bite-sized pieces

4 scallions, chopped

3 tablespoons Parmesan cheese, grated

Juice of 1 lemon

½ cup toasted walnuts, whole or chopped

1 cup cherry tomatoes, sliced

**Chill**
**Up to 1 hour**

Wild rice grains come from species of plants that grow in small lakes and streams. Wild rice is naturally high in protein and fiber and low in fat.

1. Prepare rice according to package directions. In small bowl, whisk together oil, vinegar, and lemon. When rice is ready, stir in the chicken and scallions; add the vinegar mixture and cheese. Toss well to coat. Pour into a serving dish and chill for up to 1 hour.
2. Garnish salad with walnuts and cherry tomatoes.

---

**Cooking Wild Rice**

Certain grains of wild rice take up to 45 minutes to cook. Read the package directions when purchasing to make sure you buy quick-cooking wild rice.

# Chicken Casserole with Red Bell Peppers

Serves 6

Prep time: 10 minutes
Cook time: 15 minutes
Total cost: $6.97
Calories: 270
Fat: 15g
Carbohydrates: 13g
Protein: 23g
Cholesterol: 39mg
Sodium: 680mg

2 cups cooked chicken, cubed

2 cups celery, sliced

¼ cup almonds, chopped

½ teaspoon sea salt

½ yellow onion, finely chopped

Juice of 1 lemon

1 cup low-fat mayonnaise

1 red bell pepper, seeded and diced

½ cup Cheddar cheese, shredded

1½ cups crushed potato chips

Casseroles usually take tons of time to bake. With pre-cooked chicken, you save about an hour of cooking time.

Preheat oven to 425°F. In lightly greased shallow quart baking dish, combine the chicken, celery, almonds, salt, onions, lemon juice, mayonnaise, and red bell peppers. Sprinkle with cheese and potato chips. Bake for 15 minutes or until heated through.

# Pasta with Chicken and Tomatoes

Serves 6

Prep time: 12 minutes
Cook time: 20 minutes
Total cost: $7.00
Calories: 334
Fat: 12g
Carbohydrates: 42g
Protein: 20g
Cholesterol: 31mg
Sodium: 432mg

2 tablespoons extra-virgin olive oil

6 cloves garlic, chopped

3 large boneless chicken breasts, skin removed

3 cups chicken broth

3 Roma tomatoes, diced

¼ cup fresh Italian parsley, leaves chopped

2 green onions, chopped

Sea salt and black pepper to taste

¼ cup unsalted butter, softened

1 pound penne pasta

Cooking pasta al dente means the pasta is cooked but still slightly firm. Overcooking pasta releases the starch and the pasta becomes pasty and mushy.

1. In a large, deep skillet, heat the oil over medium heat. Add the garlic and chicken and sauté until chicken is cooked through. Remove the chicken from the pan, cut it into 1-inch cubes, and reserve.
2. Pour the chicken stock into a saucepan and add the tomatoes, parsley, and green onions. Add salt and pepper to taste. Bring to a boil and reduce over high heat 5 to 10 minutes. Add the chicken to the pan and whisk in the butter. Turn heat to low to keep warm.
3. Meanwhile, bring a large pot filled ¾ with water to a boil. Add 1 tablespoon salt plus a drizzle of oil. Add the penne; stir to prevent sticking. Cook until al dente. Drain.
4. In a bowl toss the penne with the chicken mixture and serve.

The $7 a Meal Healthy Cookbook

# Lemon-Herbed Chicken

 Serves 5

Prep time: 10 minutes
Cook time: 15 minutes
Total cost: $5.65
Calories: 398
Fat: 6g
Carbohydrates: 44g
Protein: 18g
Cholesterol: 21mg
Sodium: 671mg

4 boneless chicken breasts, skin removed

1 10-ounce can cream of chicken soup

½ can water

1 teaspoon curry powder

Juice of 1 lemon

1 cup low-fat mayonnaise

1 8-ounce package herb stuffing mix

Baked chicken casseroles were a staple in my household growing up. They are easy to prepare and can be made ahead of time. Try cubing the chicken when making this for kids.

Preheat oven to 350°F. Lay chicken breasts in a 9" x 12" casserole. Combine the soup and water in a small bowl. Pour the soup mixture over chicken. Mix the remaining ingredients into the stuffing mix. Spread the stuffing mix over the chicken. Bake 1 hour. If the stuffing gets too brown, cover loosely with aluminum foil.

# Chicken and Vegetable Skewers

**Serves 4**

| | |
|---|---|
| Prep time: 15 minutes | 1 tablespoon lemon juice |
| Cook time: 8 minutes | 1 tablespoon water |
| Total cost: $6.79 | 1 tablespoon olive oil |

Prep time: 15 minutes
Cook time: 8 minutes
Total cost: $6.79
Calories: 181
Fat: 7g
Carbohydrates: 8g
Protein: 26g
Cholesterol: 72mg
Sodium: 64mg

**Marinate
20 minutes**

1 tablespoon lemon juice

1 tablespoon water

1 tablespoon olive oil

Sea salt and black pepper to taste

1 clove garlic, chopped

4 boneless chicken breasts, skin removed, cut into 1-inch cubes

1 red bell pepper, seeded and cut into 1-inch squares

2 zucchini, cut into 1-inch-thick slices

1 yellow onion, quartered, then quartered again

8 to 10 8-inch wooden skewers, soaked in water

If you are making these for a party, make some with chicken, some vegetarian, and some with shrimp. The vegetarian and shrimp skewers will cook faster, so grill the chicken skewers first.

1. In a small bowl, combine the lemon juice, water, oil, salt, and garlic. Place the chicken in a Ziploc bag and set in a deep bowl. Pour the lemon juice mixture into the bag, secure the top closed, and let the chicken stand for 20 minutes at room temperature, turning the bag frequently.

2. Preheat the broiler. Drain the chicken, reserving the marinade. Thread the chicken, bell pepper, zucchini, and onion alternately onto skewers. Arrange the skewers on a broiler pan. Slip under the broiler 4 to 5 inches from the heat source. Broil, turning once, and brush with the reserved marinade until the chicken is tender and cooked through, about 8 minutes. Serve immediately. Discard any remaining marinade.

The $7 a Meal Healthy Cookbook

# Pasta Primavera with Breast of Chicken

Serves 4

Prep time: 15 minutes
Cook time: 15 minutes
Total cost: $6.68
Calories: 382
Fat: 12g
Carbohydrates: 53g
Protein: 12g
Cholesterol: 20mg
Sodium: 266mg

1 tablespoon olive oil

2 yellow onions, chopped

2 green bell peppers, seeded and chopped

1 clove garlic, chopped

2 zucchini squash, chopped

2 yellow summer squash, chopped

3 Roma tomatoes, chopped

¼ cup fresh basil leaves, chopped

Sea salt and black pepper to taste

1 tablespoon plain flour

½ cup low-fat milk

½ cup low-fat sour cream

3 cups cooked chicken breasts, cubed

½ cup chicken broth

1 pound rotini pasta

Pasta primavera typically is made with light flavors, aromatic herbs, and colorful vegetables.

1. In a large, deep skillet, heat the oil over medium heat. Add the onions, bell peppers, and garlic and sauté 3 minutes. Add the zucchini and yellow squash and sauté 1 minute. Add the tomatoes and basil and cook briefly, just until the tomatoes soften. Season with salt and pepper to taste.
2. In a small bowl, mix together flour with 2 tablespoons of vegetable juices. Stir well so that there are no lumps and the mixture is smooth. Add flour mixture to vegetables, add milk and sour cream, stirring constantly. Add cooked vegetables, chicken, and chicken broth. Stir to combine. Bring to a simmer over low heat and cook 2 to 3 minutes until chicken is heated through.
3. Meanwhile, in a large pot, bring at least 4 quarts of water to a rolling boil. Add 1 tablespoon salt. Add the pasta, stir, and cook until al dente. Drain. Transfer the hot pasta to a serving platter and spoon the chicken and vegetable mixture over the top.

# Crispy Chicken Tenders

Serves 4

Prep time: 10 minutes
Cook time: 25 minutes
Total cost: $6.60
Calories: 470
Fat: 18g
Carbohydrates: 36g
Protein: 33g
Cholesterol: 63mg
Sodium: 378mg

12 ounces potato chips

1 teaspoon freshly ground black pepper

2 tablespoons fresh chives, chopped

1 teaspoon fresh thyme, leaves chopped

1 pound chicken tenders, cut into 1- to 2-inch cubes

⅔ cup low-fat sour cream

These tasty chicken tenders are easy to make and are perfect as appetizers or for kids' after-school snacks.

1. In a food processor, chop potato chips until you have 1 cup crumbs. Mix crumbs together with pepper, chives, and thyme.
2. Preheat oven to 350°F. Coat baking dish with butter or spray with nonstick cooking spray. Lay in chicken. Coat chicken with sour cream, then sprinkle with potato chip mixture. Bake in oven for 25 minutes or until browned and crispy.

**Healthy Tip**
Even though these chicken tenders are coated with potato chips, they are baked as opposed to fried, which saves a load of added fat, calories, and cleanup time.

# Grilled Ginger Chicken

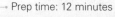 Serves 4

4 boneless, skinless chicken breasts

Juice of 3 lemons

½ cup canola oil

¼ cup soy sauce

1 teaspoon grated gingerroot or 1 tablespoon ground ginger

1 teaspoon onion salt

¼ teaspoon garlic powder

**Marinate**
4 hours

Fresh gingerroot is best for this recipe and is relatively inexpensive. Buy some fresh root and keep what you don't use in your freezer!

1. Place chicken in a shallow baking dish. In a small bowl, combine the lemon juice, oil, soy sauce, ginger, onion, and garlic powder. Pour over the chicken. Cover and refrigerate at least 4 hours or overnight, turning occasionally.
2. Grill or broil for about 20 minutes, turning after 10 minutes. Cook until the meat is no longer pink and the juices run clear.

**Food Safety Tip**
Throw away any leftover marinade as it has been contaminated by the raw chicken meat and could contain salmonella.

# Skillet Chicken with Broccoli

Serves 4

Prep time: 10 minutes
Cook time: 20 minutes
Total cost: $6.99
Calories: 382
Fat: 11g
Carbohydrates: 26g
Protein: 28g
Cholesterol: 6mg
Sodium: 760mg

1 tablespoon olive oil

4 boneless chicken breast halves, skin removed

1 10-ounce can cream of broccoli soup

¼ cup low-fat milk

Juice of 1 lemon

Pinch black pepper

1 small head of broccoli, largely chopped

4 thin lemon slices

I prefer to cook with an iron skillet—you get better flavor and iron skillets heat evenly, therefore cooking the food more evenly.

Heat the oil in a skillet. Sauté the chicken breasts about 10 minutes, until browned on both sides. Pour off the fat. Combine the soup, milk, lemon juice, and pepper. Add broccoli to chicken. Pour soup mixture over the chicken. Top each chicken piece with a slice of lemon. Reduce heat to low and cover. Simmer 5 to 10 minutes until chicken is tender, stirring occasionally.

# Kung Pao Chicken

Serves 4

Prep time: 10 minutes
Cook time: 15 minutes
Total cost: $6.90
Calories: 260
Fat: 16g
Carbohydrates: 15g
Protein: 17g
Cholesterol: 70mg
Sodium: 338mg

3 boneless chicken breasts, skin removed

1½ tablespoons peanut oil

1 dried red chili

⅓ cup peanuts

2 tablespoons water

2 tablespoons dry sherry

1 tablespoon soy sauce

1 teaspoon sugar

1 tablespoon chili sauce

1 teaspoon fresh ginger, peeled and chopped

2 cloves garlic, minced

2 scallions, chopped

2 teaspoons rice or apple cider vinegar

1 teaspoon sesame oil

4 cups cooked white rice

This recipe calls for both peanut and sesame oil, which are flavorful and healthy oils used mainly in Asian cooking. Use peanut oil for frying potatoes and sesame oil in Asian vinaigrettes.

Dice the chicken into 1-inch cubes. Heat the oil in a wok or skillet and add the chili. Add the chicken and peanuts and stir-fry until the chicken is cooked. Add the remaining ingredients, except the sesame oil and rice, and bring to a boil. Cook for a few minutes. Add the sesame oil and serve over rice.

# Chicken with Teriyaki Sauce

Serves 6

Prep time: 10 minutes
Cook time: 20 minutes
Total cost: $6.58
Calories: 195
Fat: 8g
Carbohydrates: 17g
Protein: 16g
Cholesterol: 12mg
Sodium: 722mg

½ cup Italian dressing

½ cup teriyaki sauce

5 boneless, skinless chicken breasts

**Marinate**
Overnight

This is the perfect recipe to serve over rice with a side of grilled vegetables.

Combine the Italian dressing and teriyaki sauce. Marinate the chicken in dressing mixture overnight. Grill over hot grill for about 20 minutes, turning chicken after 10 minutes. Cook until the meat is no longer pink and the juices run clear.

**Marinades**
The Italian dressing in this recipe mellows out the sometimes harsh, strong flavors of the teriyaki. Use this combination for other proteins such as steak and pork.

# Chicken with Mushrooms in Marinara

 Serves 6

Prep time: 10 minutes
Cook time: 50 minutes
Total cost: $6.89
Calories: 346
Fat: 6g
Carbohydrates: 25g
Protein: 32g
Cholesterol: 95mg
Sodium: 451mg

1 cup plain flour

Sea salt and black pepper

1 teaspoon fresh oregano, leaves chopped

¼ cup olive oil

1 teaspoon butter

1 yellow onion, diced

2 to 3 cloves garlic, minced

1 tablespoon fresh rosemary, leaves chopped

2 cups cremini or button mushrooms, brushed and chopped

5 boneless, skinless chicken breasts, cut into 2-inch pieces

1 16-ounce jar marinara sauce

½ cup red wine

½ cup Parmesan cheese

1 bunch fresh Italian parsley, chopped, for garnish

Make your own marinara sauce by combining 1 to 2 cans of diced tomatoes with a tablespoon or two of fresh herbs such as oregano and basil.

1. In mixing bowl, combine flour, salt, pepper, and oregano. Heat the oil and butter in large skillet over medium heat until butter melts. Add onion, garlic, rosemary, and mushrooms and saute for 5 minutes. Add chicken and sauté an additional 5 minutes.
2. Add the marinara sauce and red wine. Cover and simmer over low heat for 45 minutes. Remove cover and place chicken on platter; simmer sauce an additional 10 minutes. Serve by spooning sauce over chicken. Sprinkle with cheese and fresh parsley.

# Chicken and Vegetable Stir-Fry

**Serves 4**

Prep time: 15 minutes
Cook time: 10 minutes
Total cost: $6.44
Calories: 367
Fat: 11g
Carbohydrates: 21g
Protein: 29g
Cholesterol: 82mg
Sodium: 627mg

2 tablespoons red wine

1 tablespoon soy sauce

½ teaspoon cornstarch

1 teaspoon sugar

1 tablespoon sea salt

1 tablespoon peanut oil

2 cups blanched broccoli florets

1 red bell pepper, seeded and chopped

½ cup yellow onion, sliced

6 ounces boneless chicken breasts, skin removed, cut into thin strips

2 cups cooked rice

Stir-fry is a healthy way to cook. If you don't have a wok, don't worry; a skillet works fine.

1. In a small bowl, make the sauce by combining the red wine, soy sauce, cornstarch, sugar, and salt. Stir to dissolve the cornstarch. Set aside. In a wok or saucepan, heat the oil; add the broccoli, bell pepper, and onion. Cook, stirring quickly and frequently, until vegetables are tender and crisp and onions are browned. Stir in the chicken and stir-fry 2 more minutes.
2. Add the sauce to the chicken mixture and cook, stirring constantly, until the sauce is thickened, 2 to 3 minutes. Serve each portion over ½ cup cooked rice.

### Blanching Vegetables
Blanching vegetables is a process that brings out the color of the vegetable while at the same time making them tender. Be sure not to overcook them as the vegetables will become mushy and not good for stir-fry.

The $7 a Meal Healthy Cookbook

# Chicken Piccatta

Serves 4

Prep time: 12 minutes
Cook time: 20 minutes
Total cost: $5.98
Calories: 202
Fat: 9g
Carbohydrates: 7g
Protein: 24g
Cholesterol: 50mg
Sodium: 721mg

4 boneless, chicken breast halves, skin removed

Sea salt and black pepper to taste

2 tablespoons butter

1 teaspoon olive oil

½ cup chicken broth

¼ cup vermouth

Juice of 1 lemon

1 tablespoon capers, drained and rinsed

Lemon slices for garnish, if desired

Picatta is a cooking style using lemon, capers, and wine and is traditional to Italian cuisine. This recipe uses chicken, but you can also substitute veal or pork.

1. Pat chicken dry. Season with salt and pepper. Melt butter with oil in a large heavy skillet over medium-high heat. Add the chicken and cook until springy to the touch, about 4 minutes per side. Remove from the skillet; keep warm.
2. Increase heat to high. Stir the broth and vermouth into the skillet. Boil until reduced by half, scraping up any browned bits. Remove from the heat. Mix in the lemon juice and capers. Place the chicken on plates and pour the sauce over the chicken. Garnish the chicken with lemon slices.

# Grilled Turkey Cutlets with Lime

Serves 6

Prep time: 12 minutes
Cook time: 7 minutes
Total cost: $6.48
Calories: 229
Fat: 4g
Carbohydrates: 8g
Protein: 28g
Cholesterol: 75mg
Sodium: 130mg

2 large limes: 1 lime zested and juiced, 1 lime cut in wedges

⅓ cup plain yogurt

1 tablespoon canola oil

2 teaspoons fresh gingerroot, peeled, chopped

1 teaspoon ground cumin

1 teaspoon ground coriander

1 teaspoon sea salt

1 clove garlic, crushed

1½ pounds turkey cutlets

Fresh cilantro sprigs for garnish

The flavors of lime and cilantro complement one another and bring life to this simple recipe. You can also add a hint of other citrus flavors, such as lemon and orange juice or zest, for another layer of flavor.

1. Heat grill. Place zest and juice in a large bowl. Add yogurt, oil, ginger, cumin, coriander, salt, and garlic to bowl with zest and juice. Mix until blended.
2. Add the turkey cutlets to the bowl with the yogurt mixture, stirring to coat the cutlets. Do not marinate as their texture will become mealy.
3. Place the turkey cutlets on grill. Cook cutlets 5 to 7 minutes until they just lose their pink color throughout. Serve with lime wedges. Garnish with cilantro sprigs.

**Turkey Cutlets**

Turkey cutlets are a choice cut that are perfect for the grill as they are not typically as thick as chicken and, therefore, take less time to cook.

# Low-Fat Turkey Tetrazzini

 Serves 6

- Prep time: 10 minutes
- Cook time: 45 minutes
- Total cost: $6.72
- Calories: 329
- Fat: 3g
- Carbohydrates: 37g
- Protein: 17g
- Cholesterol: 30mg
- Sodium: 339mg

8 ounces linguine pasta

8 cremini or button mushrooms, brushed, stems removed, and sliced

3 cups cooked turkey, chopped

4 tablespoons unsalted butter

¼ cup plain flour

Sea salt and black pepper to taste

2¼ cups chicken broth

1 cup low-fat milk

½ cup nonfat sour cream

½ cup Parmesan cheese, grated

Chicken Tetrazzini was so named for famed Italian opera star, Luisa Tetrazzini: An executive chef at the hotel she frequented in New York created this delicious dish just for her. I substitute turkey here, along with low-fat milk and nonfat sour cream for a healthy yet still flavorful meal.

1. Break the spaghetti into pieces and cook according to package directions, but undercook slightly. Drain. In a large bowl, toss the drained noodles with the mushrooms and turkey. Preheat oven to 350°F. Melt the butter over low heat. Stir in the flour, salt, and pepper, and cook until the mixture is bubbly. Remove the pan from the heat, and stir in the broth, milk, and sour cream. Stirring constantly, heat the sauce until it boils; boil 1 minute.
2. Pour the sauce over the noodle mixture and mix thoroughly. Place mixture in an 8" x 11" baking dish. Sprinkle the Parmesan cheese on top. Bake about 45 minutes, or until hot and bubbly in the center.

# Sautéed Turkey Breast with Linguine Pasta

Serves 6

2 teaspoons olive oil

1 yellow onion, chopped

3 cloves garlic, chopped

1 pound boneless turkey breast, skin removed, cut into bite-sized pieces

1 tablespoon fresh basil, chopped

½ teaspoon fresh thyme, leaves chopped

½ teaspoon fresh rosemary, leaves chopped

12 kalamata olives, pitted and chopped

1 tablespoon capers, drained

2 tomatoes, chopped

2 cups chicken broth

1 tablespoon sea salt

¾ pound linguine pasta

½ cup Parmesan cheese, grated

Caper berries are the bud of the caper plant. When the buds are ripe, they are picked, salted, and pickled.

1. In a large, deep skillet, heat the oil over medium heat. Add the onion and garlic and cook until the onion is translucent. Add the turkey, basil, thyme, and rosemary and sauté until the turkey is lightly browned. Stir in the olives, capers, and tomatoes and cook briefly, until the tomatoes begin to give off liquid. Remove the turkey from the skillet. Add the chicken stock, bring to a boil, and simmer over medium heat until the broth is reduced by half. Return the turkey to the sauce and stir well.
2. Meanwhile, in a large pot, bring at least 4 quarts of water to a rolling boil. Add 1 tablespoon salt. Add the linguine, stir to separate, and cook until al dente. Drain.
3. Transfer the linguine to the skillet and toss with the sauce until the sauce is evenly distributed. Transfer to a warm serving dish, top with the cheese, and serve.

# Ground Turkey Sausage with Bow Tie Pasta

Serves 4

Prep time: 15 minutes
Cook time: 20 minutes
Total cost: $7.00
Calories: 483
Fat: 12g
Carbohydrates: 24g
Protein: 29g
Cholesterol: 66mg
Sodium: 1862mg

1 tablespoon olive oil

1 yellow onion, chopped

2 cloves garlic, chopped

1 green bell pepper, seeded and julienned (cut into strips)

12 ounces boneless turkey breasts, skin removed, cut into ½-inch wide pieces

½ pound sweet or hot turkey sausages, cut crosswise into ½-inch-thick pieces

1 16-ounce can Italian plum tomatoes, with juice, chopped

¼ cup dry red wine

½ teaspoon fresh oregano, leaves chopped

¼ teaspoon fresh basil, leaves chopped

1 teaspoon sugar

1 tablespoon salt

12 ounces bow tie pasta (farfalle)

½ cup low-fat milk

½ cup nonfat sour cream

Sea salt and black pepper to taste

Fresh herbs make a huge difference in cooking, as their flavors are sharp and crisp.

1. In a large, deep skillet, heat the oil over medium heat. Add the onion, garlic, and bell pepper and sauté until just softened. Add the turkey and sausage and sauté until slightly browned. Add the tomatoes with the juice, wine, oregano, basil, and sugar. Bring to a boil, lower the heat, and simmer gently, stirring occasionally, for 10 minutes or until the tomatoes cook down and thicken slightly.
2. Meanwhile, in a large pot, bring at least 4 quarts of water to a rolling boil. Add 1 tablespoon salt. Add the farfalle and stir to prevent sticking. Cook until al dente. Drain.
3. Stir in the milk, sour cream, and salt and pepper to taste to the tomato sauce and simmer for 3 minutes, or until it thickens slightly. Add pasta to tomato sauce and toss well.

# Baked Lasagna with Ground Turkey

Serves 8

Prep time: 10 minutes
Cook time: 1 hour
Total cost: $7.00
Calories: 315
Fat: 11g
Carbohydrates: 29g
Protein: 36g
Cholesterol: 185mg
Sodium: 885mg

1 8-ounce box lasagna noodles

1 tablespoon olive oil

1 large zucchini, sliced

1 large squash, sliced

1 cup broccoli florets

¾ pound ground turkey

3 cups marinara sauce

1¾ cups ricotta cheese

2 eggs, slightly beaten

½ teaspoon dried basil

½ teaspoon oregano

1 tablespoon butter for coating baking dish

16 ounces (2 cups) shredded mozzarella cheese

¼ cup Parmesan cheese

Drizzle a little olive oil on cooked noodles to prevent them from sticking together while you assemble the lasagna.

1. Boil lasagna noodles until softened. While boiling, heat oil in skillet or saucepan over medium heat. Add vegetables and sauté until they begin to brown and are tender. Remove vegetables from heat and set aside.
2. Add turkey to skillet and cook over medium heat until browned. Drain some of the fat from the pan and stir in marinara sauce.
3. In small bowl, stir together ricotta, eggs, basil, and oregano.
4. Spread ¾ cup of turkey and marinara sauce mixture into buttered 13" x 9" x 2" baking dish.
5. Place three pieces of lasagna crosswise over sauce. Spread ⅔ cup ricotta mixture, then ¾ cup turkey sauce, then ½ cup vegetables evenly over pasta. Sprinkle with 1 cup mozzarella and half of the Parmesan cheese. Repeat with remaining ingredients.
6. Cover with foil and bake for 30 minutes. Remove foil. Bake 10–15 minutes more until bubbly.

The $7 a Meal Healthy Cookbook

# Walnut-Crusted Turkey Risotto

Serves 8

Prep time: 10 minutes
Cook time: 25 to 30 mins.
Total cost: $6.98
Calories: 339
Fat: 13g
Carbohydrates: 39g
Protein: 24g
Cholesterol: 54mg
Sodium: 102mg

3 tablespoons olive oil

1½ pounds boneless turkey, cut into 1-inch pieces

Sea salt and black pepper to taste

1 egg, beaten

1 cup walnuts, finely chopped

4 cloves garlic, minced

1½ cups arborio rice

¾ cup Pinot Grigio or Sauvignon Blanc

4 cups chicken broth, plus 1 to 2 cups, if needed

½ bunch fresh Italian parsley, chopped

½ cup Parmesan cheese, grated

1 tablespoon butter, unsalted

To get the proper creaminess of risotto, add the liquid a little at a time and stir frequently.

1. Preheat oven to 375°F. Lightly grease a baking pan with 1 tablespoon of the oil. Season the turkey with salt and pepper. Dip turkey in the egg, and lightly coat with nuts. Heat 1 tablespoon of the oil in a large saucepan. Lightly brown the turkey on each side, about 3 minutes per side. Transfer turkey to baking dish and bake for about 10 minutes, or until cooked through.

2. Add the remaining 1 tablespoon of oil to the saucepan and heat to medium. Add the garlic and rice; stir for 1 minute. Pour in the wine and stir until completely absorbed. Add the broth ½ cup at a time, stirring frequently and allowing each addition to be completely absorbed before adding the next. (You will be able to tell because the rice will begin to make that "sticking" sound.) Continue until all broth is absorbed and rice is tender. This process will take about 20 minutes. Remove from heat; add turkey, parsley, cheese, and butter.

# Skillet Picadillo with Turkey

Serves 6

Prep time: 10 minutes

Cook time: 15 minutes

Total cost: $6.78

Calories: 222

Fat: 11g

Carbohydrates: 14g

Protein: 25g

Cholesterol: 35mg

Sodium: 232mg

2 tablespoons olive oil

1½ pounds ground turkey

1 clove fresh garlic, minced

½ teaspoon all-purpose seasoning

1 cup yellow onions, chopped

1 large tomato, diced

1 tablespoon tomato paste

2 teaspoons cumin

¼ cup fresh cilantro, leaves chopped

¼ cup golden raisins

1 cup baking potatoes, cut into 1-inch cubes

1 cup water

Picadillo is a Cuban dish usually made with ground beef. This lean turkey version is lower in fat and calories but maintains the delicious flavor.

1. In large skillet over medium heat, heat 1 tablespoon olive oil. Add turkey, olive oil, garlic, and all-purpose seasoning to skillet. Cook on medium-high for 5 to 8 minutes, using a spatula to stir and chop turkey meat.
2. Add onions, tomatoes, tomato paste, cumin, and cilantro to skillet. Cook for 5 minutes on medium heat.
3. Add raisins, potatoes, and water. Simmer for another 8 to 10 minutes or until potatoes are tender.

The $7 a Meal Healthy Cookbook

# Oven-Baked Turkey with Fresh Herbs

 Serves 6

Prep time: 10 minutes
Cook time: 25 minutes
Total cost: $6.72
Calories: 263
Fat: 11g
Carbohydrates: 22g
Protein: 17g
Cholesterol: 51mg
Sodium: 500mg

1 clove fresh garlic, minced

½ teaspoon all-purpose seasoning

1 cup yellow onions, chopped

4 cups bread stuffing

½ cup carrots, chopped

½ cup celery, chopped

1 cup cremini or button mushrooms, sliced

2 cups turkey sausage, sliced

1 cup chicken broth

1 tablespoon fresh Italian parsley, chopped

1 teaspoon fresh sage, leaves chopped

1 teaspoon fresh thyme, leaves chopped

2 large eggs

You can also remove the sausage from the casing, mix with the other ingredients and use it as a stuffing for a whole chicken. Or after baking, use this mix to stuff tomatoes or red bell peppers.

1. Preheat oven to 375°F. Mix all ingredients together well in a large bowl.
2. Coat a 9" x 13" baking dish with nonstick spray. Pour mixture into the dish and cover with foil. Bake for 25 minutes.
3. Remove foil and bake for another 5 minutes or until top is golden brown.

# Turkey Scallopini with Mascarpone

● Serves 5

Prep time: 10 minutes
Cook time: 35 minutes
Total cost: $6.98
Calories: 340
Fat: 11g
Carbohydrates: 27g
Protein: 32g
Cholesterol: 49mg
Sodium: 364mg

1 tablespoon olive oil

2 pounds boneless, skinless turkey breasts

Sea salt and black pepper to taste

2 yellow onions, chopped

1 stick unsalted butter

½ cup plain flour

4 cups low-fat milk

2 cups nonfat sour cream

1 cup mascarpone cheese

Mascarpone is Italian-style cream cheese and is most commonly used in making Italian desserts such as tiramisu.

1. Preheat oven to 400°F. Grease a large roasting pan with oil. Slice the turkey into thin scaloppini-like portions, and season with pepper. Place onions and turkey in roasting pan. Cover and roast for 20 minutes. Uncover and continue roasting for another 10 to 15 minutes.
2. While turkey is roasting, make the cheese sauce by melting butter in large saucepan over medium heat. Sprinkle in flour and stir with a wooden spoon. Whisk in the milk and sour cream, stirring constantly. Simmer until the sauce thickens, about 10 minutes. Remove from heat and stir in mascarpone cheese.
3. To serve, place roasted turkey on platter and drizzle with cheese sauce. Serve remaining sauce on the side.

# Grilled Turkey with Toasted Almonds

 Serves 6

Prep time: 10 minutes

Cook time: 10 minutes

Total cost: $5.32

Calories: 278

Fat: 9g

Carbohydrates: 14g

Protein: 16g

Cholesterol: 8mg

Sodium: 528mg

2 tablespoons olive oil

1 cup sliced carrots

2 cups grilled turkey breast, from Citrus-Glazed Turkey Tenderloin (page 132)

1 14-ounce jar turkey gravy

½ cup low-fat milk

½ cup nonfat sour cream

Sea salt and black pepper to taste

½ cup whole almonds, toasted

Gravy can be tricky to make, so using premade gravy is an easy way to get the flavor and consistency you desire without going through a great hassle. Premade gravy is also a good trick to use for your Thanksgiving turkey. Use it as a base, adding drippings from your cooked turkey before serving.

In heavy saucepan over medium heat, heat oil. Add carrots and cook until crisp-tender, about 5 minutes. Add chopped turkey and stir. Add gravy, milk, sour cream, salt, and pepper, and stir to combine. Bring to a simmer and cook for 5 minutes until turkey is heated through. Top with almonds and serve.

**Money-Saving, Time-Saving Tip**
This is a perfect recipe for leftover Thanksgiving turkey. Not only do you get at least two meals in one, using leftovers saves on cooking time!

# Citrus-Glazed Turkey Tenderloin

Serves 6

Prep time: 10 minutes
Cook time: 10 minutes
Total cost: $7.00
Calories: 227
Fat: 5g
Carbohydrates: 2g
Protein: 22g
Cholesterol: 70mg
Sodium: 180mg

1 pound turkey tenderloin

½ cup orange juice

2 tablespoons Dijon mustard

¼ cup honey

2 garlic cloves, chopped

Sea salt and black pepper to taste

Citrus and mustard are two ingredients you can add to almost anything. The flavors work well together and are delicious on pork, beef, and even in salads. The combination of sweet and sour balance equally to enhance the flavors of the recipe you are preparing.

1. Preheat grill to medium-high heat. Butterfly tenderloin by cutting in half lengthwise, being careful not to cut all the way through. Spread tenderloin open, cover with plastic wrap, and pound out using a meat mallet to about ½-inch thick.
2. In a bowl, mix remaining ingredients and blend well. Transfer turkey to large Ziploc bag and pour in mustard mixture. Knead the bag, pressing the marinade into the turkey. Let stand at room temperature for 10 minutes.
3. Place turkey on grill for 5 minutes, brushing with any leftover marinade. Turn turkey and cook for 4 to 6 minutes on second side, until thoroughly cooked. Discard any remaining marinade as it has been contaminated by the raw turkey meat.

# CHAPTER 8

## PORK ENTRÉES

# Pork Ribs with Herb Cabernet Sauce

Serves 5

Prep time: 10 minutes
Cook time: 60 minutes
Total cost: $7.00
Calories: 230
Fat: 8g
Carbohydrates: 13g
Protein: 25g
Cholesterol: 65mg
Sodium: 482mg

6 Roma tomatoes, diced

1 tablespoon fresh thyme, leaves finely chopped

1 orange, zested and juiced

2 cups beef broth

4 sprigs fresh oregano, leaves chopped

1 cup cabernet wine

½ cup honey

1 tablespoon olive oil

1 yellow onion, chopped

2 pounds thick pork ribs

Sea salt and black pepper to taste

Smoking ribs is also a great way to infuse flavor into the ribs; however, it takes much longer and requires a bit more attention than baking them.

1. Preheat oven to 400°F. In small bowl, combine tomatoes, thyme, orange zest and juice, broth, oregano, wine, and honey. Mix well.
2. Heat oil in large ovenproof saucepan over medium-high heat. Add the onions and ribs. Brown together, about 5 minutes per side for the ribs. Add remaining ingredients and cook for about 3 minutes. Cover the pan and place in oven for 45 minutes. Uncover and cook an additional 15 minutes or until done. Serve.

### Zesting Fruit
Zesting fruit means to use a grater (or zester) and scrape the peel from the fruit, stopping when you reach the white (or pith) part as the pith tastes bitter. Use zest in everything from dressings to desserts!

The $7 a Meal Healthy Cookbook

# Oven-Roasted Pork Shoulder with Apples and Fennel

 Serves 4

Prep time: 10 minutes
Cook time: 3 to 4 hours
Total cost: $6.92
Calories: 340
Fat: 7g
Carbohydrates: 18g
Protein: 32g
Cholesterol: 128mg
Sodium: 281mg

1 2-pound boneless pork shoulder roast

1 bulb fennel, cleaned and chopped

1 yellow onion, chopped

2 Granny Smith apples, cored and chopped (substitute pears, if you prefer)

1 tablespoon olive oil

Sea salt and black pepper to taste

1 cup vegetable broth

Fennel is a vegetable that is often confused with the herb star anise because they each have a mild licorice flavor. Dice or chop the fennel bulb as you would an onion and use the more bitter stalks for soups and stews.

Preheat oven to 375°F. Cut the roast in half sideways, creating a top and bottom, and place "insides" up. Layer bottom half with fennel, onion, and apples. Place top half on and tie securely with butcher's twine. Coat with olive oil, salt, and pepper. Place in small roasting pan and pour in broth. Cover with foil and roast (bake) for 1 hour. Uncover and roast an additional ½ hour longer until the pork is thoroughly cooked, reaching an internal temperature of 160°F. Untie, slice, and serve.

**Cut of Pork Shoulder**

Pork shoulder is a lean muscle that can be purchased bone in or bone out. Cooking a bone-in pork shoulder takes a little more time than boneless, but the bone adds extra flavor to the recipe.

# Herb-Crusted Bone-In Pork Chops

● Serves 4

Prep time: 10 minutes
Cook time: 18 minutes
Total cost: $6.40
Calories: 220
Fat: 7g
Carbohydrates: 16g
Protein: 27g
Cholesterol: 67mg
Sodium: 210mg

2 tablespoons fresh rosemary, leaves chopped

2 tablespoons fresh thyme, leaves chopped

2 tablespoons olive oil

4 pound bone-in pork chops

Sea salt and black pepper to taste

1 yellow onion, chopped

½ cup apple juice

Substitute boneless pork chops if you prefer, but you'll miss the added flavor that comes from the marrow of the bone.

1. In small mixing bowl, combine herbs and mix together. Lightly coat chops using 1 tablespoon olive oil. Season chops with salt and pepper, then coat with herb mixture.
2. In large saucepan, heat 1 tablespoon olive oil over medium-high heat. Add chops and brown on both sides, turning once. Transfer the chops to a plate and set aside. Add the onions and cook over medium heat until soft, about 3 minutes. Return chops to skillet and add apple juice. Reduce heat to low and cover with lid. Cook until tender, about 15 minutes.

**Fresh Herbs**
The combination of fresh rosemary and thyme were very popular at the restaurant I worked at in Florence.

The $7 a Meal Healthy Cookbook

# Dijon-Crusted Broiled Pork Chops

Serves 4

Prep time: 10 minutes
Cook time: 12 minutes
Total cost: $6.24
Calories: 198
Fat: 4g
Carbohydrates: 21g
Protein: 25g
Cholesterol: 61mg
Sodium: 247mg

2 tablespoons honey

¼ cup Dijon mustard

1 tablespoon fresh thyme, leaves chopped

Sea salt and black pepper to taste

4 boneless pork chops, about 1-inch thick

Chefs use honey as a sweetener for all kinds of dishes. Substitute for sugar in vinaigrettes for a healthier option with great flavor.

Preheat broiler. In bowl, combine honey, mustard, thyme, and salt and pepper and whisk to combine. Brush over the chops, and place chops on aluminum foil. Then place under broiler and cook for about 5 minutes, turn once, baste with mustard mixture, and cook an additional 5 to 6 minutes or until pork reaches 160°F and is cooked through but still pinkish in color.

# Wine-Poached Pork Chops with Sage

Serves 4

Prep time: 10 minutes
Cook time: 35 minutes
Total cost: $6.96
Calories: 217
Fat: 5g
Carbohydrates: 16g
Protein: 24g
Cholesterol: 65mg
Sodium: 175mg

2 tablespoons fresh sage, finely chopped

2 cloves garlic, chopped

Sea salt and black pepper to taste

4 bone-in pork chops

2 tablespoons butter

¾ cup dry white wine

¼ cup apple juice

Apple juice is a great substitute for white wine when you are cooking just about anything. The sweetness of the apple juice compares to the sweetness of the wine, the only difference beign that the alcohol in wine actually helps to extract flavors.

1. Combine sage, garlic, salt, and pepper. Press mixture firmly into both sides of the pork chops. In large saucepan, melt butter over medium heat. Add chops and brown on both sides. Remove chops and set aside.
2. Add about ⅔ of the wine and 1 tablespoon of the apple juice, and bring to a boil. Return chops to pan, cover, and reduce heat. Simmer until chops are tender when pressed with the tip of a knife, about 25 to 30 minutes. When done, remove chops. Add remaining wine and juice to saucepan and boil down to a syrupy glaze, about 4 minutes. Pour over chops.

# Italian-Seasoned Pork Cutlets with Lemon

 Serves 4

Prep time: 10 minutes
Cook time: 5 minutes
Total cost: $6.08
Calories: 345
Fat: 17g
Carbohydrates: 15g
Protein: 35g
Cholesterol: 50mg
Sodium: 336mg

4 boneless pork cutlets

Sea salt and black pepper to taste

½ cup plain flour

2 eggs, beaten

1¼ cups Italian-seasoned bread crumbs

2 cups canola oil, as needed

1 lemon, halved

Chef Wolfgang Puck made a similar dish famous as this recipe is native to his homeland of Austria.

1. Using meat pounder, cover cutlets with parchment or wax paper, and pound cutlets as thin as possible. Sprinkle with salt and pepper. Set up an assembly line with flour on one plate, eggs on another, and crumbs on a third. Coat each cutlet with flour, then egg, then bread crumbs.
2. Heat ¼ inch of oil in a large skillet over medium heat. Add as many cutlets as will fit without crowding. Cook until golden brown on each side, about 1½ minutes per side. Drain cutlets on paper towels. When serving, squeeze a little lemon juice over top, removing any seeds.

### Cooking Tip

Reading a recipe all the way through before beginning is an essential and basic rule for cooking. This helps you know what to organize before you begin the actual cooking process and prevents lots of frustration when you find halfway through cooking you are missing an ingredient or have used up all of one ingredient or another.

# Sautéed Pork Sausage with Herbs and Peppers

Serves 4

Prep time: 8 minutes

Cook time: 15 minutes

Total cost: $6.75

Calories: 391

Fat: 31g

Carbohydrates: 5g

Protein: 21g

Cholesterol: 65mg

Sodium: 1371mg

1 tablespoon olive oil

1 shallot, chopped

1 pound ground pork sausage, mild or medium

1 red bell pepper, seeded and chopped

2 garlic cloves, chopped

2 stalks celery, chopped

1 orange, zested and juiced

½ tablespoon fresh thyme, leaves chopped

1 teaspoon fresh rosemary, leaves chopped

1 bay leaf

Sea salt and black pepper

Feel free to add other ingredients to this delicious recipe, such as mushrooms or even spinach. Add them after you brown the sausage along with the other ingredients.

In large saucepan, heat oil over medium-high heat. Add shallots and sauté until tender, about 2 minutes. Add sausage and cook until browned, about 3 minutes. Add the remaining ingredients, reduce heat to medium low, adjust salt and pepper seasoning as needed, and simmer, uncovered, about 10 minutes. Serve with rice, if desired.

# Cornmeal-Crusted Pork Tenderloin with Dried Apricots and Cranberries

 Serves 6

Prep time: 15 minutes
Cook time: 30 to 35 mins.
Total cost: $6.88
Calories: 297
Fat: 5g
Carbohydrates: 28g
Protein: 32g
Cholesterol: 38mg
Sodium: 96mg

3 dried apricots, chopped

¼ cup dried cranberries

¾ cup warm water

Juice of ½ lemon

1½ pounds pork tenderloins

1 tablespoon Worcestershire sauce

1 cup cornmeal

Sea salt and black pepper to taste

¼ cup olive oil

Cooking with dried fruits is an easy way to enhance both flavor and color in recipes. They are easy to cook with, versatile, and add a natural sweetness.

1. Place dried fruit in a mixing bowl with warm water and lemon juice. Let stand until most water is absorbed.
2. Preheat oven to 350°F. Make a tunnel through each tenderloin by using the handle of a wooden spoon, knife handle, or knitting needle. Stuff the fruit into the tunnels. Sprinkle tenderloins with Worcestershire. Make a paste with cornmeal, salt, pepper, and olive oil. Spread it on the pork and roast for 30 minutes. The crust should be golden brown and the pork a healthy, cooked pink.

### Pork Tenderloins

Pork tenderloin is logically named because it is the most tender muscle of the pork and should be cooked to an internal temperature of 160°F. When cooking, use a thermometer tested for accuracy by placing it in ice with a little water. If your thermometer reaches 32°F in the freezing water, you know your thermometer is accurate.

# Oven-Roasted Pork Tenderloin with Sautéed Shallots and Herbs

Serves 4

Prep time: 15 minutes
Cook time: 35 minutes
Total cost: $6.96
Calories: 232
Fat: 6g
Carbohydrates: 1g
Protein: 39g
Cholesterol: 112mg
Sodium: 79mg

¼ cup olive oil

½ cup shallots, minced

2 cloves garlic, minced

2 tablespoons fresh rosemary, leaves chopped

1 tablespoon fresh basil, chopped

1½ pounds pork tenderloin, sliced in half lengthwise

Sea salt and black pepper to taste

For a Tuscan-inspired feast, thread pork loins through the center with fresh rosemary, stems and all, along with whole cloves of garlic and then roast.

1. Preheat oven to 475°F. In large saucepan, heat 1 tablespoon olive oil over medium heat. Add the shallots and garlic, and sauté until softened, about 4 minutes. Add herbs and sauté an additional 1 minute. Remove from pan and spread in center of tenderloin. Tie with cooking twine to secure.
2. Rub tenderloin with remaining olive oil, salt, and pepper. Cover with foil and place on parchment-lined baking sheet. Bake for 30 minutes, or until internal temperature reaches 160°F.

# Sautéed Pork Medallions with Fresh Spinach Leaves

Serves 4

Prep time: 10 minutes
Cook time: 11 minutes
Total cost: $6.04
Calories: 325
Fat: 19g
Carbohydrates: 4g
Protein: 42g
Cholesterol: 119mg
Sodium: 275mg

¼ cup plain flour

Pinch nutmeg

Sea salt and black pepper to taste

1½ pounds pork tenderloin, sliced into ½- to 1-inch medallions

¼ cup olive oil

1 yellow onion, chopped

Juice from 1 lemon

1 teaspoon Worcestershire sauce

1 large bunch fresh spinach, washed, dried, stems trimmed

Try not to overcook pork, as it becomes tough. Properly cooked pork should have a very slight pink hue to it and be firm, but not hard, to the touch.

1. In large mixing bowl, combine flour, nutmeg, salt, and pepper, and mix well. Coat pork with flour mixture.
2. Heat olive oil in large saucepan over medium heat. Add onions and sauté until tender, about 5 minutes. Add pork medallions and sauté about 2 minutes, turn and sauté an additional 2 minutes. Add lemon juice, Worcestershire sauce, and spinach, and sauté an additional 3 to 4 minutes, until pork is cooked through and spinach leaves are wilted.

# Pan-Grilled Pear-Stuffed Pork Chops

Serves 4

Prep time: 10 minutes
Cook time: 30 minutes
Total cost: $6.92
Calories: 315
Fat: 8g
Carbohydrates: 12g
Protein: 41g
Cholesterol: 105mg
Sodium: 86mg

½ cup olive oil

2 pears, cored and chopped

1 yellow onion, chopped

1 tablespoon fresh rosemary, leaves chopped

¼ cup fresh Italian parsley, chopped

Sea salt and black pepper to taste

4 thick-cut pork rib chops

1 pinch lemon pepper

4 garlic cloves, chopped

Zest and juice of 1 lemon

½ cup chicken broth

½ cup dry white wine

1 teaspoon cornstarch mixed in 1 tablespoon water

Even at your local grocery store, the butcher often provides helpful services at no charge. Ask the butcher to cut bone-in chops about 1½ inches to 2 inches thick.

1. In large saucepan, heat 1 tablespoon olive oil. Add pears, onion, and herbs and sauté until softened, about 5 minutes. Season with salt and pepper. Remove from heat and let cool slightly. Then, using 1 to 2 tablespoons of mixture, stuff into chops.
2. Lightly coat stuffed chops with olive oil and season with a little lemon pepper. Heat 2 tablespoons olive oil in saucepan over medium heat. Add the stuffed chops and brown on each side. Add the remaining ingredients, except for the cornstarch-water mixture, and cover. Simmer for 20 minutes over low heat, or until chops are cooked through.
3. Place the chops on a warm platter and add the cornstarch-water mixture to the remaining liquid in the saucepan. Stir to thicken. Season with salt and pepper as desired. Spoon sauce over chops when serving.

The $7 a Meal Healthy Cookbook

# Pork Meatballs with Sautéed Apples

Serves 4

Prep time: 12 minutes
Cook time: 30 minutes
Total cost: $6.88
Calories: 267
Fat: 5g
Carbohydrates: 16g
Protein: 37g
Cholesterol: 138mg
Sodium: 563mg

1 pound ground pork

1 yellow onion, finely chopped

2 teaspoons fresh oregano, leaves chopped

1 egg, lightly beaten

Sea salt and black pepper to taste

1 cup Italian-seasoned bread crumbs, plus an additional ½ cup if needed

2 tablespoons olive oil

2 Granny Smith apples, cored and diced

¼ cup apple juice

Meatballs are great for appetizer buffets. They are filling, appeal to large groups of people, and are delicious. Pork meatballs are a leaner alternative to beef.

1. Preheat oven to 400°F. Line baking sheet with parchment paper.
2. In bowl, combine pork, onion, oregano, egg, salt, and pepper. Mix well. Add bread crumbs as needed to bind ingredients. Form mixture into 1½- to 2-inch balls. Place meatballs on baking sheet. Bake for about 15 minutes. Remove from oven and set aside.
3. When meatballs are cooked but not done, heat oil in large saucepan over medium heat; add meatballs, apples, and apple juice. Cover and reduce heat. Simmer for about 8 minutes or until meatballs are cooked through. Serve meatballs with a side of pasta tossed with salt, pepper, and olive oil.

# Oven-Roasted Pork with Potatoes and Onions

Serves 6

Prep time: 10 minutes
Cook time: 1 hour
Total cost: $7.00
Calories: 389
Fat: 5g
Carbohydrates: 36g
Protein: 38g
Cholesterol: 37mg
Sodium: 227mg

1 2½-pound boneless pork roast

2 cloves garlic, chopped

1 tablespoon fresh rosemary, leaves chopped

Sea salt and black pepper to taste

1 tablespoon olive oil

1 yellow onion, quartered

2 large baking potatoes, cut into 2-inch chunks

½ cup vegetable broth

Food that looks amazing tastes amazing. Adding red potatoes to this recipe enhances color to the overall presentation.

Preheat oven to 375°F. Pierce the pork with a sharp knife in several places and insert garlic cloves and rosemary. Season with salt and pepper. Prepare roasting pan by pouring in oil. Place the pork roast in a roasting pan with onions, potatoes, vegetable broth, and any remaining rosemary. Cover and roast for 40 minutes. Uncover and continue roasting for ½ hour or until pork reaches an internal temperature of 160°F.

**Time-Saving Tip**
Use the roasting time to make your side dishes or dessert. Just be sure to keep the roast on a timer so you don't overcook it.

The $7 a Meal Healthy Cookbook

# Slow-Cooked Pork Roast with Chili Peppers

Serves 6

Prep time: 8 minutes
Cook time: 3 hours
Total cost: $6.98
Calories: 293
Fat: 7g
Carbohydrates: 13g
Protein: 41g
Cholesterol: 112mg
Sodium: 84mg

1 2-pound pork shoulder (fat trimmed)

1 yellow onion, quartered

2 whole cloves

1 cinnamon stick

1 tablespoon whole peppercorns

2 garlic cloves, chopped

1 teaspoon cumin seeds

5 whole, fresh chili peppers, chopped

3 large new potatoes, quartered

Water as needed

The peppers are left whole so you gain maximum flavor without having to worry about the super-spicy pepper seeds.

In large-quart boiler, place pork, onions, cloves, cinnamon, peppercorns, garlic, cumin, and chili peppers. Add enough water to cover all. Cover and cook on low heat for 1½ to 2 hours. Stir and add the potatoes. Cook about 1½ hours longer. Remove cloves, cinnamon stick, peppercorns, and chili peppers.

**Slow-Cooking Tip**
This is easiest when cooked in a crock pot and left to simmer all day. If you don't have a crock pot, check water every hour or so to be sure it doesn't evaporate. Add water as needed to maintain water level.

# Skillet-Braised Pork with Horseradish

Serves 6

Prep time: 10 minutes

Cook time: 1½ to 2 hours

Total cost: $7.00

Calories: 210

Fat: 6g

Carbohydrates: 4g

Protein: 34g

Cholesterol: 89mg

Sodium: 322mg

2 tablespoons olive oil

1½ pounds boneless pork roast, cut into 1- to 2-inch cubes

1 yellow onion, chopped

1 carrot, peeled and chopped

1 rib celery, chopped

2 cans beef broth

Sea salt and lemon pepper to taste

¼ cup cider vinegar

¼ cup prepared horseradish

Fresh horseradish is a root related to mustard. Prepared horseradish is fresh horseradish that has been grated and mixed with vinegar to preserve flavor and color.

In large saucepan, heat oil over medium heat. Add pork and cook until browned, about 3 minutes. Add vegetables and cook until onions are softened, about 3 minutes. Add beef broth, salt, lemon pepper, vinegar, and horseradish and bring to a boil. Reduce the heat, cover, and simmer for 1½ hours or until pork is tender.

# Baked Pork Chops with Sweet Raisin Crust

Serves 6

Prep time: 10 minutes
Cook time: 35 minutes
Total cost: $6.87
Calories: 215
Fat: 5g
Carbohydrates: 5g
Protein: 20g
Cholesterol: 82mg
Sodium: 191mg

3 slices raisin bread, toasted
 and well crushed

¼ cup plain flour

Sea salt and black pepper to
 taste

1 cup milk

1 egg, beaten

6 pork chops

Bread crumbs don't have to be plain and boring. Using varieties of bread to add flavor to foods is a great way to maximize flavor without extra ingredients, which translates to less work for you and a more cost-effective recipe.

Preheat oven to 375°F. Line baking sheet with parchment paper. In medium mixing bowl, combine bread crumbs, flour, salt, and pepper. In a separate bowl, whisk together milk and egg. Dredge chops in milk mixture, then in bread crumb mixture. Place on baking sheet and bake for 15 minutes, turn, and continue baking for an additional 10 minutes or until chops reach an internal temperature of 160°F.

# Sautéed Pork with Broccoli

Serves 6

Prep time: 10 minutes
Cook time: 28 minutes
Total cost: $6.87
Calories: 226
Fat: 9g
Carbohydrates: 7g
Protein: 22g
Cholesterol: 96mg
Sodium: 195mg

2 tablespoons olive oil

2 garlic cloves, chopped

1 yellow onion, chopped

4 boneless pork chops, cut into 2-inch chunks

2 cups chicken broth

Juice of ½ lemon

2 teaspoons Worcestershire sauce

1½ cups broccoli florets, largely chopped

1½ cups nonfat sour cream

¼ cup Italian parsley, chopped

Sea salt and black pepper to taste

Worcestershire sauce originated in England and was made by two English chemists. Aren't we glad they discovered this little bit of heaven? Worcestershire sauce is a blend of spices with malt vinegar, sugar, molasses, and even anchovies. It can be used in cooked or fresh foods and is commonly used in caesar salads and bloody marys!

In large saucepan, heat oil over medium heat and add garlic and onion. Cook until tender, about 3 minutes. Add pork, broth, lemon juice, Worcestershire, and broccoli. Bring to a boil, reduce heat, cover, and simmer for 20 minutes, stirring occasionally. Gradually stir in sour cream and parsley. Season with salt and pepper. Cook an additional 5 minutes or until sour cream is well incorporated.

**Serving Tip**
This pork recipe is delicious served over rice or with a side of pasta.

# Cayenne Pork Chops with Banana

**Serves 4**

Prep time: 7 minutes
Cook time: 23 minutes
Total cost: $6.79
Calories: 463
Fat: 23g
Carbohydrates: 33g
Protein: 49g
Cholesterol: 105mg
Sodium: 105mg

4 thick pork chops, boneless
Sea salt to taste
1 teaspoon cayenne pepper
1 tablespoon olive oil
1½ cups dry white wine
¼ cup honey
1 cup red bell pepper, chopped

1 yellow onion, chopped
1 clove garlic, chopped
¼ cup apple juice
1 banana, peeled and sliced
2 cups hot cooked rice

As you can tell from the pork recipes I have shared, pork pairs nicely with all types of fruits. Feel free to experiment with other fruits such as pineapple, strawberries, and even mango!

Sprinkle chops with salt and cayenne pepper. In a large saucepan, heat 1 tablespoon oil over medium heat. Add pork chops and brown them on each side, about 2 minutes per side. Add wine, honey, bell pepper, onion, and garlic. Cover and simmer for 10 minutes. Stir in ¼ cup apple juice. Simmer, about 5 minutes. Add bananas and cook until pork is cooked through, about 4 minutes. Serve pork chops and bananas over cooked rice.

# Citrus-Glazed Ham over Rice

Serves 4

Prep time: 8 minutes
Cook time: 28 minutes
Total cost: $6.38
Calories: 342
Fat: 11g
Carbohydrates: 24g
Protein: 25g
Cholesterol: 72mg
Sodium: 1695mg

1 cup uncooked rice

2 cups water

½ cup orange marmalade

Sea salt and black pepper to taste

¼ cup orange juice

2 tablespoons balsamic vinegar

½ teaspoon fresh marjoram, leaves chopped

1 pound cooked ham, cut into cubes

This citrus-sweet ham is also delicious served chilled with mixed greens and balsamic vinaigrette.

1. In medium-quart boiler, combine rice and 2 cups of water. Bring to a boil over high heat. Cover and reduce heat to low and simmer for about 18 minutes. Remove from heat and set aside.
2. Meanwhile, in large saucepan, combine all remaining ingredients except ham and bring to a boil. Reduce heat to low and simmer for about 4 minutes. Add ham and stir to combine. Cook until ham is heated through and sauce has thickened to a glaze, about 4 minutes. Serve over rice and drizzle with any remaining glaze.

The $7 a Meal Healthy Cookbook

# Penne Pasta with Ham, Broccoli, and Cauliflower

 Serves 6

Prep time: 8 minutes
Cook time: 20 minutes
Total cost: $6.90
Calories: 302
Fat: 11g
Carbohydrates: 24g
Protein: 23g
Cholesterol: 46mg
Sodium: 365mg

2 cups penne pasta

2 tablespoons olive oil

1½ cups frozen broccoli and cauliflower blend

2 tablespoons water

Sea salt to taste

2 cups cubed ham

1 10-ounce container four-cheese or Alfredo sauce

Black pepper to taste

Other vegetable combinations are also delicious in this recipe. Use sugar snap peas and shaved carrots, for example.

1. Bring a large pot of water to boil; cook penne according to package directions. Meanwhile, heat olive oil in large saucepan over medium heat. Add frozen vegetables; sprinkle with 2 tablespoons water and season lightly with salt. Cover and cook over medium heat for 4 to 5 minutes until vegetables are almost hot, stirring once during cooking time. Add ham and Alfredo sauce; bring to a simmer.
2. Drain pasta when cooked and add to saucepan with ham mixture. Stir gently, then simmer for an additional 4 minutes until vegetables and ham are hot. Season with pepper and serve.

# Panko-Crusted Pork Chops

Serves 4

Prep time: 8 minutes
Cook time: 18 minutes
Total cost: $6.28
Calories: 381
Fat: 14g
Carbohydrates: 12g
Protein: 28g
Cholesterol: 62mg
Sodium: 367mg

1 egg, beaten

½ cup milk

1 cup panko bread crumbs

1 teaspoon Italian seasoning

Sea salt and black pepper to taste

½ cup Parmesan cheese, grated

4 boneless pork chops, 1-inch thick

¼ cup canola oil

If you don't have Italian seasoning, substitute cayenne pepper, herbs de provence, or spice it up with chili powder.

1. Preheat oven to 375°F. In small mixing bowl, whisk together egg and milk to combine. In separate bowl, combine panko, Italian seasoning, salt, pepper, and cheese. Blend well.
2. Place pork chops between two pieces of plastic wrap and pound out to about ⅓-inch thick with mallet or rolling pin. Dredge pounded chops in egg mixture, then into panko mixture. Place on wire rack, if you have one. If not, just set aside.
3. On grill pan over medium heat, heat oil. Add chops and grill about 4 minutes on each side, or until crisp and golden on each side. Transfer chops to parchment-lined baking sheet and bake for about 10 minutes, or until chops are cooked through.

### Panko Bread Crumbs

Panko bread crumbs are Japanese-style bread crumbs. They are very light, dry, and coarse. Usually they are located in your grocer's Asian food aisle. Use them anywhere your recipe calls for bread crumbs.

# Grilled Polish Sausages with Slaw

 Serves 4

Prep time: 8 minutes
Cook time: 18 minutes
Total cost: $6.98
Calories: 425
Fat: 19g
Carbohydrates: 45g
Protein: 28g
Cholesterol: 49mg
Sodium: 681mg

5 Polish sausages

1 cup beer

3 cups coleslaw mix

¾ cup Italian dressing

5 4-inch sourdough rolls,
  if desired

Polish sausage is also known as kielbasa and can be purchased smoked or fresh. In North America, the term *polish sausage* refers to any Eastern European sausage.

1. Prepare and preheat grill. Prick sausages with fork and place in saucepan with beer. Bring to a boil over high heat, then reduce heat to low and simmer for 5 minutes, turning frequently. Drain sausages and place on grill over medium coals; grill until hot and crisp, turning occasionally, about 5 to 7 minutes.
2. Meanwhile, combine coleslaw mix and dressing in medium bowl and toss. Toast rolls, cut side down, on grill. Make sandwiches using sausages, coleslaw mix, and buns.

# Asparagus Wrapped with Ham and Cream Cheese

Serves 4

Prep time: 15 minutes
Cook time: 7 minutes
Total cost: $6.87
Calories: 201
Fat: 6g
Carbohydrates: 2g
Protein: 14g
Cholesterol: 32mg
Sodium: 649mg

16 asparagus spears

½ tablespoon salt (for blanching)

8 ¼-inch-thick slices ham

¾ cup Neufchâtel cheese

1 teaspoon fresh cilantro, finely chopped

¾ cup Parmesan cheese, grated

Neufchâtel cheese is a softened style of cream cheese. It is a lighter cheese that is more easily spreadable than traditional cream cheese.

1. In large-quart boiler over high heat filled ¾ with water, add ½ tablespoon salt. Bring to a boil. When boiling, add fresh asparagus spears and let boil for 20 seconds. Remove asparagus immediately and transfer to an ice bath, then drain well.
2. Preheat oven to 375°F. Place ham on work surface and spread each piece with some of the cream cheese, then sprinkle with cilantro. Top each with two spears of asparagus and roll up. Sprinkle with Parmesan cheese. Bake for 5 to 7 minutes, or until cheese is melted.

### Sliced Ham

For recipes that require you to enclose other ingredients in ham slices, do not use the thin slices of boiled ham meant for making sandwiches. You can use slices from spiral-sliced hams or go to the deli and ask for ham to be sliced from the whole ham.

The $7 a Meal Healthy Cookbook

# CHAPTER 9

# BEEF ENTRÉES

# Grilled Flank Steak

Serves 4

Prep time: 4 minutes
Cook time: 25 minutes
Total cost: $6.25
Calories: 182
Fat: 7g
Carbohydrates: 0g
Protein: 29g
Cholesterol: 77mg
Sodium: 107mg

2 garlic cloves, minced

1 tablespoon steak seasoning
such as Lawry's or Emeril's

1 pound flank steak

Steak seasoning contains lots of spices, usually including cumin, oregano, pepper, garlic, and sugar. Although you could make your own, it's usually less expensive to buy premade seasonings for small amounts.

1. Preheat grill to medium heat. In small bowl, mash garlic and seasoning together and rub onto steak. Prick both sides of steak with fork and rub garlic mixture into the steak.
2. Place steak on grill and cook for 5 minutes. Turn once and cook an additional 5 minutes, until medium rare or rare. When cooked, remove steak from grill and let rest about 5 minutes. Slice against the grain and serve.

**Steak Cuts**
Flank steak refers to the steak from the belly portion of the cow. It is best when marinated or braised and is most widely used in steak fajitas.

# Asian Beef with Sugar Snap Peas

 Serves 4

Prep time: 8 minutes

Cook time: 11 minutes

Total cost: $6.85

Calories: 328

Fat: 14g

Carbohydrates: 12g

Protein: 31g

Cholesterol: 44mg

Sodium: 842mg

¾ pound round sirloin steak, cut into 2-inch cubes

1 tablespoon steak seasoning

1 tablespoon olive oil

1 yellow onion, quartered

1 clove fresh garlic, minced

3 tablespoons low-sodium soy sauce

1 cup chicken broth

½ cup hoisin sauce

1 tablespoon sesame oil

1½ tablespoons ground ginger

2 cups sugar snap peas, fresh or frozen

Sugar snap peas are different than snow peas as their pods are round versus flat. They are a young variety of pea where both the pea and the pod are edible.

On cutting board, coat steak with steak seasoning. In large skillet over medium heat, heat olive oil and add onion and garlic. Sauté until fragrant, about 3 minutes. Add beef and brown about 1 minute. Add remaining ingredients, stir to combine, cover, and let simmer for 5 to 8 minutes, or until steak is cooked. Remove from heat and serve.

# Grilled Sirloin with Blue Cheese and Basil

Serves 4

Prep time: 8 minutes
Cook time: 15 minutes
Total cost: $6.99
Calories: 371
Fat: 12g
Carbohydrates: 14g
Protein: 41g
Cholesterol: 72mg
Sodium: 322mg

2 bone-in sirloin steaks

3 tablespoons olive oil

Sea salt and lemon pepper
  to taste

¼ cup blue cheese

¼ cup fresh basil leaves,
  chopped

Sirloin is a quality cut of beef that is usually less expensive than filet mignon. Sirloin is great marinated and grilled or served chopped over mixed greens with a mustard vinaigrette.

Coat steaks with 2 tablespoons olive oil, and season with salt and lemon pepper as desired. In large saucepan over medium heat, heat 1 tablespoon oil. When hot, place steaks in pan. Cook about 5 minutes, turn once, and cook an additional 5 minutes. Top each steak with cheese and cook until steaks are cooked through and cheese is beginning to melt, about 4 minutes. Serve with fresh basil.

### Grilling Steaks

One of the toughest things about cooking is learning not to fidget with the food while it's cooking, and meats are an especially good example of that. Place meats on hot grill or grill pan and do not move! Let the meat naturally release from the heated surface. This is called searing the meat. Turn once and cook the other side, again, without moving it until done.

# Pan-Fried Cube Steak with Tomatoes and Green Chilies

**Serves 4**

Prep time: 8 minutes
Cook time: 36 minutes
Total cost: $6.49
Calories: 283
Fat: 10g
Carbohydrates: 5g
Protein: 26g
Cholesterol: 98mg
Sodium: 166mg

3 tablespoons plain flour

1 tablespoon chili powder

Sea salt and lemon pepper to taste

¾ pound beef cube steaks

2 tablespoons olive oil

1 large can (28 to 32 ounces) diced tomatoes with green chilies

Cube steaks are round steaks that have been run through a machine that pierces the steak, breaking up the connective tissue and making the meat more tender. You can pound your own round steaks using the pointed side of a meat mallet. Just be sure the meat is covered when you pound it.

In mixing bowl, combine flour, chili powder, salt, and pepper. Rub flour mixture onto steak. In large saucepan, heat olive oil over medium-high heat. Add steak and sauté for 3 minutes, then turn and sauté for 3 minutes. Remove steaks from saucepan. Pour tomatoes into pan; cook and stir until simmering, scraping browned bits. Add steaks back to pan and simmer for 15 to 20 minutes, until tender.

# Grilled Sirloin with Black Bean Salsa

Serves 4

Prep time: 5 minutes
Cook time: 21 minutes
Total cost: $7.00
Calories: 240
Fat: 9g
Carbohydrates: 4g
Protein: 37g
Cholesterol: 77mg
Sodium: 149mg

¾ pound top round sirloin, cut into 2-inch cubes

2 teaspoons steak seasoning

1 tablespoon olive oil

1 clove fresh garlic, minced

1 yellow onion, chopped

1 cup frozen corn

1 tablespoon fresh cilantro, chopped

½ cup beef broth

1 stalk celery, chopped

1 cup salsa, mild or hot

1 14-ounce can black beans, drained

Sea salt and black pepper to taste

Salsas are a great way to give steaks a unique twist and flavor. Black beans are naturally high in protein, but other tasty, healthy salsas include mango, tomato with cilantro, and avocado. All are delicious with steaks as well as chicken, pork, and even fish!

Rub steak with steak seasoning. In large skillet over medium heat, heat olive oil. When hot, add garlic and onion. Sauté until fragrant, about 3 minutes. Add steak and grill about 4 minutes on one side, then turn and grill an additional 3 to 4 minutes. Add remaining ingredients to skillet, then cover and simmer for about 8 to 10 minutes.

The $7 a Meal Healthy Cookbook

# Sautéed Spicy Beef with Cilantro

Serves 4

Prep time: 10 minutes
Cook time: 15 minutes
Total cost: $6.89
Calories: 243
Fat: 9g
Carbohydrates: 6g
Protein: 38g
Cholesterol: 61mg
Sodium: 202mg

1 tablespoon olive oil

1 clove fresh garlic, minced

½ yellow onion, diced

¾ pound top sirloin, cut into 2-inch cubes

1 teaspoon steak seasoning

1 cup frozen corn

½ red bell pepper, seeded and diced

1 tablespoon fresh cilantro, chopped

Juice of ½ lemon

2 teaspoons brown sugar

1 teaspoon oregano

½ teaspoon paprika

½ teaspoon red pepper

½ teaspoon cumin

Sea salt and lemon pepper to taste

1 cup beef broth

The sugar and spices in this recipe can be used as a dry rub for other proteins such as chicken or pork. Combine the mixture, rub the chicken or pork, and then place on a hot grill.

In large skillet over medium heat, add oil. When hot, but not smoking, add garlic and onion. Sauté until fragrant, about 3 minutes. Toss steak with steak seasoning. Add to skillet and sauté until browned, about 2 minutes. Add remaining ingredients and simmer for 8 to 10 minutes, uncovered. Add additional beef broth if needed to prevent burning.

# Flat Iron Enchiladas

Serves 6

Prep time: 10 minutes
Cook time: 25 minutes
Total cost: $6.99
Calories: 474
Fat: 17g
Carbohydrates: 24g
Protein: 21g
Cholesterol: 57mg
Sodium: 939mg

1 pound flat iron steak

Pinch sea salt

Pinch cayenne pepper

1 tablespoon chili powder

1 teaspoon ground cumin

3 tablespoons olive oil

1 16-ounce can pinto beans, drained

1 16-ounce can enchilada sauce

6 10-inch corn tortillas

1 cup pepper jack cheese, shredded or grated

This is the perfect recipe to prepare the day before and then bake. Or, freeze leftovers for a quick meal on a busy day.

1. Preheat oven to 400°F. Cut the steak, against the grain, into thin strips. Sprinkle steak with salt, pepper, chili powder, and cumin. Heat large saucepan or skillet over medium-high heat and add oil; heat oil until hot and add steak, then cook for 3 minutes or until steak is cooked through. Add beans and ½ enchilada sauce and stir to combine.
2. Divide mixture among tortillas and top with half of cheese. Fold and roll up tortillas to enclose tortillas and filling. Place in ovenproof baking dish or aluminum pan, drizzle with remaining enchilada sauce, and sprinkle with remaining cheese. Bake for 15 to 18 minutes, or until heated through.

**Flat Iron Steak**
Flat iron steak is a tender cut of the shoulder, also called chuck roast. The shape of the cut is similar to that of an old flat iron, hence its name.

The $7 a Meal Healthy Cookbook

# Oven-Baked Artichokes with Beef

Serves 4

Prep time: 10 minutes
Cook time: 1 hour
Total cost: $6.76
Calories: 378
Fat: 8g
Carbohydrates: 23g
Protein: 36g
Cholesterol: 80mg
Sodium: 649mg

4 artichokes

1 tablespoon salt

¾ pound ground beef

1 yellow onion, chopped

2 cloves garlic, chopped

½ tablespoon fresh oregano, leaves chopped

1 tablespoon fresh basil, leaves chopped

Sea salt and black pepper to taste

¼ cup Parmesan cheese, grated

Artichokes can be prickly, so wear thick kitchen gloves if you have sensitive hands.

1. Preheat oven to 375°F. Cut the artichokes in half, lengthwise, leaving stems on but peel them with a vegetable peeler. Remove and discard the chokes (the prickly white and purple center). Bring a large boiler ¾ filled with water to a boil; add 1 tablespoon salt. Add artichokes and boil them for 2 minutes. Remove artichokes and transfer to a large bowl filled with ice water. Drain and set aside.
2. In large mixing bowl, combine beef, onion, garlic, oregano, basil, salt, pepper, and cheese. Stuff the artichoke leaves with the beef mixture and place cut side down in a deep roasting pan.
3. Bake, covered, for 45 minutes. Uncover and bake for an additional 10 to 15 minutes.

# BBQ Sirloin Skewers

**Serves 4**

Prep time: 10 minutes
Cook time: 20 minutes
Total cost: $6.87
Calories: 204
Fat: 8g
Carbohydrates: 5g
Protein: 26g
Cholesterol: 56mg
Sodium: 360mg

¾ pound sirloin steak

¾ cup BBQ sauce

2 tablespoons Coca-Cola

2 cloves garlic, chopped

1 to 2 pinches of black pepper

8 cremini mushrooms, halved

1 red bell pepper, seeded and
cut into 1-inch squares

The sugar acids in both the BBQ sauce and cola blend well to add spice, flavor, and actually help cook the steak. Use as both a marinade and a basting sauce.

1. Cut steak into 1-inch cubes and combine with BBQ sauce, cola, garlic, and black pepper. Mix well. Massage the sauce, or marinade, into the meat. Let stand for 10 minutes.
2. Meanwhile, prepare vegetables and preheat grill. Thread steak cubes, mushrooms, and bell peppers onto wooden or metal skewers. Place on grill over medium heat. Grill skewers and brush frequently with basting marinade for 7 to 10 minutes, until steak is desired doneness. Discard any remaining marinade when done.

# Meatloaf with Olives and Herbs

 Serves 6

Prep time: 10 minutes
Cook time: 60 minutes
Total cost: $6.97
Calories: 293
Fat: 9g
Carbohydrates: 34g
Protein: 18g
Cholesterol: 80mg
Sodium: 328mg

3 slices bread, soaked in milk and squeezed

2 Roma tomatoes, seeded and diced

1 yellow onion, chopped

4 cloves garlic, chopped

2 tablespoons fresh Italian parsley, chopped

1 teaspoon fresh thyme leaves, chopped

6 green olives, chopped

6 black olives, chopped

2 slices Swiss cheese, chopped

1½ pounds ground beef

1 egg

1 tablespoon honey

Sea salt and black pepper to taste

Meatloaf often gets a bad rap, but it tastes great and is easy to make.

Preheat oven to 375°F. In mixing bowl, soak bread in water for up to 1 minute, then squeeze out liquid. In large mixing bowl, combine remaining ingredients with the bread. Mix together well and form into desired loaf shape. Place in greased loaf pan and bake for 45 to 60 minutes or until internal temperature reaches 170°F. Slice and serve.

### Meatloaf Glaze
Make a glaze for your meatloaf by combining ketchup, brown sugar, and a bit of Worcestershire sauce. Coat the meatloaf during the last 15 minutes of baking and allow to bake uncovered.

# Herb-Crusted Roast Beef with Potatoes

 Serves 6

Prep time: 12 minutes
Cook time: 35 minutes
Total cost: $6.96
Calories: 339
Fat: 5g
Carbohydrates: 35g
Protein: 29g
Cholesterol: 94mg
Sodium: 537mg

1½ pounds bottom round roast

Sea salt and lemon pepper to taste

1 teaspoon fresh thyme, leaves chopped

½ teaspoon fresh sage, leaves chopped

3 garlic cloves, chopped

2 carrots, peeled and chopped

2 medium baking potatoes, cut into 2-inch cubes

2 cups beef broth

1 yellow onion, quartered

1 bay leaf

Roasting meats may take a little while in the oven, but it is too simple to pass up. Use the roasting time to make a side dish or perhaps just relax!

Preheat oven to 350°F. Coat roast with salt, lemon pepper, thyme, and sage. Place in a roasting pan or aluminum pan. Add remaining ingredients, then cover and roast for 1 to 1½ hours, or until internal temperature reaches 145°F.

# Grilled Flank Steak with Merlot Reduction

 Serves 4

Prep time: 5 minutes
Cook time: 15 minutes
Total cost: $7.00
Calories: 259
Fat: 13g
Carbohydrates: 3g
Protein: 37g
Cholesterol: 84mg
Sodium: 142mg

1½ cups dry red wine such as Merlot

½ teaspoon ground cloves

½ teaspoon fresh thyme, leaves chopped

¾ pound flank steak

Sea salt and lemon pepper to taste

1 tablespoon olive oil

1 yellow onion, chopped

If you prefer not to cook with wine, make a sauce using canned cranberry sauce (with whole or crushed berries) mixed with a little orange juice.

1. In small saucepan, combine wine, cloves, and thyme leaves. Simmer over low heat until mixture is reduced by half, about 30 minutes.
2. Meanwhile, coat steak lightly with salt and pepper. Heat oil on grill pan over medium heat. Add onion and sauté about 4 minutes, until tender. Add steak and grill until flesh releases from grill pan, about 4 to 5 minutes. Do not tear the meat off the grill pan, gently lift when ready (seared) and turn to grill other side. When cooked to desired doneness, slice steak against the grain and serve with Merlot reduction sauce.

### Cooking with Wine

Have you heard that you should never cook with a wine you would not drink? That is true to some degree; however, do not take that to mean that you should cook with your best bottle of vintage Bordeaux. Simple table wine is fine, even if it is not your preferred drinking wine.

# Jalapeño Beef with Onions

**Serves 4**

Prep time: 10 minutes
Cook time: 15 minutes
Total cost: $6.99
Calories: 146
Fat: 8g
Carbohydrates: 5g
Protein: 35g
Cholesterol: 63mg
Sodium: 302mg

¾ pound bottom round sirloin, cut into 2-inch cubes

Sea salt and lemon pepper to taste

1 tablespoon olive oil

1 clove fresh garlic, minced

1 yellow onion, chopped

1 teaspoon ground ginger

1 teaspoon jalapeño pepper, finely chopped

2 tomatoes, diced

1 tablespoon curry powder

1 cup beef broth

1 cup nonfat sour cream

When cooking beef, the leaner cuts are top sirloin, eye of round, and bottom round, which have less than 3 grams of saturated fats per serving.

Season beef with salt and pepper. In large skillet, heat oil over medium heat. Add garlic and onion. Sauté until fragrant, about 3 minutes. Add beef and brown about 3 minutes. Add remaining ingredients except sour cream, cover, reduce heat, and simmer for 10 minutes. Stir in sour cream and mix well. Cover and simmer an additional 5 minutes over low heat. Add extra broth a little at a time, if needed.

**Curry Powder**

Curry is a blend of other seasonings. There are many varieties, but the most common spices used to create it are coriander, cumin, turmeric, and fenugreek. Ginger, nutmeg, black pepper, and garlic are also commonly used.

# Thyme-Crusted Fillet with Feta Cheese

 Serves 2

Prep time: 10 minutes
Cook time: 25 to 30 mins.
Total cost: $6.49
Calories: 385
Fat: 12g
Carbohydrates: 14g
Protein: 41g
Cholesterol: 75mg
Sodium: 325mg

½ pound beef tenderloin

¼ cup extra-virgin olive oil plus 2 tablespoons

Sea salt and black pepper to taste

1 tablespoon fresh thyme, leaves chopped

¼ cup balsamic vinegar

2 cloves garlic, chopped

½ red onion, chopped

½ cup feta cheese, crumbled

Thyme is a mildly flavorful herb and blends well with a variety of foods.

1. Coat fillets with 1 tablespoon olive oil. Season lightly with salt and pepper. Press thyme onto steaks. In mixing bowl, whisk together vinegar, ¼ cup oil, and garlic. Place steaks in baking pan and pour vinegar mixture over steaks. Let stand at room temperature for 10 minutes.
2. Meanwhile, in heavy saucepan or iron skillet, heat 1 table-spoon olive oil over medium heat and add onion. Sauté until just tender, about 5 minutes. Add in steaks and grill about 3 to 4 minutes. Turn and grill other side an additional 3 minutes. While grilling this side, add cheese and continue cooking until desired level of doneness. Serve with onions.

**How to Know When It's Done**
Put your hand palm up and touch your thumb and index finger together. Feel the pad at the base of your thumb; that's what rare steaks feel like. Touch your thumb and middle finger together; the pad will feel like a medium-rare steak. Ring finger and thumb is medium, and thumb and pinkie feels like a well-done steak.

# Meatballs with Julienned Vegetables

Serves 5 to 6

Prep time: 4 minutes
Cook time: 35 minutes
Total cost: $6.99
Calories: 345
Fat: 33g
Carbohydrates: 25g
Protein: 10g
Cholesterol: 74mg
Sodium: 225mg

3 tablespoons olive oil

1 yellow onion, chopped

2 cloves garlic, chopped

1 pound package frozen meatballs

1 16-ounce package frozen julienned vegetables

½ cup beef broth

Sea salt and lemon pepper to taste

Serve this recipe tossed with cooked spaghetti for a different version of traditional spaghetti and meatballs.

In large saucepan, heat oil over medium-high heat. Add onion and garlic, and cook for 5 minutes. Add meatballs, vegetables, and beef broth, then cover, reduce heat, and simmer for 7 minutes. Uncover, season with salt and pepper, and cook an additional 5 to 7 minutes, until meatballs are hot.

**Julienned Vegetables**

*Julienne* is a French term meaning to slice about ⅛-inch thick and about 2 inches long. You don't have to worry about exact dimensions when you julienne vegetables, just be aware that julienned vegetables are cut into thin strips.

# Texas Ground Beef Bake

Serves 4

Prep time: 10 minutes
Cook time: 35 minutes
Total cost: $6.64
Calories: 336
Fat: 10g
Carbohydrates: 15g
Protein: 28g
Cholesterol: 134mg
Sodium: 472mg

2 baking potatoes, chopped into 1-inch cubes

1 tablespoon olive oil

1 yellow onion, chopped

1 pound ground beef

1 package taco seasoning

¼ cup beef broth

1 16-ounce package frozen broccoli, cauliflower, and carrots

½ cup nonfat sour cream

½ cup Parmesan cheese, grated

The potatoes make this recipe super-filling. It's pretty inexpensive to make, so this recipe is great for a crowd.

1. Fill large-quart boiler halfway with water and place over high heat. Add potatoes and boil until tender, about 10 to 15 minutes. Drain and mash with fork or potato masher. Set aside.
2. Preheat oven to 400°F. In large saucepan over medium heat, heat oil. Add onion and sauté for 5 minutes. Add ground beef and taco seasoning and cook for approximately 7 minutes or until beef is browned. Add frozen vegetables and cook an additional 3 minutes. Add in potatoes, ½ cup sour cream, and beef broth. Let cook for 5 more minutes.
3. Grease casserole dish with butter. Transfer beef mixture to casserole dish. Top with Parmesan cheese and bake for 15 minutes or until casserole is heated through.

# Meatloaf Spaghetti

Serves 6

Prep time: 8 minutes
Cook time: 15 minutes
Total cost: $6.72
Calories: 492
Fat: 19g
Carbohydrates: 29g
Protein: 31g
Cholesterol: 65mg
Sodium: 1044mg

1 pound spaghetti pasta noodles

2 tablespoons olive oil

1 yellow onion, chopped

1 pound leftover Meatloaf with Cheese and Brown Sugar Glaze (page 178), or 1 pound frozen meatballs

1 14-ounce can tomato sauce

1 28-ounce jar pasta sauce

¼ cup fresh Italian flat-leaf parsley, leaves chopped

1 cup grated Parmesan cheese

Don't let good meatloaf go to waste! If you froze your leftover meatloaf, bring it out for a super-quick and nutritious meal.

1. Fill large-quart boiler ¾ with water, heat over high heat until boiling. Add pasta, drizzle of olive oil, and pinch of salt.
2. Meanwhile, in large saucepan, heat olive oil over medium heat. Add onions and cook for 5 minutes, until tender. Add leftover meatloaf, tomato sauce, pasta sauce, and parsley. Cook for 7 to 9 minutes or until sauce is hot. Drain pasta and serve with Parmesan cheese.

The $7 a Meal Healthy Cookbook

# Jalapeño Chili

Serves 6

Prep time: 8 minutes
Cook time: 20 minutes
Total cost: $6.81
Calories: 333
Fat: 11g
Carbohydrates: 14g
Protein: 23g
Cholesterol: 47mg
Sodium: 978mg

¾ pound ground beef

2 cloves garlic, minced

1 yellow onion, chopped

2 14-ounce cans diced tomatoes, undrained

1 4-ounce can chopped jalapeños, undrained

1 can red kidney beans, undrained

1 tablespoon chili powder

2 8-ounce cans tomato sauce with seasonings

Water as desired

Jalapeño peppers vary in degree of heat. If yours are overly spicy, cut back on the amount you use in the recipe. You can always serve extra jalapeños on the side for those who like it extra spicy.

1. In large saucepan, cook ground beef, garlic, and onion over medium heat, stirring frequently to break up the meat, about 4 to 5 minutes. When beef is browned, drain off half the liquid and grease.
2. Add remaining ingredients, bring to a simmer, and simmer for 20 minutes, until flavors are blended and liquid is thickened. Serve immediately.

**Extra Ingredients**

If your budget allows, add seeded and chopped red bell pepper and kernel corn.

# Pasta with Beef and Cheese

Serves 4

Prep time: 5 minutes
Cook time: 18 minutes
Total cost: $6.14
Calories: 434
Fat: 9g
Carbohydrates: 32g
Protein: 21g
Cholesterol: 22mg
Sodium: 452mg

1 16-ounce package pasta
  shells

1 pound ground beef

1 yellow onion, chopped

1 10-ounce jar or package
  four-cheese Alfredo sauce

1 tablespoon fresh Italian flat-
  leaf parsley, finely chopped

Alfredo sauce is named for Italian restaurateur, Alfredo di Lelio, from Rome. A largely American dish now, *Alfredo* refers to a sauce made with melted cheese and butter.

1. Bring large-quart boiler filled ¾ with water to boil over high heat. Add pasta and cook as directed, about 5 to 8 minutes for fresh or fresh frozen pasta.
2. While waiting to boil, in large saucepan over medium-high heat, cook beef and onion, stirring to break up beef, about 5 minutes until beef is browned. Drain off grease. Combine beef with cooked and drained pasta and add Alfredo sauce to saucepan. Cook over medium heat for 5 minutes, stirring occasionally until mixture is combined and sauce bubbles. Stir in parsley, cover, remove from heat, let stand for 5 minutes, and serve.

**Healthy Tip**
Substitute chicken or turkey in this recipe for a lower-fat meal.

# New York Strip with Mustard Marinade

Serves 4

Prep time: 10 minutes
Cook time: 15 minutes
Total cost: $7.00
Calories: 262
Fat: 13g
Carbohydrates: 0g
Protein: 34g
Cholesterol: 97mg
Sodium: 455mg

4 4- to 5-ounce New York strip steaks

Sea salt and lemon pepper to taste

2 tablespoons olive oil

2 tablespoons Worcestershire sauce

2 tablespoons fresh thyme leaves, chopped

½ teaspoon dried oregano leaves

¼ cup balsamic vinegar

2 tablespoons dry mustard

Worcestershire sauce is used a lot in steak recipes. It is a blend of different spices and ingredients, including anchovies.

1. Season steaks with salt and pepper. In small bowl, combine remaining ingredients and mix well. Pour over steaks, turning to coat, rubbing marinade into steaks with hands. Let marinate for 30 minutes or up to 2 hours in refrigerator.
2. Heat grill pan. When hot, place steaks on pan and grill for 5 minutes; drizzle with marinade, if desired. Turn steaks and cook for 5 minutes longer, drizzling again with any remaining marinade. Cook to desired doneness. Remove from heat and let rest for 5 minutes, then serve.

---

**Cooking Temperature Guide**

An instant-read meat thermometer is a good utensil to have on hand. When grilling steaks, 140°F is rare, 145°F is medium rare, 160°F is medium, and 170°F is well done. Be sure to let the steak stand for a few minutes before carving and serving to let the juices redistribute.

---

# Meatloaf with Cheese and Brown Sugar Glaze

Serves 6

Prep time: 10 minutes
Cook time: 30 minutes
Total cost: $6.76
Calories: 359
Fat: 23g
Carbohydrates: 19g
Protein: 18g
Cholesterol: 75mg
Sodium: 719mg

1 egg

2 teaspoons Italian seasoning

1 yellow onion, chopped

¼ teaspoon garlic pepper

¾ cup soft bread crumbs

¾ cup ketchup

1 pound ground beef

½ cup shredded jack cheese

¼ cup brown sugar

If you have a large cupcake pan, make individual meat-loaves by cooking them like cupcakes. Be sure to grease the cupcake tins if you don't have a nonstick pan.

1. Preheat oven to 350°F. In large bowl, combine egg, Italian seasoning, onion, garlic pepper, bread crumbs, ½ cup ketchup, beef, and cheese. Mix gently but thoroughly to combine.
2. Press meat mixture into nonstick meatloaf pan. In small bowl, combine ¼ cup ketchup with brown sugar. Mix together well. Spread on top of meatloaf. Cover loaf with aluminum foil and bake for 25 minutes. Uncover and bake an additional 15 to 20 minutes or until loaf is cooked through.

# Classic Beef Stroganoff

Serves 4

Prep time: 5 minutes
Cook time: 20 minutes
Total cost: $6.84
Calories: 352
Fat: 15g
Carbohydrates: 5g
Protein: 17g
Cholesterol: 65mg
Sodium: 283mg

2 tablespoons olive oil

1 yellow onion, chopped

2 cloves garlic, chopped

1 pound ground beef

2 stalks celery, chopped

1 pound uncooked egg noodles

2 cups nonfat sour cream

Egg noodles are the traditional noodle for stroganoff. They are lighter, thinner, and cook faster than regular pasta noodles.

1. In large-quart boiler filled ¾ with water, bring water to a boil over high heat. Meanwhile, heat olive oil in large saucepan over medium heat. Add onion and garlic, and cook for 4 minutes, until tender. Add beef and celery. Bring to a simmer and cook for 7 minutes, until beef is cooked and celery is tender.
2. When water is boiling, add egg noodles and cook until tender but not mushy, about 5 minutes. Drain and set aside.
3. Stir sour cream into beef mixture, cover, and remove from heat. Place noodles on serving platter and spoon beef mixture over.

# Classic Swedish Meatballs

Serves 4

Prep time: 10 minutes
Cook time: 2 hrs., 45 mins.
Total cost: $5.80
Calories: 416
Fat: 12g
Carbohydrates: 12g
Protein: 25g
Cholesterol: 135mg
Sodium: 305mg

1½ cups plain bread crumbs

1 cup milk

½ pound ground beef

½ pound ground pork

2 eggs

1 yellow onion, chopped

Pinch sea salt

½ teaspoon steak seasoning

¼ teaspoon cardamom

1 10½-ounce can beef broth

Black pepper to taste

2 tablespoons butter, melted

2 tablespoons plain flour

Swedish meatballs are most commonly known as meatballs made with both beef and pork.

1. Soak bread crumbs in milk for 5 minutes in large mixing bowl. Preheat oven to 400°F. Add beef, pork, eggs, onion, pinch of salt, steak seasoning, and cardamom to bread crumbs. Mix well. Shape into 1-inch balls. Place on parchment-lined baking sheet and bake for 15 minutes.
2. In large-quart boiler, place cooked meatballs, ½ can beef broth, and pepper. Simmer over low heat for about 2 hours, adding broth or water as needed.
3. In small bowl, mix together melted butter and flour. Mix until a smooth paste forms. Add paste to ½ can beef broth and add to meatball mixture. Cook until thickened, about 25 minutes.

The $7 a Meal Healthy Cookbook

# Spicy Joes

Serves 4

- Prep time: 10 minutes
- Cook time: 1 hour
- Total cost: $6.12
- Calories: 328
- Fat: 10g
- Carbohydrates: 40g
- Protein: 19g
- Cholesterol: 46mg
- Sodium: 493mg

1 pound ground beef

1 yellow onion, chopped

2 cloves garlic, minced

1 cup tomato sauce

1 small can tomato paste

1 cup green bell pepper, seeded and chopped

½ cup water

¼ cup brown sugar

¼ cup spicy mustard

¼ cup apple cider vinegar

2 tablespoons chili powder

8 hamburger buns

To cut back on the spice, use regular mustard rather than hot, spicy mustard instead of cutting back on the chili powder.

In large saucepan, over medium heat, add beef, onion, and garlic. Cook until meat is browned and onion is tender. Drain off fat. In large-quart boiler, combine remaining ingredients, except buns. Stir in meat mixture, then cover and simmer over low heat for about 45 minutes, adding water if necessary to prevent from drying. Serve by spooning over hamburger buns.

# Curried Apricot Beef over Rice

Serves 4

Prep time: 10 minutes
Cook time: 15 minutes
Total cost: $6.68
Calories: 330
Fat: 14g
Carbohydrates: 16g
Protein: 36g
Cholesterol: 121mg
Sodium: 398mg

1 tablespoon olive oil

1 yellow onion, chopped

2 cloves garlic, chopped

1 pound ground beef

½ cup dried apricots, chopped

2 teaspoons curry powder

Sea salt and black pepper to
    taste

½ cup orange juice

¼ cup Italian flat-leaf parsley,
    chopped

4 cups cooked rice

This is another great recipe to use as a stuffing for bell peppers. Make the mixture first then prepare peppers by chopping off the stems and removing the seeds. Spoon in the beef/rice mixture and bake in a 400° oven for about 12 minutes. This recipe should make 6 to 8 stuffed peppers. Enjoy!

In large saucepan over medium heat, add olive oil, onion, and garlic and cook until tender, about 5 minutes. Add ground beef and cook until browned, about 4 minutes. Add apricots, curry, salt, pepper, orange juice, and parsley. Bring to a boil, reduce heat, and simmer until sauce is reduced, about 5 minutes. Serve over rice.

# Chopped Beef with Peppers and Onions

 Serves 4

Prep time: 10 minutes
Cook time: 25 minutes
Total cost: $6.84
Calories: 362
Fat: 13g
Carbohydrates: 9g
Protein: 25g
Cholesterol: 71mg
Sodium: 252mg

¾ pound bottom round steak, chopped

Sea salt and black pepper

1 tablespoon olive oil

1 yellow onion, chopped

1 red bell pepper, seeded and chopped

1 green bell pepper, seeded and chopped

1 celery stalk, chopped

2 cups beef broth

4 cups cooked white rice

Chopping the beef helps reduce cooking time making this dish great for a busy midweek meal.

Season beef with salt and pepper. In large saucepan or skillet, heat oil over medium heat. Add onions, peppers, and celery. Mix well. Sauté for 3 minutes. Add beef and broth. Stir well and reduce heat to low. Cover and cook until the meat is cooked through, about 20 minutes. Serve with rice and gravy from the saucepan.

# CHAPTER 10

# FISH AND SEAFOOD ENTRÉES

# Sautéed Shrimp with Artichokes

**Serves 4**

Prep time: 8 minutes
Cook time: 6 minutes
Total cost: $7.00
Calories: 251
Fat: 5g
Carbohydrates: 42g
Protein: 17g
Cholesterol: 120mg
Sodium: 220mg

1 tablespoon olive oil

¼ cup scallions, chopped

¾ pound shrimp

Pinch chili powder

½ cup chili sauce

½ can artichoke hearts, drained and chopped

Sea salt and black pepper to taste

Use these same ingredients to make shrimp dip. Just substitute cooked bay shrimp for the uncooked, large shrimp here and add a cup of mayonnaise. Mix all the ingredients together and don't cook, as the shrimp are already cooked! Just be sure the shrimp are drained before combining.

In large skillet over medium heat, add oil and heat until fragrant. Add scallions and sauté for 1 minute. Add shrimp and cook for 2 minutes. Add chili powder, chili sauce, and artichoke hearts. Cook an additional 3 minutes or until sauce is heated through. Season with salt and pepper as desired. Serve with rice.

**Cooking Shrimp**

If your budget allows, buy peeled and deveined shrimp. If not, peel shrimp and remove tails before cooking.

# Penne Pasta with Basil Cream Sauce and Crab

Serves 4

Prep time: 5 minutes
Cook time: 20 minutes
Total cost: $7.00
Calories: 239
Fat: 8g
Carbohydrates: 8.43g
Protein: 17g
Cholesterol: 122g
Sodium: 559mg

½ tablespoon salt

1 pound penne pasta, uncooked

Drizzle olive oil

2 cups nonfat sour cream

1 tablespoon fresh basil, chopped

1 teaspoon Jane's Krazy Mixed-Up Salt or other salt seasoning

½ pound canned crab meat, drained

Believe it or not, there really is a seasoning called Jane's Krazy Mixed-Up Salt. It is usually found in the herbs and seasoning section of the grocery store. Use it for dips, stews, or anywhere you would use seasoned salt.

1. Fill large-quart boiler ¾ with water and add ½ tablespoon salt. Bring to a boil and add pasta. Add a drizzle of olive oil. Cook until al dente, then drain.
2. In large saucepan over medium heat, add sour cream, basil, and seasoned salt. Heat until just bubbling. Reduce heat and add drained crabmeat. Cook until heated. Toss with pasta and serve.

The $7 a Meal Healthy Cookbook

# Risotto with Shrimp and Asparagus Tips

 Serves 6

Prep time: 10 minutes
Cook time: 25 minutes
Total cost: $7.00
Calories: 452
Fat: 13g
Carbohydrates: 52g
Protein: 32g
Cholesterol: 52mg
Sodium: 410mg

1 tablespoon olive oil

1 yellow onion, chopped

3 cloves garlic, minced

½ cup asparagus tips, coarsely chopped

1½ cups arborio rice

¼ cup dry white wine

3½ cups vegetable or chicken broth

¾ pound cooked shrimp, peeled, tails off

½ bunch fresh Italian parsley, chopped

¼ cup Parmesan cheese

Sea salt and black pepper to taste

Arborio rice is used in "reboiled" or risotto recipes. It is a short, thick-grain rice that absorbs almost all liquid it comes in contact with. The secret to creamy risotto is to stir continuously and wait until most liquid is absorbed before adding more.

In large saucepan, heat oil over medium heat and add onion. Cook for 3 minutes. Add the garlic and asparagus, and cook an additional 1 minute. Add the rice and stir into the mixture, combining well. Pour in the wine and let reduce by half. Add the broth, ½ cup at a time, stirring each addition until liquid is fully incorporated before adding more. Continue the process until all liquid is used. Remove from heat. Stir in shrimp, parsley, and cheese. Season with salt and pepper and serve.

### Quick-Cooking Risotto
Partially cook risotto the day before to save time. When doing so, stop after 10 minutes, reserving liquid for continued cooking the next day.

# Mussels in Garlic White Wine Sauce

Serves 4

- Prep time: 8 minutes
- Cook time: 18 minutes
- Total cost: $6.98
- Calories: 227
- Fat: 5g
- Carbohydrates: 7g
- Protein: 12g
- Cholesterol: 43mg
- Sodium: 386mg

½ pound fettuccini noodles

¼ cup olive oil

6 cloves garlic, chopped

½ yellow onion, chopped

1 red bell pepper, seeded and chopped

½ teaspoon dried oregano leaves

½ cup dry white wine

1 cup low-fat milk

2 tablespoons butter

½ cup chicken broth

Sea salt and black pepper to taste

2 pounds cleaned mussels

Cleaned mussels means to "debeard" and rinse them. If you don't care for mussels, substitute clams or shrimp.

1. Bring large pot of water with a small drizzle of olive oil to a boil; cook pasta until tender, drain, do not rinse, and set aside.
2. In large stockpot, heat olive oil over medium-high heat. Add onion and garlic and cook until fragrant, about 1 minute. Add bell pepper and cook for 3 to 4 minutes, until tender. Add oregano, white wine, milk, butter, and broth. Bring to a boil. Season with salt and pepper, then add mussels. Cover and reduce heat to medium-low. Cook for about 7 minutes or until all mussels are opened (some mussels may not open; discard them).
3. Remove mussels from pot and place in mixing bowl. Add cooked fettuccini to pot with liquid, then toss and transfer to serving platter. Place mussels on top of fettuccini and serve.

### All about Mussels
Saltwater mussels are the variety most commonly used in cooking. Before cooking, test mussel quality by tapping lightly on any open shells. If the shell does not close, the mussel has died and should be instantly discarded as it will become toxic.

The $7 a Meal Healthy Cookbook

# Wine-Poached Salmon with Tomatoes and Zucchini

● Serves 4

Prep time: 10 minutes

Cook time: 15 minutes

Total cost: $6.97

Calories: 239

Fat: 15g

Carbohydrates: 8g

Protein: 17g

Cholesterol: 40mg

Sodium: 359mg

¾ cup chicken stock

¼ cup white wine such as Sauvignon Blanc

2 large tomatoes, chopped

1 yellow onion, chopped

1 zucchini, sliced

1 clove garlic, chopped

2 teaspoons Italian seasoning

Sea salt and black pepper to taste

4 4-ounce skinless salmon fillets

2 tablespoons grated Parmesan cheese (optional)

You can enjoy salmon smoked, grilled, baked, poached, or marinated with vegetables, rice, or on salads.

1. Combine the broth, wine, tomatoes, onions, zucchini, garlic, Italian seasoning, salt, and pepper in a large saucepan, and heat over medium-high heat. Cover and bring to a boil.
2. Using wooden spoon, move vegetables aside and add the salmon fillets. Reduce heat to medium, cover, and gently simmer until the fish is opaque and firm throughout, about 8 to 10 minutes. Transfer salmon to serving plates, spoon vegetables over salmon, and sprinkle with Parmesan cheese, if desired.

**Health Benefits of Salmon**
When cooked properly, salmon doesn't taste fishy and it's great for your skin as it is high in omega-3 fatty acids.

# Lime-Poached Halibut with Cilantro

Serves 4

¾ pound halibut fillet

Sea salt and black pepper to taste

2 tablespoons extra-virgin olive oil

2 cloves garlic, chopped

2 limes, zested and juiced

1 tablespoon fresh cilantro, stems removed, leaves chopped

¼ cup white wine such as Sauvignon Blanc

¼ cup chicken or vegetable broth

This dish is especially light and healthy, as halibut is naturally low in fat, high in protein, and contains no carbs. The lime, cilantro, and other ingredients greatly enhance the flavor of the fish without adding fat or calories.

Season halibut with salt and pepper. In large saucepan, heat oil over medium heat and add garlic. Sauté until fragrant, about 1 minute. Add remaining ingredients, including halibut, then cover and cook until halibut is flaky, about 8 minutes.

**Halibut**
Halibut is a type of flatfish from the northern waters of the Pacific and the Atlantic. It is a meaty fish that becomes flaky when cooked properly. Pay attention not to overcook as the fish becomes dry and tough.

The $7 a Meal Healthy Cookbook

# Mussels with Leeks in Red Wine Broth

 Serves 4

Prep time: 10 minutes
Cook time: 12 minutes
Total cost: $6.89
Calories: 263
Fat: 9g
Carbohydrates: 12g
Protein: 27g
Cholesterol: 47mg
Sodium: 820mg

1 tablespoon olive oil

2 shallots, chopped

3 cloves garlic, chopped

1 leek, cleaned and finely chopped

1 pound mussels, cleaned and rinsed

1 cup dry red wine

½ cup fish broth, canned

Juice of 1 lemon

2 teaspoons fresh thyme, leaves chopped

If you prefer, substitute white wine for the red wine. It is equally delicious.

In large-quart boiler, heat oil over medium heat. Add shallots, garlic, and leeks. Cook for 5 minutes. Add mussels, wine, broth, lemon, and thyme; simmer until mussels open. Serve with your favorite crusty bread.

**Cleaning Mussels**
To debeard mussels, just yank down on the fibers showing on the outside shell, then rinse them. Keep them chilled, however, so they don't die on you.

# Tuna Salad with Red Seedless Grapes on Whole-Grain Toast

Serves 4

Prep time: 12 minutes
Chill time: 1 hour
Total cost: $6.78
Calories: 288
Fat: 3g
Carbohydrates: 35g
Protein: 27g
Cholesterol: 20mg
Sodium: 483mg

1 hard-boiled egg, diced

½ red onion, chopped

1 cup red seedless grapes, halved

Zest of 1 lemon

1½ cups canned tuna

¼ cup chopped walnuts

¾ cup low-fat mayonnaise

1 tablespoon balsamic vinegar

Sea salt and black pepper to taste

1 head green or red leaf lettuce

8 slices whole-grain bread, toasted

Chopped celery and apples are also natural additions to tuna salad, which can be served chilled or warmed.

In mixing bowl, combine all ingredients except lettuce and bread. Toss well. Cover with plastic wrap and refrigerate about an hour. When ready to serve, layer lettuce on 1 slice of bread, mound the tuna mixture on top, and top with other slice of bread. Or skip the bread and serve tuna salad on lettuce leaf.

# Tilapia Fillets with Creamed Spinach

🥄 Serves 4

Prep time: 8 minutes
Cook time: 20 minutes
Total cost: $6.26
Calories: 261
Fat: 6g
Carbohydrates: 24g
Protein: 26g
Cholesterol: 4mg
Sodium: 921mg

1 package frozen spinach, thawed and drained

1 shallot, minced

⅓ cup chicken broth

Pinch nutmeg

2 tablespoons olive oil

1 pound tilapia fillets

½ cup buttermilk

Dash hot pepper sauce such as Tabasco

2 tablespoons butter

2 tablespoons Romano cheese, grated

Sea salt and black pepper to taste

For a lighter alternative, skip the buttermilk and cheese and just sauté the spinach.

1. In large saucepan over medium heat, combine spinach, shallots, broth, and nutmeg. Cook, covered, for about 4 minutes, stirring occasionally. Transfer to mixing bowl and set aside.
2. In same saucepan, heat oil over medium heat. Add tilapia fillets and cook until done, about 6 minutes. Transfer to side dish. Return pan to heat and add buttermilk and pepper sauce. Over medium-low heat, heat milk mixture, stirring occasionally. Do not let boil. Add butter and cheese and stir until cheese is melted.
3. Return spinach mixture to saucepan and cook, slowly, until heated through. Add tilapia fillets, and cook until heated through. Serve by placing spinach mixture on plate and topping with tilapia. Season as desired with salt and pepper.

**Tilapia**
Tilapia is a thin whitefish with a slightly pinkish color. Native to Africa, tilapia can now be found around the world. It is a light, flaky fish when cooked and is low in fat.

# Scallops Sautéed in White Wine and Butter

Serves 4

Prep time: 5 minutes
Cook time: 10 minutes
Total cost: $7.00
Calories: 343
Fat: 9g
Carbohydrates: 12g
Protein: 40g
Cholesterol: 75mg
Sodium: 212mg

2 tablespoons olive oil

4 cloves garlic, chopped

2 scallions, chopped

1 cup dry white wine such as Sauvignon Blanc

¾ pound sea scallops

Pinch sea salt and lemon pepper

Zest and juice of ½ lemon (zest first, then juice)

2 tablespoons butter

As an appetizer, substitute small bay scallops, add some finely chopped apple, and serve on spoons arranged on a platter.

1. In large saucepan, heat olive oil over medium heat. Add garlic and scallions. Cook for 2 to 3 minutes, stirring occasionally. Add wine, reduce heat to low, and simmer for 2 minutes. Add scallops, pinch of salt and pepper, and lemon zest and juice. Cover and simmer for 3 minutes or until scallops turn opaque in color and are slightly firm. Be careful not to overcook as the scallops will become tough.
2. When scallops are cooked, stir in butter until melted and serve.

### Scallops
Scallops are bivalve mollusks, some of which have beautiful shells. They can be found in waters all over the world. The three major kinds of scallops are sea scallops, which are the largest; bay scallops, which are smaller and more sweet in flavor; and calico scallops, which are the smallest of the scallop family and are not widely used in cooking as they are darker in color and tougher in texture.

# Pan-Grilled Salmon with Baby Bok Choy

Prep time: 10 minutes

Cook time: 12 minutes

Total cost: $6.98

Calories: 263

Fat: 6g

Carbohydrates: 2g

Protein: 34g

Cholesterol: 89mg

Sodium: 125mg

¾ pound salmon fillet, cut into 4 equal portions

4 tablespoons olive oil

Sea salt and lemon pepper

1 green onion, chopped

2 baby bok choy, finely sliced lengthwise

¼ cup white wine

Juice of ½ lemon

Bok choy is also known as Chinese cabbage or snow cabbage and is part of the turnip family. It should not be confused with napa Chinese cabbage, which is lighter in texture and color than bok choy.

Coat salmon fillets with 3 tablespoons olive oil, then season with salt and lemon pepper. Heat remaining 1 tablespoon oil in large saucepan over medium heat. Add green onion and sauté for 1 minute. Add salmon, bok choy, wine, and lemon juice. Cover, reduce heat to medium low, and cook salmon for 10 minutes, or until cooked through.

# Grilled Whitefish BLTs on Sourdough

Serves 4

Prep time: 12 minutes
Cook time: 10 minutes
Total cost: $6.97
Calories: 251
Fat: 11g
Carbohydrates: 21g
Protein: 6g
Cholesterol: 11g
Sodium: 361mg

2 slices bacon, cooked crisp then crumbled, drippings reserved

¾ pound grilled whitefish

8 mini sourdough rolls, sliced in half

3 tablespoons extra-virgin olive oil

4 green or red leaf lettuce leaves, torn into large pieces

½ red onion, chopped

1 tomato, sliced

The term *whitefish* can refer to a variety of white flesh fish but is most commonly associated with Atlantic whitefish and other whitefish varieties.

1. In large saucepan, heat bacon drippings. Add fish and cook for about 3 minutes per side, depending upon thickness. Turn once.
2. Lightly toast bread slices, then brush with olive oil. Layer one bread slice with lettuce, onion, bacon, tomatoes, and fish. Top with additional bread slice.

# Spiced Tuna with Mustard and Crushed Peppercorns

 Serves 2

Prep time: 8 minutes
Cook time: 6 minutes
Total cost: $6.84
Calories: 150
Fat: 2g
Carbohydrates: 12g
Protein: 15g
Cholesterol: 17mg
Sodium: 610mg

½-pound tuna steak, sliced into 2 equal portions

3 tablespoons prepared mustard

Pinch sea salt

4 tablespoons freshly cracked peppercorns, crushed

1 tablespoon olive oil

4 lemon wedges

Fresh tuna is naturally low in fat and high in protein. The meatiness of the flesh makes it more filling than other lighter fish, such as tilapia. Fresh fish can get a little expensive, so look for specials and freeze it for later use.

Coat tuna with mustard on both sides. Season lightly with salt. Press the cracked peppercorns firmly into each side of tuna steak. Heat 1 tablespoon oil in a large nonstick skillet over medium-high heat and cook the fish, peppered side down, until seared, about 2 minutes. Turn fish and cook for 2 minutes, until the fish is seared on the outside yet still very pink in the center. Transfer the fish to a plate and cover loosely with foil to keep warm. Serve with lemon wedges.

**Crushed Peppercorns**

An easy way to crush peppercorns without making a huge mess is to place peppercorns in a Ziploc bag and crush them using a rolling pin.

# Fish Chowder with Potatoes and Corn

🥄 Serves 4

Prep time: 10 minutes
Cook time: 35 minutes
Total cost: $6.99
Calories: 323
Fat: 12g
Carbohydrates: 25g
Protein: 28g
Cholesterol: 77g
Sodium: 1080mg

1 tablespoon olive oil

½ yellow onion, diced

2 large baking potatoes, peeled and cut into 1- to 2-inch cubes

2 ears corn, kernels cut off cob

1 leek, trimmed and sliced

½ pound cod, skin removed

16 ounces chicken broth

16 ounces low-fat milk

Sea salt and lemon pepper to taste

When making a chowder, it is best to use a less expensive fish such as cod because you are combining it with so many other layers of flavors. If you don't care for cod, substitute shrimp, clams, or mussels.

In large-quart boiler, heat oil on medium heat. Add onion and sauté until just tender, about 3 minutes. Add the potatoes, then stir in corn, leeks, and fish; sauté until leeks begin to wilt, about 6 minutes. Add broth and milk, and season with salt and pepper. Let simmer for 30 minutes, adding broth and milk as needed.

# Wonton Shrimp with Fresh Ginger

 Serves 4

Prep time: 15 minutes
Cook time: 5 minutes
Total cost: $6.99
Calories: 345
Fat: 11g
Carbohydrates: 39g
Protein: 22g
Cholesterol: 115mg
Sodium: 926mg

½ pound cooked shrimp, peeled and chopped

1 bunch scallions, chopped

3 cloves garlic, chopped

1 tablespoon fresh ginger, peeled and chopped

½ cup white wine such as Sauvignon Blanc

Juice of 1 lemon

1 cup vegetable broth

2 tablespoons soy sauce

1 package square wonton wrappers

Wontons are very versatile. For parties, brush them with olive oil, sprinkle with Parmesan cheese, and bake until golden for easy Parmesan crisps that are perfect by themselves or for dips.

1. In mixing bowl, combine shrimp and half the scallions, garlic, and ginger. Spoon mixture into wonton wrappers. Seal edges by wetting slightly with water, then fold wonton in half and press to seal.
2. In large saucepan, combine remaining garlic and ginger. Heat over medium heat and add in wine, lemon juice, broth, and soy sauce. Bring to a simmer. Add the filled wontons and simmer about 2 minutes. Serve with remaining broth, and garnish with remaining scallions.

### Fresh Gingerroot
Ginger is an edible root that has healing qualities. To peel, simply scrape outer layer with the edge of a spoon, then chop as needed. Freeze remaining ginger in freezer for up to 3 months.

# Cheese Ravioli with Shrimp

Serves 4

Prep time: 8 minutes

Cook time: 15 minutes

Total cost: $7.00

Calories: 498

Fat: 6g

Carbohydrates: 85g

Protein: 45g

Cholesterol: 43mg

Sodium: 410mg

1 tablespoon olive oil

½ pound frozen shrimp, peeled and deveined

1 9-ounce package refrigerated or frozen cheese ravioli

¾ cup pesto sauce

½ cup grated Parmesan cheese

Make your own ravioli by using wonton wrappers. Place cheese or other filling in the center of one wrapper and top with a second wrapper. Seal the edges by coating them lightly with water and pressing together. Buying premade ravioli saves time.

1. In large saucepan over medium heat, heat olive oil. Add shrimp and cook for about 4 minutes, until shrimp turn pinkish. Remove all from skillet and set aside.
2. Add ravioli with 2 cups water to skillet. Bring to a boil over high heat. Reduce heat to medium, cover, and simmer for 5 minutes, until ravioli are hot, stirring occasionally. Drain pasta. Return pasta and shrimp to skillet. Stir in pesto sauce, mixing gently so as not to break ravioli. Cook until heated, about 1 to 2 minutes, then top with Parmesan cheese.

The $7 a Meal Healthy Cookbook

# Whitefish with Peppered Polenta

 Serves 4

Prep time: 10 minutes
Cook time: 25 minutes
Total cost: $6.96
Calories: 265
Fat: 12g
Carbohydrates: 32g
Protein: 5g
Cholesterol: 5mg
Sodium: 222mg

2½ tablespoons olive oil

½ serrano chili pepper, seeded and diced

1 quart vegetable broth

1½ cups cornmeal or masa meal

¾ pound whitefish such as cod or tilapia

Sea salt and black pepper to taste

3 ounces Parmigiano-Reggiano cheese or Parmesan

2 tablespoons extra-virgin olive oil, for drizzling when serving

1 tablespoon apple cider vinegar

Polenta is synonymous with cornmeal. Once prepared, spread it onto a baking sheet in a 1- to 1½-inch thickness and bake for about 20 minutes at 375°. Cut into squares and top with roasted peppers, sundried tomatoes, or other toppings for a great appetizer.

1. Heat olive oil in a stockpot on medium. Lightly sauté the serrano pepper, then add the broth and bring to a boil.
2. Whisk in the cornmeal slowly and cook for about 20 to 30 minutes, stirring frequently, adding more broth if necessary.
3. While polenta cooks, heat remaining tablespoon of oil in large saucepan over medium heat. Add fish and season with salt and pepper. Cook until light and flaky, about 3 minutes per side.
4. When polenta is cooked, remove from heat and stir in cheese until thoroughly combined. To serve, place ½ cup serving of polenta on plate, top with fish, and drizzle with extra-virgin olive oil and vinegar.

# New Orleans–Style Jambalaya

● Serves 4

Prep time: 6 minutes
Cook time: 30 minutes
Total cost: $6.86
Calories: 366
Fat: 19g
Carbohydrates: 45g
Protein: 26g
Cholesterol: 40mg
Sodium: 952mg

1 8-ounce package yellow rice mix

2 tablespoons olive oil

1 yellow onion, chopped

1 14-ounce can diced tomatoes with green chilies, undrained

½ pound frozen cooked shrimp, thawed

1 Italian or Polish sausage, cooked and sliced into ½-inch slices

Other flavorful additions to this recipe are chopped celery, sliced okra, and canned or fresh corn. If you use canned corn, be sure to drain the liquid.

Prepare rice mix as directed on package. Meanwhile, in large saucepan, heat olive oil over medium heat. Add onion; cook and stir for 4 to 5 minutes, until tender. Add tomatoes, shrimp, and sliced sausages; bring to a simmer, and cook for 20 minutes. When rice is cooked, add to saucepan; stir and cook for 8 to 10 minutes, until blended. Serve immediately.

**Jambalaya**
Jambalaya is a blend of both Spanish and French culture and is the New World answer to Old World paella. Unlike paella, however, jambalaya does not usually contain saffron.

The $7 a Meal Healthy Cookbook

# Oven-Baked Freshwater Bass with Red Bell Pepper

**Serves 4**

Prep time: 10 minutes
Cook time: 20 minutes
Total cost: $6.87
Calories: 127
Fat: 3g
Carbohydrates: 2g
Protein: 19g
Cholesterol: 91mg
Sodium: 86mg

1 shallot, peeled and chopped

1 red bell pepper, seeded and chopped

2 cloves garlic, chopped

¼ teaspoon fresh-grated lemon zest

Sea salt and black pepper to taste

1 pound freshwater bass fillet

½ cup dry white wine

1 cup fish broth or vegetable broth

The bass used here is black bass or freshwater bass. Chilean sea bass can be used, but it is significantly more expensive.

Preheat oven to 400°F. In ovenproof baking dish, add shallots, bell pepper, garlic, and lemon zest to bottom of dish. Sprinkle with salt and pepper. Place fish on top and add the wine and broth. Cover and bake for 15 to 20 minutes.

# Pan-Grilled Halibut with Jalapeño Lime Butter

**Serves 4**

- Prep time: 8 minutes
- Cook time: 10 to 12 mins.
- Total cost: $7.00
- Calories: 225
- Fat: 24g
- Carbohydrates: 6g
- Protein: 36g
- Cholesterol: 34mg
- Sodium: 420mg

½ stick (¼ cup) unsalted butter, room temperature

2 tablespoons jalapeños, seeded and chopped

Juice of 1 lime

Sea salt and black pepper to taste

¾ pound halibut fillets

3 tablespoons olive oil

Pan-grilling is an easy alternative to grilling fish and can be done any time of year and in any weather! I usually use a cast-iron skillet or grill pan which adds a little flavor, is easy to clean, and provides an even heat.

1. In small bowl, combine butter, jalapeños, lime juice, and salt (for a smoother butter, combine in food processor). Set aside. Season fillets with salt and pepper. Place flour in a small bowl and coat the fish in the flour.
2. Heat oil in a large saucepan over medium-high heat, then add the fish and cook until browned, about 3 to 5 minutes. Carefully turn the fish and cook for an additional 3 to 4 minutes or until fish is golden on both sides and texture is flaky. When serving, dollop fish with jalapeño butter.

**Seeding Jalapeños**

When seeding jalapeños, be sure to wear gloves as the fire is in the seeds. If you do accidentally seed them without gloves, soak your hands in milk to calm the burn.

The $7 a Meal Healthy Cookbook

# Breaded Tilapia Fillet with Balsamic Syrup

Serves 4

Prep time: 5 minutes
Cook time: 25 minutes
Total cost: $6.79
Calories: 285
Fat: 11g
Carbohydrates: 3g
Protein: 27g
Cholesterol: 91mg
Sodium: 251mg

3 cups balsamic vinegar

½ cup plain flour

¼ cup cornmeal

¾ pound tilapia fillet

1 tablespoon olive oil

Black pepper to taste

Balsamic syrup is an easy and inexpensive way to add unique flavor to fish. It is not limited to fish, however, as it tastes great with other proteins such as chicken and even with fresh berries. See the dessert recipe Strawberries with Toasted Pecans and Balsamic Syrup, page 318.

1. In small-quart boiler, add balsamic vinegar and simmer over medium heat until liquid is reduced by two-thirds, about 15 minutes.
2. While vinegar is reducing, in mixing bowl combine flour and cornmeal and coat the tilapia. In large saucepan over medium heat, heat oil. Add tilapia and cook about 5 minutes on each side. Serve fish by drizzling with balsamic reduction and sprinkle with pepper.

# Cornmeal-Crusted Trout

Serves 4

Prep time: 10 minutes
Cook time: 12 minutes
Total cost: $7.00
Calories: 189
Fat: 5g
Carbohydrates: 7g
Protein: 23g
Cholesterol: 158mg
Sodium: 233mg

½ cup plain flour
¼ cup cornmeal
½ teaspoon garlic powder
Black pepper to taste
2 egg whites

1 tablespoon cold water
4 small prepared trout
¼ cup olive oil
¼ bunch fresh Italian parsley
Sea salt to taste

Trout is usually cooked whole. Be careful when eating to discard any bones.

1. In small bowl, combine flour, cornmeal, garlic powder, and pepper. In a separate bowl, mix together egg whites and water. Coat trout with cornmeal mixture, then dip in egg mixture, then dip again in cornmeal mixture. Shake off excess.
2. Heat oil to medium temperature in large skillet. Cook trout about 5 minutes on each side until golden brown and cooked through. Remove trout from pan and drain on rack covered with paper towels. Sprinkle with parsley and salt before serving.

**Smoked Trout**
A popular way to enjoy trout is smoked. If you have a stovetop smoker, smoke trout for 20 to 25 minutes using cherry wood chips.

The $7 a Meal Healthy Cookbook

# Baked Salmon with Horseradish Mustard

 Serves 2

Prep time: 7 minutes
Cook time: 12 minutes
Total cost: $6.96
Calories: 245
Fat: 15g
Carbohydrates: 2g
Protein: 35g
Cholesterol: 80mg
Sodium: 228mg

½ pound salmon fillets, skin on

2 tablespoons olive oil

Pinch sea salt and black pepper

2 tablespoons prepared horseradish

1 tablespoon Dijon grainy mustard

1 large shallot, peeled and minced

1 tablespoon fresh chives, chopped

Most chefs consider the skin side of fish to be the presentation side. I prefer skin side down when serving.

1. Preheat oven to 375°F. Line baking sheet with parchment paper and place salmon skin side up. Drizzle with olive oil and season with salt and pepper. Bake salmon for about 12 minutes.
2. Separately, combine horseradish, mustard, and shallot in small bowl and blend well. Season with salt and pepper. Serve salmon with a dollop of horseradish mustard. Top with chopped chives.

# Whitefish with Lemon-Caper-Dijon Sauce

Serves 4

Prep time: 7 minutes

Cook time: 9 minutes

Total cost: $6.93

Calories: 258

Fat: 10g

Carbohydrates: 2g

Protein: 27g

Cholesterol: 91mg

Sodium: 247mg

¾ stick unsalted butter

2 tablespoons shallots, chopped

Juice of ½ lemon

2 tablespoons capers

2 tablespoons Dijon mustard

Pinch sea salt and black pepper

¾ pound whitefish or cod fillets

1 tablespoon fresh Italian parsley, chopped

Both capers and mustard contain high amounts of sodium, so be careful not to oversalt your fish.

1. Preheat broiler. In small saucepan over medium-low heat, heat butter and add in shallots. Cook until soft, about 2 minutes. Add lemon juice, capers, mustard, salt, and pepper. Remove from heat and whisk until creamy and well blended. Transfer the butter sauce to a small bowl.
2. Dip the fillets in butter sauce, coating both sides. Place the fillets in a single layer in shallow broiler pan. Spoon any remaining butter sauce over tops of fillets.
3. Broil the fish until browned and cooked through, about 4 to 5 minutes. Baste with pan juices several times during the cooking process. To serve, transfer fillets to a platter and pour pan juices over the fish. Top with parsley.

**Choosing Fish**

When buying fish—whether fresh frozen, wild caught, or farm raised—be sure the color of the fish is bright and the texture firm. If not, don't buy it! Buy frozen fish from the freezer section instead.

The $7 a Meal Healthy Cookbook

# CHAPTER 11

# VEGETARIAN ENTRÉES

# Sautéed Squash with Mushrooms and Goat Cheese

Serves 4

Prep time: 5 minutes
Cook time: 12 minutes
Total cost: $6.95
Calories: 122
Fat: 3g
Carbohydrates: 14g
Protein: 11g
Cholesterol: 5mg
Sodium: 201mg

2 tablespoons olive oil

1 yellow onion, chopped

3 yellow squash, sliced

1 zucchini squash, sliced

2 cups cremini or button mushrooms, cleaned and sliced

1 red bell pepper, seeded and chopped

Salt and lemon pepper to taste

4 ounces goat cheese

Use a medley of mushrooms such as baby portobellos, shiitake, and morel, if your budget allows.

In large sauté pan over medium heat, add olive oil. Heat oil until fragrant, then add onion and sauté for 3 minutes. Add both kinds of squash, mushrooms, and peppers. Season with salt and pepper. Cover and reduce heat to medium-low. Simmer for about 5 to 6 minutes. Uncover, stir, and stir in goat cheese. Cook until heated through. If too much liquid, cook uncovered about 1 to 2 minutes longer, or leave liquid and serve over brown or white rice.

**Goat Cheese**
Goat cheese is a delicious cheese made from goat's milk. The tart flavor comes from its unique chain of fatty acids.

# Frittata with Asparagus, Broccoli, and Red Bell Peppers

 Serves 8

Prep time: 12 minutes
Cook time: 12 minutes
Total cost: $6.75
Calories: 225
Fat: 15g
Carbohydrates: 23g
Protein: 21g
Cholesterol: 298mg
Sodium: 240mg

2 tablespoons butter, unsalted

¼ cup red onion, chopped

½ cup fresh asparagus tips

½ cup fresh broccoli florets, chopped

½ red bell pepper, seeded and diced

Sea salt and black pepper to taste

6 eggs

1 tablespoon fresh cilantro, leaves chopped

Fine zest of 1 lemon

¼ cup Monterey jack cheese, shredded

Frittatas are typically enjoyed for breakfast but can be served for lunch, dinner, or even as an appetizer!

1. In large ovenproof saucepan over medium heat, heat butter. Add onion and sauté about 1 minute. Continue cooking and add asparagus, broccoli, and red bell pepper. Season with salt and pepper and cook about 2 to 3 minutes. In separate bowl, whisk eggs until combined. Add cilantro and lemon zest, and whisk again. Pour egg mixture over vegetables, tilting pan to coat evenly. Top with cheese.

2. Preheat broiler. Reduce heat, cooking slowly for about 5 minutes, or until eggs are setting. To finish cooking, place saucepan under broiler for about 1 minute to finish cooking and brown very slightly on top.

### No Ovenproof Skillet? No Worries

If you do not have an ovenproof skillet, don't worry. When cooking the frittata, use a spatula to run around the sides of the frittata to lift. Tilt the pan and let some of the runny egg mixture in the center of the frittata run to the sides. You can also cover the pan with a lid to help cook the center.

# Baked Stuffed Artichokes

Serves 4

Prep time: 12 minutes
Cook time: 35 minutes
Total cost: $6.32
Calories: 153
Fat: 9g
Carbohydrates: 12g
Protein: 3g
Cholesterol: 1mg
Sodium: 156mg

4 large artichokes, trimmed and split lengthwise

½ fresh lemon

4 quarts water

¾ cup Parmesan cheese, grated

10 pitted black olives, chopped

1 red bell pepper, seeded and chopped

1 clove garlic, finely chopped

1 teaspoon fresh thyme, leaves chopped

1 yellow squash, finely chopped

Sea salt and lemon pepper to taste

1 tablespoon olive oil

If artichokes aren't your thing or you are pressed for time, use this mixture to stuff red bell peppers or large tomatoes. If you do, it is not necessary to boil the peppers or tomatoes.

1. Boil the artichokes in 4 quarts of water, squeezing in lemon juice, then placing in lemon half. Boil for 20 to 25 minutes. Drain and place on a parchment-lined baking sheet, cut side up.
2. Preheat oven to 350°F. Scoop out choke, using any heart pieces in vegetable mixture. In a large mixing bowl, combine remaining ingredients, tossing with the olive oil. Divide filling into artichokes, pressing between the leaves where needed. Bake for 15 minutes or until hot.

**Artichoke Tip**
Artichokes can be a little tricky to work with because they have prickly little tips like roses. Wear gloves to tear off the outer leaves and trim the stem. Either steam, boil, or bake them to make them tender. Enjoy them alone with some melted butter or dipping sauce.

The $7 a Meal Healthy Cookbook

# Crepes with Snow Peas and Green Onions

**Serves 4**

Prep time: 7 minutes
Cook time: 15 minutes
Total cost: $4.60
Calories: 203
Fat: 7g
Carbohydrates: 22g
Protein: 12g
Cholesterol: 125mg
Sodium: 263mg

4 eggs

2¼ cups milk

2 cups plain flour

¼ cup (½ stick) melted butter, plus 2 to 3 tablespoons for cooking

Pinch sea salt

¼ cup peanut oil

½ pound snow pea pods, ends trimmed slightly

1 green onion, chopped

½ fresh lemon, zested and juiced

1 8-ounce can sliced water chestnuts, drained

2 tablespoons soy sauce

1 tablespoon fresh gingerroot, minced

Tabasco or other red pepper sauce as desired

Water chestnuts are an aquatic vegetable that grow in marshes and are native to China.

1. In medium mixing bowl, whisk together eggs, milk, flour, butter, and salt. Mix to combine well, but don't overly mix. In nonstick skillet, add ½ to 1 tablespoon of the butter and heat over medium heat. Swirl pan to coat. Pour in ¼ cup of batter and swirl to cover pan. Cook for 1 to 1½ minutes, lifting edges with spatula. Crepe should easily slide out of pan. As crepes are cooked, transfer to plate to hold; stacking them is okay.
2. In large saucepan or nonstick skillet, heat oil over medium-high heat. Add snow pea pods and green onion; stir to coat. Add lemon zest, lemon juice, and water chestnuts; cook for 5 minutes, stirring occasionally. Add remaining ingredients and mix well.
3. To wrap crepes, place crepe flat on plate, add ⅓ cup filling, fold crepe in half, then fold again.

# Two-Cheese Twice-Baked Potatoes with Spinach

Serves 4

Prep time: 12 minutes
Cook time: 1 hour
Total cost: $5.45
Calories: 249
Fat: 3g
Carbohydrates: 53g
Protein: 5g
Cholesterol: 2mg
Sodium: 422mg

4 baking potatoes, wrapped in foil

1 tablespoon olive oil

½ yellow onion, chopped

1 10-ounce package frozen chopped spinach, thawed, excess water squeezed out

Pinch nutmeg

1 cup nonfat sour cream

1 cup white American cheese, grated

Sea salt and black pepper to taste

½ cup Parmesan cheese, grated

Cheddar, provolone, and Gruyère cheeses also work well for this recipe. If you are looking to add a few calories and fat, top with crispy, crumbled bacon.

1. Preheat the oven to 350°F. Bake the potatoes for 40 minutes. While baking, heat oil in large saucepan over medium heat. Add onion and sauté until just tender, about 2 minutes. Then add spinach and nutmeg, and sauté until heated and moisture has cooked out, about 4 minutes. Add sour cream and American cheese. Cook until cheese is just melting, about 1 minute. Turn off heat.
2. Cool the potatoes and split them in half lengthwise. Spoon out the insides of the potatoes, leaving skin intact. Place potato filling in saucepan with spinach mixture, season with salt and pepper, and combine well. Restuff the potato skins and arrange Parmesan cheese on top. Bake for another 20 minutes, and serve hot.

The $7 a Meal Healthy Cookbook

# Roasted Rosemary Beets

 Serves 4

Prep time: 10 minutes
Cook time: 45 to 55 mins.
Total cost: $5.62
Calories: 181
Fat: 4g
Carbohydrates: 12g
Protein: 3g
Cholesterol: 12mg
Sodium: 125mg

2 pounds fresh beets, washed and cut into 2-inch cubes

3 tablespoons olive oil

2 tablespoons fresh rosemary, leaves chopped

Zest of 1 lemon

Sea salt and black pepper to taste

1 cup feta cheese

Beets are root vegetables, which means they grow in the ground. Be careful when slicing or chopping fresh beets as the juices are dark in color and will stain your clothes!

1. Heat oven to 375°F. Toss beets with olive oil, rosemary, lemon zest, salt, and pepper. Spread onto parchment-lined baking sheet in single layer. Roast in middle rack of oven for 45 minutes or until tender. Check about halfway through cooking and toss if needed.
2. Remove from oven, toss with feta, and serve.

**Beets**

Beets are packed full of nutrients, and the juice has been known to help lower blood pressure. Also, sugar beets are used for making table sugar.

# Baked Eggplant Rolls with Ricotta and Fresh Herbs

Serves 4

- Prep time: 15 minutes
- Cook time: 40 minutes
- Total cost: $5.56
- Calories: 196
- Fat: 6g
- Carbohydrates: 14g
- Protein: 6g
- Cholesterol: 4mg
- Sodium: 124mg

2 medium eggplants, cut into 16 round slices and salted

1 cup corn flour

Black pepper to taste

¼ cup olive oil, or as needed

2 cups tomato sauce

1 pound (16 ounces) ricotta cheese

1 cup Parmesan cheese, grated

2 eggs

½ tablespoon fresh oregano, leaves chopped

½ tablespoon fresh thyme, leaves chopped

1 cup mozzarella cheese, shredded

1 tablespoon fresh Italian flat-leaf parsley, leaves chopped

Add chicken or turkey to this recipe, which is similar to eggplant parmesan.

1. Stack salted eggplant slices on a plate and place another plate on top. Place something of weight on top plate to press out the brown liquid. Separately, in medium mixing bowl, mix flour and pepper. Dredge the eggplant slices in the flour mixture. In large saucepan over medium-high heat, heat olive oil. When hot but not burning, add eggplant and fry until browned, about 5 minutes.
2. Preheat oven to 325°F. Prepare a 2-quart casserole dish with nonstick spray and spread a thin layer of tomato sauce. In large bowl, mix ricotta cheese, ½ cup of Parmesan cheese, eggs, oregano, and thyme. Place a tablespoon of the egg-cheese mixture on each slice of eggplant and roll, placing seam side down in baking dish.
3. Spread with sauce, sprinkle with remaining Parmesan and mozzarella, and top with parsley. Bake, uncovered, for 35 minutes.

# Oven-Roasted Sweet Potatoes with Carrots

 Serves 6

Prep time: 5 minutes
Cook time: 30 minutes
Total cost: $6.51
Calories: 189
Fat: 3g
Carbohydrates: 27g
Protein: 2g
Cholesterol: 0mg
Sodium: 14mg

2 pounds peeled sweet potatoes

1 pound carrots, peeled

Sea salt and lemon pepper to taste

2 tablespoons olive oil

Kids love sweet potatoes and carrots, so this recipe is a natural for family dinners. If you have leftovers, save them for your kids' after-school snacks.

1. Preheat oven to 450°F. Cut potatoes and carrots into matchsticks, about ½-inch thick. Toss potatoes, carrots, salt, pepper, and olive oil in a bowl.
2. Line baking sheet with parchment paper. Bake for 25 to 30 minutes or until potatoes and carrots are tender and fairly crispy, turning once if necessary.

**Roasting Vegetables**

Roasting vegetables is a low-cal, low-fat way to add flavor to vegetables while at the same time maintaining their nutrients. Plus it's simple and easy on cleanup! Keep some in your refrigerator for a quick, healthy, and tasty snack.

# Mashed Sweet Potatoes with Candied Ginger and Cilantro

Serves 4

Prep time: 10 minutes
Cook time: 25 minutes
Total cost: $5.36
Calories: 249
Fat: 3g
Carbohydrates: 53g
Protein: 5g
Cholesterol: 1mg
Sodium: 422mg

4 large sweet potatoes, peeled and cut into 2- to 3-inch cubes

¼ cup low-fat milk

2 tablespoons butter

1 tablespoon mashed candied ginger or 1 tablespoon brown sugar plus ½ teaspoon ground ginger

1 tablespoon fresh cilantro, leaves chopped

The candied ginger pairs nicely with the natural sugars found in sweet potatoes, which are native to South America. You can also substitute yams, which are less sweet but similar in flavor and texture and are native to North America.

Place potatoes in large-quart boiler filled ¾ with water. Bring to a boil and cook potatoes until tender, about 20 minutes. Drain and return to pan. In small saucepan, heat the milk with the butter. Add milk mixture to potatoes, along with candied ginger and cilantro. Mash by hand using potato masher or with a hand mixer.

**Gingerroot**
Fresh ginger is the underground stem of the ginger plant. This root can be candied and eaten as a snack or combined with other foods as a spice. Look for candied ginger where you find specialty nuts at the grocery store.

The $7 a Meal Healthy Cookbook

# Sautéed Asian Vegetables with Peanuts

 Serves 4

Prep time: 8 minutes
Cook time: 18 minutes
Total cost: $5.42
Calories: 228
Fat: 4g
Carbohydrates: 55g
Protein: 9g
Cholesterol: 9mg
Sodium: 379mg

1 tablespoon sesame oil

1 green onion, chopped

1 cup broccoli florets, largely chopped

1 cup sugar snap peas

½ cup sliced water chestnuts, drained

½ cup baby corn, drained

1 cup cauliflower, chopped

1 cup cremini or button mushrooms, sliced

½ cup roasted, salted peanuts, finely chopped

2 tablespoons soy sauce

Peanuts are often used in preparing Asian cuisine. However, feel free to substitute walnuts, hazelnuts, pecans, or almonds, depending upon your flavor preference.

Heat oil in large saucepan over medium heat. Add onion and sauté about 1 minute. Add remaining ingredients, then cover and reduce heat. Simmer vegetables until tender, about 15 minutes.

# Stuffed Mushrooms with Fresh Herbs, Garlic, and Parmesan

Serves 6

Prep time: 7 minutes

Cook time: 12 minutes

Total cost: $5.05

Calories: 125

Fat: 11g

Carbohydrates: 9g

Protein: 6g

Cholesterol: 5mg

Sodium: 145mg

1 pound cremini mushrooms, stems removed and reserved

3 tablespoons butter, unsalted

1 yellow onion, chopped

2 cloves garlic, chopped

¾ cup bread crumbs

Sea salt and black pepper to taste

1 teaspoon fresh thyme, leaves chopped

½ cup Parmesan cheese, grated, plus 2 tablespoons

2 tablespoons fresh Italian parsley, chopped

Stuffed mushrooms are great as a side dish or an appetizer. They are easy to make and mushrooms combine well with most flavors. This recipe incorporates the entire mushroom for maximum cost benefit.

1. Preheat broiler. Chop mushroom stems. In large saucepan over medium heat, melt butter. Add onion and garlic. Cook for 2 minutes. Add mushroom stems and cook 2 to 3 minutes more. Stir in bread crumbs, salt, pepper, thyme, and cheese. Cook an additional 2 minutes.
2. Using a small spoon, fill each mushroom cap with mushroom mixture. Place filled mushrooms on baking sheet, top with remaining 2 tablespoons of Parmesan. Broil mushrooms for 6 minutes, or until tops are browned and caps have softened slightly and become juicy. Sprinkle tops with parsley.

# Jicama Salad with Mango

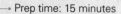 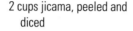 Serves 4

- Prep time: 15 minutes
- Cook time: none
- Total cost: $6.05
- Calories: 102
- Fat: 1g
- Carbohydrates: 14g
- Protein: 1g
- Cholesterol: 0mg
- Sodium: 3mg

**Chill**
**20 minutes**

2 cups jicama, peeled and diced

⅓ cup mango, diced

½ cup canned black beans, drained and rinsed

½ cup red onion, diced

⅓ cup mandarin oranges, drained

2 tablespoons fresh lime juice

2 tablespoons fresh orange juice

2 tablespoons fresh cilantro, chopped

Pinch sea salt and black pepper

If you want to lose or maintain a certain weight level, this is a great salad for you. Plus, it is satisfying to your palate, as you get a perfect balance of flavors and textures.

1. Combine the jicama, mango, black beans, red onion, and mandarin oranges in a medium bowl and toss to mix.
2. Separately, mix together the lime juice, orange juice, cilantro, salt, and pepper in a bowl. Pour over jicama mixture and toss well. Refrigerate for 10 to 20 minutes.

**Jicama**

Jicama is a Mexican vine, and the edible part is the root. It is high in fiber and up to 90 percent water. Jicama makes for a terrific healthy, crunchy snack and kids love it!

# Fresh Fennel with Pecorino Romano Cheese

Serves 4

Prep time: 7 minutes
Cook time: none
Total cost: $6.78
Calories: 65
Fat: 3g
Carbohydrates: 6g
Protein: 3g
Cholesterol: 1mg
Sodium: 345mg

2 bulbs fresh fennel, cleaned

½ fresh lemon

½ cup Pecorino Romano cheese, shaved

2 tablespoons extra-virgin olive oil

Fennel is actually an herb. Harvested for many culinary uses, the fresh fennel bulb may be eaten raw, as in this recipe, or stewed, sautéed, grilled, or braised. Fennel seeds are used in rye bread and fennel is the primary ingredient used in absinthe.

Trim fennel stems and wispy fronds from fennel tops. Break the bulbs apart, layer by layer, using your hands to make long, bite-size pieces. Discard the core. Arrange the pieces onto a serving platter. Squeeze lemon over fennel. Sprinkle with cheese and drizzle olive oil.

**Pecorino Romano Cheese**
Pecorino Romano is a hard, salty sheep's milk cheese from the region of Sardinia, Italy, one of the most beautiful places on earth! Because of its salty nature, it is not necessary to add salt to this fennel recipe.

The $7 a Meal Healthy Cookbook

# Roasted Red Pepper Omelet with Fresh Mint Leaves

Serves 2

Prep time: 10 minutes
Cook time: 5 minutes
Total cost: $2.83
Calories: 325
Fat: 28g
Carbohydrates: 4g
Protein: 15g
Cholesterol: 471mg
Sodium: 480mg

2 tablespoons unsalted butter

½ yellow onion, chopped

½ red bell pepper, seeded and chopped

½ tablespoon fresh mint leaves, chopped

4 eggs, well beaten

2 ounces Gorgonzola cheese, crumbled

Sea salt and black pepper to taste

Gorgonzola is an Italian blue cheese originally from the town of Gorgonzola near Milan, in northern Italy. Made from cow's milk, it is typically firm yet crumbly and has a strong, salty flavor.

1. Heat a 10-inch nonstick pan over medium-high heat; add 1 tablespoon butter and heat until just melted. Add onion and sauté about 1 minute. Add bell pepper and sauté an additional 1 minute. In small bowl, whisk in mint leaves with eggs. Remove onion mixture from pan and set aside.
2. Place pan over medium heat and add remaining tablespoon of butter. Pour egg mixture into pan and tilt pan to distribute evenly. Place onion mixture on one side of omelet. Top the mixture with cheese. Season with salt and pepper. Cook until the consistency is like custard. Run spatula along sides of omelet, tilting pan to let liquid eggs in center drain off to bottom of omelet. Then carefully but quickly flip plain side of omelet over side with cheese and peppers. Cut in half and serve.

# Egg Custard with Port Wine Shallots

Serves 4

Prep time: 10 minutes
Cook time: 50 minutes
Total cost: $5.79
Calories: 391
Fat: 35g
Carbohydrates: 25g
Protein: 18g
Cholesterol: 130mg
Sodium: 437mg

1 tablespoon unsalted butter

1 shallot, chopped

1 cup carrots, peeled and thinly sliced

1 cup asparagus tips, finely chopped

2 tablespoons Port wine

Pinch sea salt and black pepper

Pinch nutmeg

1 tablespoon fresh tarragon, chopped

1 cup whipping cream, lightly whipped with wire whisk

3 large eggs

¼ cup Parmesan cheese, grated

Adding water to a pan to cook foods is called a bain-marie and helps to ensure an even cooking temperature.

1. Preheat oven to 375°F. Butter 4 6-ounce ramekins or custard cups. In a medium saucepan over medium heat, melt 1 tablespoon butter; add the shallots and cook until just tender, about 2 minutes. Add carrots and asparagus, cook an additional 3 to 4 minutes, or until vegetables are becoming soft. Reduce heat and add Port wine, salt, pepper, nutmeg, and tarragon. Let simmer for 2 minutes.
2. In separate saucepan heat the cream until hot but not boiling. Quickly whisk the cheese and eggs into the carrot mixture, then gradually whisk in the cream.
3. Divide the entire mixture into the prepared ramekins. Place them in a shallow baking dish. Add enough hot tap water to come two-thirds up the sides of the ramekins. Cover entire dish with foil and place in center of oven. Bake for 30 minutes, until almost set. Open oven door and bake an additional 10 minutes. Remove from oven and allow to rest for 10 minutes before serving. Unmold by loosening with a knife and turning over, or serve in ramekins.

The $7 a Meal Healthy Cookbook

# Parsnips and Leeks with Fresh Herbs

 Serves 4

Prep time: 12 minutes
Cook time: 21 minutes
Total cost: $5.35
Calories: 215
Fat: 1g
Carbohydrates: 46g
Protein: 5g
Cholesterol: 0mg
Sodium: 50mg

1½ pounds parsnips, cut into 1-inch pieces

2 tablespoons olive oil

1 red onion, thinly sliced

1 leek, cleaned, trimmed, and chopped

2 Bosc pears, unpeeled, cored, and thinly sliced

1 teaspoon fresh thyme, leaves chopped

Sea salt and lemon pepper to taste

Italian parsley, fresh rosemary, or flavored fresh thyme such as lemon thyme are also great herbs for this recipe.

1. Partially boil the parsnips, about 5 minutes. Drain and set aside.
2. Heat oil in large saucepan over medium heat. Add onion and leeks. Sauté for 4 minutes. Add pears, thyme, and parsnips. Season with salt and pepper. Cover and cook about 10 minutes, stirring regularly. Uncover and cook an additional 2 minutes or until parsnips are tender.

**Parsnips**

Parsnips are root vegetables related to carrots. They typically grow in cold climates, not warm, as frost enhances their flavor.

# Potato Latkes with Basil

Serves 4

Prep time: 12 minutes
Cook time: 12 minutes
Total cost: $4.56
Calories: 274
Fat: 8g
Carbohydrates: 24g
Protein: 4g
Cholesterol: 20mg
Sodium: 310mg

2 large eggs

3 large baking potatoes, peeled and grated

1 yellow onion, grated

Sea salt and lemon pepper to taste

½ tablespoon fresh basil, chopped

2 tablespoons plain flour, plus a little extra if needed

Canola oil for frying

Overworking the potato mixture will result in overly wet "dough" and will require more flour. Try to avoid this, as adding more flour will cause your latkes to taste more like flour than potatoes.

1. Beat eggs in large bowl. After grating potatoes, squeeze out as much excess water from potatoes as possible. Combine potato, onion, salt, pepper, and basil. Mix well. Add in flour and toss together, being careful not to overwork the mixture.

2. In a large saucepan over medium-high heat, pour in oil about ¼-inch deep. Heat oil to hot but not burning. From potato batter, make 8 pancakes. Gently squeeze out any excess water and place pancakes in batches into hot oil. Cook slowly, without moving them for the first 5 minutes. Loosen with spatula and turn after about 8 minutes. When the top appears to be about ⅓ cooked, flip pancake and finish cooking, about 4 more minutes. Drain on paper towels and serve.

# Oven-Broiled Portobello Mushrooms with Fresh Herbs and Provolone

 Serves 4

Prep time: 15 minutes

Cook time: 8 minutes

Total cost: $6.20

Calories: 120

Fat: 1g

Carbohydrates: 4g

Protein: 7g

Cholesterol: 26mg

Sodium: 123mg

4 large portobello mushrooms, stems removed

½ cup extra-virgin olive oil, plus more if needed

Sea salt and black pepper to taste

½ cup variety fresh herbs, chopped, such as parsley, thyme, rosemary, chives

½ cup provolone cheese, sliced

If you are unable to locate portobello mushrooms, buy a variety of mushrooms and broil them together. Because they will most likely be smaller in size than the portobellos, your cooking time may be shortened.

1. Preheat broiler. Brush any dirt from the mushrooms, but do not wash them. Place mushrooms on parchment-lined baking sheet, stem side down to start. Drizzle with olive oil and season lightly with salt and pepper. Place under broiler for 4 minutes.
2. Remove mushrooms from broiler and place pan on stovetop. Turn mushrooms over, drizzle with additional olive oil, and top with herbs, seasoning lightly with salt and pepper. Top with cheese slices. Return to broiler and broil until cheese melts.

### Portobello Mushrooms
Portobello mushrooms are really just super-large cremini mushrooms! They are so large and meaty they are like eating a vegetarian burger. Being the Bikini Chef with a focus on figure-flattering flavors, I use them as "bread" for a portobello mushroom sandwich (see Grilled Portobello Mushroom Panini, page 295).

# Risotto with Morel Mushrooms

Serves 6

Prep time: 10 minutes
Cook time: 30 minutes
Total cost: $6.93
Calories: 250
Fat: 6g
Carbohydrates: 31g
Protein: 10g
Cholesterol: 11mg
Sodium: 641mg

2 tablespoons butter, unsalted

2 ounces dried morel mushrooms, soaked in water, liquid reserved, chopped

Sea salt and black pepper to taste

2 tablespoons olive oil

1 medium yellow onion, chopped

2 cloves garlic, chopped

½ cup cremini (or button) mushrooms, chopped

1½ cups arborio rice

½ cup dry white wine such as Sauvignon Blanc

3 cups vegetable broth

¼ cup Parmesan cheese, plus 2 tablespoons

½ fresh lemon

¼ cup fresh Italian flat-leaf parsley, leaves chopped

Morel mushrooms are sponge-like and absorb moisture. If you buy fresh morels, there is no need to soak them. If you have extras, simply dry them out and freeze them. When needed, reconstitute them in water for about 20 minutes.

1. In large saucepan over medium heat, heat 1 tablespoon butter and add morel mushrooms with liquid. Season with salt and pepper and let cook for 5 minutes. Set aside.
2. In large-quart boiler, heat 1 tablespoon olive oil over medium heat and add onion, garlic, and cremini mushrooms and cook for about 3 minutes. Then add rice and stir with wooden spoon to coat with other ingredients, about 1 minute. Pour in wine and stir constantly until all wine is absorbed.
3. Add 1 cup broth, and stir constantly until absorbed. Repeat with remaining stock, adding ½ cup to 1 cup at a time, until rice is mostly tender. Remove from heat and stir in cheese and remaining butter and mix well. Add morel mushrooms, lemon, and season to taste. Serve with any remaining Parmesan cheese.

The $7 a Meal Healthy Cookbook

# Tomatoes, Basil, and Camembert with Linguine

Serves 4

- Prep time: 5 minutes
- Cook time: 15 minutes
- Total cost: $6.49
- Calories: 241
- Fat: 8g
- Carbohydrates: 28g
- Protein: 5g
- Cholesterol: 12mg
- Sodium: 180mg

1 12-ounce box linguine pasta

¼ cup olive oil

5 large tomatoes, seeded and diced

Sea salt and black pepper to taste

¼ fresh basil, chopped

1 cup Camembert cheese, chopped, room temperature

Camembert is a softer cheese made from cow's milk and is traditionally from the Normandy region of France. It has a mild but distinctive flavor and creamy texture. It is one of my favorite cheeses to cook with as it pairs nicely with many types of foods.

1. Fill large-quart boiler ¾ with water, adding in pinch of salt and a drizzle of olive oil. Bring to a boil and cook linguine pasta until al dente. Drain and set aside.
2. In large saucepan over medium heat, heat oil. Add tomatoes and simmer 1 minute; season with salt and pepper. Return pasta to large-quart boiler. Add tomato mixture, basil, and cheese. Toss well and serve.

# CHAPTER 12

# PASTA, RICE, AND OTHER GRAINS

# Black Beans with Cilantro over Rice

● Serves 6

Prep time: 12 minutes
Cook time: 15 minutes
Total cost: $5.60
Calories: 198
Fat: 3g
Carbohydrates: 25g
Protein: 12g
Cholesterol: 0mg
Sodium: 366mg

1 tablespoon olive oil

½ yellow onion, diced

2 cloves garlic, minced

2 16-ounce cans black beans, undrained

½ cup medium salsa

Fine zest of 1 lemon

1 tablespoon fresh cilantro, chopped

Sea salt and black pepper to taste

4 cups cooked long-grain white rice

Black beans are good for you as they are low in fat and have no cholesterol. However, as with most canned products, they are high in sodium. To reduce the sodium content, rinse the beans. If you rinse the beans for use here, you will need to add about ¼ cup of water to the recipe.

In large saucepan over medium heat, heat oil and add onions and garlic. Sauté until tender, about 5 minutes. Stir in beans, salsa, and lemon zest. Mix well, cover, and simmer about 10 minutes, stirring occasionally. Add cilantro and season with salt and pepper. Stir to combine. Serve over rice in a bowl.

# Risi e Bisi with Fresh Italian Parsley

 **Serves 6**

Prep time: 5 minutes
Cook time: 25 minutes
Total cost: $5.75
Calories: 192
Fat: 2g
Carbohydrates: 38g
Protein: 4g
Cholesterol: 0mg
Sodium: 301mg

2 tablespoons olive oil

1 onion, finely chopped

2 cups long-grain white rice

4 cups chicken broth

1½ cups frozen peas

Sea salt and pepper to taste

1 tablespoon fresh Italian flat-leaf parsley

1 tablespoon unsalted butter (optional)

When I tell my family we are having rice and peas for dinner they don't appear so thrilled. Yet, when I announce we are having "risi e bisi," they become overjoyed! It's all in the presentation, remember? Risi e bisi is a traditional Italian dish and this is the traditional recipe. Feel free to spruce it up by adding red bell pepper or diced tomatoes.

1. In heavy saucepan, heat olive oil over medium heat. Add onion; cook and stir until onion is tender, about 5 minutes. Add rice; stir to combine and cook about 2 minutes. Add chicken broth and bring to a boil. Cover pan, reduce heat, and simmer for an additional 15 minutes, until rice is almost tender.
2. Add peas, cover, and cook over medium-low heat until peas are hot and rice is tender, about 3 to 4 minutes. Season with salt and pepper, stir in parsley and butter (optional), and serve.

# Pasta Salad with Lemon Balsamic Vinaigrette and Red Bell Peppers

Serves 8

Prep time: 15 minutes
Chill time: 2 hours
Total cost: $6.35
Calories: 199
Fat: 6g
Carbohydrates: 28g
Protein: 6g
Cholesterol: 22mg
Sodium: 349mg

¼ cup extra-virgin olive oil

¼ cup balsamic vinegar

Sea salt and black pepper to taste

2 cloves garlic, chopped

Fine zest of 1 lemon

1 pound rotini pasta, cooked and drained

1 red onion, chopped

2 red bell peppers, seeded and chopped

½ cup grated Parmesan cheese

1 tablespoon fresh basil, leaves chopped

This recipe for pasta salad is a great base for any pasta salad. Add chopped prosciutto, fresh kernel corn, chopped asparagus tips or green beans, chopped black olives . . . creating your own recipes in the kitchen is part of the fun of cooking!

In large bowl, whisk together oil, vinegar, salt, pepper, garlic, and lemon zest. Mix well. Add pasta, onion, peppers, Parmesan, and basil and toss well to coat.

# Tortellini Pasta with Tomatoes and Kalamata Olives

Serves 8

Prep time: 10 minutes

Cook time: 10 minutes

Total cost: $6.57

Calories: 389

Fat: 8g

Carbohydrates: 29g

Protein: 5g

Cholesterol: 62mg

Sodium: 410mg

1 8-ounce package frozen or fresh cheese tortellini

¼ cup extra-virgin olive oil

¼ cup Parmesan cheese, grated

2 large tomatoes, seeded and diced

1 cup kalamata olives, chopped

Sea salt and pepper to taste

Tortellini pasta is typical to the north-central region of Italy and is customarily filled with a meat such as prosciutto. Tortelloni pasta is of the same shape but larger in size.

Cook tortellini as directed on package. Drain well. Separately, in medium bowl, whisk together oil and cheese. Add in tomatoes and olives, season as desired with salt and pepper. Add pasta and toss well to coat. Cover and refrigerate for 20 minutes.

# Penne Pasta with Mushrooms

 Serves 8

Prep time: 8 minutes
Cook time: 23 minutes
Total cost: $5.35
Calories: 318
Fat: 10g
Carbohydrates: 47g
Protein: 13g
Cholesterol: 88mg
Sodium: 432mg

2 slices bacon, chopped

½ yellow onion, chopped

2 cups fresh cremini or button mushrooms, sliced

1 teaspoon unsalted butter

Sea salt and black pepper to taste

1 tablespoon salt for pasta water

Drizzle of oil for cooking the pasta

1 pound pasta shells or penne pasta

½ cup Parmesan cheese, grated

The bacon in this recipe is optional. If you choose and your budget allows, add a variety of mushrooms such as lobster, porcini, and morel. If the mushrooms are purchased dried, soak them in water for about 20 minutes before cooking with them using some of the water when sautéing.

1.  Heat large skillet or saucepan over medium heat. Add bacon and onion and cook until bacon is crisp and onion is tender. Drain off some of the bacon grease, then add mushrooms and cook until tender, about 5 minutes. Add butter and season with salt and pepper to taste.
2.  Meanwhile, in large pot, bring at least 4 quarts of water to a rolling boil. Add 1 tablespoon salt and a drizzle of olive oil. Add the pasta, stir to separate, and cook until not quite al dente, about 8 minutes. Drain and return pasta to pot. Add mushroom mixture to pasta, add in Parmesan, and toss to coat.

# Polenta with Fresh Basil and Garlic

Serves 6

Prep time: 10 minutes
Cook time: 15 minutes
Total cost: $6.72
Calories: 156
Fat: 2g
Carbohydrates: 32g
Protein: 4g
Cholesterol: 5mg
Sodium: 222mg

¼ cup olive oil

2 cloves fresh garlic, chopped

Sea salt and black pepper to taste

2 cups finely ground cornmeal

4 tablespoons unsalted butter, room temperature

1 tablespoon fresh basil, leaves chopped

½ cup Parmesan cheese, grated

Making polenta is easy and it tastes great. Cooked polenta can be shaped into balls, sticks, or patties, and fried in oil. Although this method tastes great, I don't recommend it regularly if you desire to consume fewer calories and fat. You can enjoy it fried on occasion, though. Everything in moderation!

Bring 8½ cups water to a boil in large heavy boiler. Add olive oil, garlic, salt, and pepper. Slowly add cornmeal (polenta) and stir continuously. After all cornmeal has been added, cook and stir over low heat until polenta pulls away from sides of boiler. This should only take a few minutes as the water is absorbed quickly. Polenta should be thick, smooth, and creamy. Stir in basil, butter, and cheese.

## Polenta

Polenta is a dish made from cornmeal and is popular in many European cuisines, especially northern Italian foods. When I worked at Beccofino Ristorante and Wine Bar in Florence, Italy, we served a similar baked version with sun-dried tomatoes.

# Red Bell Pepper Couscous with Fresh Thyme

 Serves 6

Prep time: 8 minutes

Cook time: 15 minutes

Total cost: $6.10

Calories: 244

Fat: 6g

Carbohydrates: 24g

Protein: 8g

Cholesterol: 1mg

Sodium: 376mg

2 tablespoons olive oil

1 yellow onion, finely chopped

1 red bell pepper, seeded and diced

2 cups chicken broth

1 teaspoon fresh thyme, leaves chopped

1 cup couscous

If you find your couscous is overly wet, simply spread onto a baking sheet and dry it out in the oven for 5 minutes.

In large saucepan, heat oil over medium heat. Add onion and cook until tender, about 5 minutes. Add bell pepper and cook an additional 1 minute. Add chicken broth and thyme. Mix well and bring to a boil. Stir in couscous, cover pan, and remove from heat. Let stand for 5 to 10 minutes, until liquid is absorbed. Fluff couscous with fork and serve.

**Couscous**

Couscous is actually not a grain. It is ground semolina pasta that is usually precooked. Because the ground pasta is precooked, it absorbs hot liquid extra fast, making for super-fast cooking when combined with other ingredients.

# Barley Casserole with Root Vegetables

Serves 6

Prep time: 10 minutes
Cook time: 1 hour
Total cost: $6.76
Calories: 218
Fat: 3g
Carbohydrates: 46g
Protein: 14g
Cholesterol: 10mg
Sodium: 401mg

1 large yellow onion, chopped

1 leek, cleaned, rinsed and chopped

1 carrot, peeled and chopped

1 beet, peeled and chopped

1 parsnip, peeled and chopped

2 tablespoons fresh cilantro, chopped

1 tablespoon olive oil

1 cup barley

½ teaspoon ground cumin

4 cups vegetable stock

Sea salt and black pepper to taste

Root vegetables, such as beets and parsnips, are typically a winter food but enjoy them anytime. In this recipe they are prepared baked, but root vegetables are also terrific in soups and stews.

Preheat oven to 350°F. Combine all the ingredients in a large casserole dish greased with oil. Cover tightly and bake for 60 minutes.

# Sautéed Vegetables with Quinoa

 Serves 6

Prep time: 10 minutes
Cook time: 32 minutes
Total cost: $5.36
Calories: 318
Fat: 9g
Carbohydrates: 31g
Protein: 6g
Cholesterol: 1mg
Sodium: 258mg

1 tablespoon olive oil

1 yellow squash, chopped

1 zucchini squash, chopped

1 eggplant, chopped

4 cloves garlic, chopped

¾ cup quinoa

2½ cups vegetable broth

½ tablespoon tarragon, leaves chopped

Black pepper to taste

1 teaspoon capers, smashed

Healthy grains don't have to be boring and this recipe proves just that! Tarragon has a slightly licorice flavor, so use basil if you prefer a lighter flavor.

Heat the oil to medium temperature in a medium-size saucepan, then add the vegetables and garlic; sauté for 3 minutes. Add the quinoa, and stir for 1 minute. Add the stock and simmer for approximately 30 minutes with lid slightly ajar, until the quinoa is thoroughly cooked. Remove from heat and add the tarragon, black pepper, and capers.

## Quinoa

Quinoa is a grain that is popular in South American and Mediterranean cooking. It is high in protein and contains all 9 essential amino acids.

# Zucchini and Tomatoes with Penne Pasta

 Serves 8

Prep time: 10 minutes
Cook time: 18 minutes
Total cost: $6.82
Calories: 382
Fat: 25g
Carbohydrates: 53g
Protein: 12g
Cholesterol: 20mg
Sodium: 266mg

2 tablespoons olive oil, plus a drizzle for cooking pasta

3 cloves garlic, chopped

3 cups chicken broth

6 Roma tomatoes, chopped

1 zucchini, chopped

¼ fresh Italian parsley, chopped

4 scallions, white part and half the green tops, chopped

Sea salt and black pepper to taste

¼ cup unsalted butter, softened

1 tablespoon salt (for pasta water)

1 pound penne pasta

This recipe is super delicious and perfect for a light dinner.

1. In large saucepan over medium heat, heat olive oil and add garlic; sauté until golden. Add chicken broth, tomatoes, zucchini, parsley, and scallions. Add salt and pepper as desired. Bring to a boil and reduce over medium high heat, about 5 to 8 minutes. Whisk in butter, a little at a time, to thicken sauce. Remove from heat and keep warm.
2. Meanwhile, in large pot filled ¾ with water, bring water to a boil. Add 1 tablespoon of salt and a drizzle of oil. Add pasta and stir to prevent sticking. Cook until al dente, about 8 to 10 minutes. Drain. Transfer pasta to serving bowl and toss with sauce.

# Gnocchi of Barley and Spinach

 **Serves 6**

- Prep time: 18 minutes
- Cook time: 8 minutes
- Total cost: $3.86
- Calories: 326
- Fat: 6g
- Carbohydrates: 42g
- Protein: 8g
- Cholesterol: 13mg
- Sodium: 265mg

¼ cup cooked spinach

¼ cup cooked barley

1 whole egg

1 egg white

½ teaspoon extra-virgin olive oil

1 teaspoon dry white wine

½ cup semolina

½ cup unbleached all-purpose flour

Sea salt and pepper to taste

Gnocchi is an Italian dumpling usually made from semolina flour or potato. The barley used here is a healthy, lighter version of this Italian favorite.

1. In a blender or food processor, purée the spinach and barley, then add the eggs, oil, and wine; continue to blend until thoroughly smooth.
2. Sift together the semolina, flour, salt, and pepper. Incorporate the spinach mixture with the flour mixture.
3. Bring 1 gallon water to a boil. While the water comes to a boil, form the gnocchi with a fork if you like.) Drop the gnocchi into the boiling water and cook for approximately 8 minutes, until al dente.

### Preparing Dough

Whenever preparing any type of dough, use a little flour to prevent sticking. However, you don't want a lot of excess flour on the final product, so be certain to brush all the flour off before cooking.

# Vegetable Tamale with Epazote

**Serves 6**

Prep time: 15 minutes
Cook time: 45 minutes
Total cost: $7.00
Calories: 275
Fat: 5g
Carbohydrates: 47g
Protein: 8g
Cholesterol: 2mg
Sodium: 264mg

2 tablespoons extra-virgin olive oil

1 red bell pepper, seeded and chopped

1 yellow onion, chopped

1 zucchini, sliced lengthwise

¼ cup whole button mushrooms, stems removed

½ cup chicken broth

1 cup masa harina

Sea salt and black pepper to taste

½ tablespoon chopped epazote (marjoram or cilantro can be substituted)

6 corn husks, soaked in water for at least 1 hour, then drained

The flavor of epazote is similar to anise, fennel, and tarragon but stronger. It is most commonly used with black beans.

1. Lightly oil the pepper, onion, zucchini, and mushrooms with 1 tablespoon of oil, then grill or roast them until al dente, approximately 10 minutes.
2. In a medium-size bowl, mix together the stock, masa, remaining tablespoon oil, salt, pepper, and epazote.
3. Lay out the corn husks. Place a layer of the masa mixture in the husks, then add the vegetables, and then another layer of masa mix. Roll up the tamales tightly and tie the ends closed with small strips of husk.
4. Bring water to boil in a steamer pan. Place the tamales in the perforated pan and steam for 20 to 30 minutes.

### Masa Harina
Masa harina is a very fine corn flour and is available at most health food stores or in Spanish markets.

# Moroccan Couscous Chili

 Serves 6

- Prep time: 15 minutes
- Cook time: 2 hrs., 10 mins.
- Total cost: $6.99
- Calories: 353
- Fat: 11g
- Carbohydrates: 42g
- Protein: 22g
- Cholesterol: 1mg
- Sodium: 778mg

1 tablespoon olive oil

1 large yellow onion, chopped

1 carrot, peeled and chopped

1 jalapeño or serrano chili pepper, seeded and chopped

3 cloves garlic, chopped

2 cans kidney beans, undrained

4 cups chicken broth

1 cup brewed strong coffee, decaf or regular

4 plum tomatoes, seeded and chopped

½ teaspoon red pepper flakes

Black pepper to taste

1 tablespoon chili powder

1 teaspoon curry powder

1 teaspoon honey

1 cup vegetable stock

1 cup couscous

¼ bunch fresh cilantro, leaves chopped

If you love couscous, skip the chili part and add drained kidney beans, chili powder, tomato, and cilantro to the couscous!

1. Heat the oil to medium temperature in a large stockpot. Add the onions, carrots, chili pepper, and garlic; sauté for 5 minutes. Reduce heat to low and add the beans, chicken broth, coffee, tomatoes, red pepper flakes, black pepper, chili and curry powder, and honey; simmer slowly uncovered for 2 hours, adding broth if necessary and stirring occasionally.
2. Fifteen minutes before the chili is done, in a small saucepan, bring the vegetable stock to a boil. Add the couscous and cook for 2 to 3 minutes. Cover, let sit for 1 minute, then fluff. Keep warm. Adjust seasonings to taste. Serve chili, top with the couscous, and sprinkle with cilantro.

# Tabbouleh

Serves 6

Prep time: 15 minutes
Cook time: none
Total cost: $6.39
Calories: 124
Fat: 11g
Carbohydrates: 12g
Protein: 3g
Cholesterol: 1mg
Sodium: 75mg

**Rest**
2 hours,
15 minutes

1 cup cracked (bulgur) wheat

1 quart water

1 small cucumber, chopped

3 scallions, finely chopped

2 ripe tomatoes, seeded and chopped

2 tablespoons chopped chives

1 cup chopped Italian parsley

½ cup extra-virgin olive oil

Juice of 2 lemons

Sea salt and black pepper to taste

Other great ingredients for this recipe are red or yellow bell pepper, yellow squash, and fresh peas.

1. Soak the wheat in 1 quart water for 15 minutes (or overnight). Drain and squeeze out excess moisture by tying up in a cheesecloth or clean kitchen towel.
2. Combine wheat with cucumber, scallions, tomatoes, chives, and parsley in a mixing bowl. Toss with olive oil, lemon juice, salt, and pepper. Set aside to marinate for 2 to 3 hours before serving.

**Tabbouleh**
The Middle Eastern bulgur wheat used in this recipe absorbs water quickly, giving it a pliable and chewy texture unlike anything else in the world. Tabbouleh is an everyday dish in Egypt, and it goes perfect with stuffed grape leaves.

# Barley Corn Salad

 Serves 8

Prep time: 5 minutes
Cook time: 35 minutes
Total cost: $5.84
Calories: 127
Fat: 6g
Carbohydrates: 36g
Protein: 4g
Cholesterol: 2mg
Sodium: 129mg

1 cup barley

2 quarts lightly salted water

1 16-ounce package frozen sweet corn kernels

1 carrot, chopped finely

2 ribs celery, chopped finely

1 medium red onion, chopped finely

1 tablespoon red wine vinegar or cider vinegar

2 tablespoons extra-virgin olive oil

½ cup chopped fresh herbs, such as parsley, chives, basil, oregano, mint, and cilantro

Salt and freshly ground black pepper to taste

Barley can be substituted for brown rice, white rice, or another of your favorite grains.

1. Boil the barley in 2 quarts lightly salted water until it is very tender, about 30 minutes. Drain and spread on a platter to cool. Heat a dry cast-iron pan or skillet over a high flame for 1 minute. Add the corn and cook without stirring until some kernels attain a slight char and the corn has a smoky aroma, about 5 minutes.
2. Combine the barley, corn, carrot, celery, and onion in a mixing bowl. Add remaining ingredients and toss well to coat.

**Whole-Grain Nutrients**
Whole grains like barley provide many of the B vitamins vegetarians need to fight off diseases and are higher in protein, vitamin E, zinc, phosphorus, and other phytonutrients than refined grains.

# CHAPTER 13

# VEGETABLE AND SIDE DISHES

# Yellow Squash Croquettes

Serves 6 people

Prep time: 10 minutes
Cook time: 4 minutes
Total cost: $3.81
Calories: 156
Fat: 5g
Carbohydrates: 10g
Protein: 2g
Cholesterol: 35mg
Sodium: 200mg

2 cups yellow squash, skin on, finely chopped

1 large yellow onion, chopped

1 egg, beaten

Sea salt and black pepper to taste

Pinch of cayenne pepper

½ cup plus 1 tablespoon plain flour

Canola oil for frying

Another way to test the heat of oil is to place the tip of a wooden spoon into the hot oil. If the oil bubbles around the spoon, the oil is hot and ready for frying.

Combine first 5 ingredients and mix well. Stir in flour, being careful not to overmix. In iron skillet or other deep saucepan, heat canola oil (about ½ to 1 inch deep) until hot. Test by placing a small pinch of squash mixture into hot oil. If bubbling rapidly, oil is hot. Drop mixture by teaspoonfuls into the hot oil. Cook until browned, turning once. Remove from oil with slotted spoon and transfer to paper towels. Once drained, serve hot.

# Winter Greens Salad with Green Beans and Blue Cheese Vinaigrette

Serves 4

Prep time: 15 minutes
Cook time: 5 minutes
Total cost: $7.00
Calories: 102
Fat: 4g
Carbohydrates: 14g
Protein: 4g
Cholesterol: 6mg
Sodium: 129mg

1 bunch watercress

2 heads Belgium endive

1 small red onion

½ pound green beans

**Vinaigrette**

⅓ cup balsamic vinegar

⅓ cup vegetable oil

⅓ cup extra-virgin olive oil

1 tablespoon chopped chives

¼ pound blue cheese

Sea salt and ground black pepper

Fresh asparagus tips also taste great with this salad. Prepare them the same way as the green beans.

1. Rinse watercress and break into bite-size pieces. Cut endives diagonally into 3 or 4 sections each, discarding cores. Slice red onion into thin rings.
2. In 3 quarts of rapidly boiling salted water, cook green beans in 2 separate batches until just tender, about 5 minutes, then plunge them into salted ice water to stop the cooking process. Drain them and then combine with greens and onions.
3. Whisk together vinegar, vegetable oil, olive oil, and chives. Roughly break the blue cheese into vinaigrette; stir with a spoon, leaving some large chunks. Season with salt and pepper. Pour ⅓ cup of vinaigrette onto greens. Reserve remaining vinaigrette in refrigerator for up to 2 weeks. Arrange salad onto 4 plates, with onions and green beans on top.

# Tatsoi Greens with Orange-Sesame Vinaigrette

 Serves 4

Prep time: 10 minutes
Cook time: none
Total cost: $4.21
Calories: 89
Fat: 2g
Carbohydrates: 4g
Protein: 2g
Cholesterol: 0mg
Sodium: 64mg

6 cups tatsoi

¼ cup Orange-Sesame Vinaigrette (see below)

½ cup red onion, sliced paper-thin

Wash and dry the tatsoi leaves, then toss gently with one half of the vinaigrette. Distribute onto 4 salad plates. Arrange sliced onions atop each salad, and finish with a final spoonful of vinaigrette.

# Orange-Sesame Vinaigrette

Yields about 1¼ cups

Prep time: 10 minutes
Cook time: none
Total cost: $2.55
Calories: 64
Fat: 2g
Carbohydrates: 4g
Protein: 2g
Cholesterol: 0mg
Sodium: 64mg

Zest of ½ orange

Zest of ½ lime

1 pickled jalapeño pepper, with juice, chopped

¼ cup Japanese rice wine vinegar

¼ cup orange juice concentrate

1½ teaspoons Dijon mustard

Few drops sesame oil

¼ cup peanut oil

¼ cup olive oil

Salt and freshly ground black pepper

Combine zests, pickled jalapeño and brine, rice vinegar, orange concentrate, Dijon mustard, and sesame oil in a blender. Blend on medium speed, slowly drizzling in the peanut and olive oils. Season to taste with salt and pepper.

# Classic Potato Salad

Serves 8

Prep time: 8 minutes
Cook time: none
Total cost: $5.54
Calories: 272
Fat: 6g
Carbohydrates: 22g
Protein: 3g
Cholesterol: 22mg
Sodium: 400mg

¾ cup mayonnaise

1 teaspoon sugar

2 teaspoons Dijon-style mustard

2 pounds potatoes (any variety), peeled, cut into 2-inch cubes, and boiled

1 small carrot, peeled and grated

Salt and white pepper to taste

1 tablespoon roughly chopped Italian parsley

When making potato salad, don't overboil the potatoes, as they become mushy and will cause your potato salad to have a consistency similar to mashed potatoes.

Whisk together mayonnaise, sugar, and mustard in a small bowl. Add potatoes and carrots; toss them gently to coat. Season to taste with salt and white pepper. Garnish with chopped parsley.

# Asian Cucumber Salad

Serves 4

Prep time: 10 minutes

Cook time: none

Total cost: $2.79

Calories: 103

Fat: 7g

Carbohydrates: 10g

Protein: 1g

Cholesterol: 1mg

Sodium: 170mg

¼ cup rice wine vinegar

1 teaspoon sugar

1 teaspoon chopped jalapeño pepper

1 European-style long cucumber or 1 large regular cucumber

Sesame oil

Chopped tomatoes are also a good addition to this healthy, flavorful salad.

Whisk together rice vinegar, sugar, and chopped jalapeño. If using a European cucumber, it is not necessary to peel, but if using an American cucumber, peel it. Halve the cucumber lengthwise; remove seeds. Slice seeded cucumber very thinly into half-moons. Combine with vinegar mixture, drizzle in a few drops of sesame oil, and toss to coat. Marinate for at least 10 minutes before serving.

# Slaw of Summer Vegetables

Serves 8

Prep time: 15 minutes
Cook time: none
Total cost: $6.98
Calories: 158
Fat: 3g
Carbohydrates: 9g
Protein: 2g
Cholesterol: 0mg
Sodium: 158mg

1 small head napa Chinese cabbage, grated or chopped

1 carrot, peeled and chopped

¼ pound snow peas, sliced

1 red bell pepper, seeded and chopped

12 green beans, ends trimmed, chopped

1 small red onion, chopped

1 ear fresh sweet corn, shucked, kernels cut off cob

½ teaspoon sugar

¼ cup apple cider vinegar

1 tablespoon olive oil

Pinch celery seeds

Salt and black pepper to taste

This vegetable combination is great served fresh, as with this recipe, or heat the tablespoon of olive oil in a large skillet and sauté the ingredients for about 5 minutes.

Combine all vegetables in a large mixing bowl; toss with sugar, vinegar, oil, celery seeds, salt, and pepper. Allow to sit at least 10 minutes before serving.

**Napa Cabbage**
Napa, or, Chinese cabbage is lighter in texture and flavor than American cabbage.

# Wild Mushroom Ragout in Puff Pastry Shells

 Serves 8

Prep time: 5 minutes
Cook time: 25 minutes
Total cost: $7.00
Calories: 192
Fat: 2g
Carbohydrates: 38g
Protein: 4g
Cholesterol: 44mg
Sodium: 301mg

24 pieces frozen puff pastry hors d'oeuvre shells

1 tablespoon unsalted butter

2 cups cremini mushrooms, chopped

½ teaspoon salt

2 sprigs fresh rosemary, leaves picked and chopped

¼ cup vegetable stock or water

1 teaspoon cornstarch dissolved in 1 tablespoon cold water

Freshly ground black pepper to taste

Squeeze of lemon

Sea salt to taste

If you love cheese, add a little grated Parmesan cheese to the top or in the ragout.

Bake puff pastry shells according to package directions. In a medium skillet over medium heat, melt the butter. Add the mushrooms and cook, without stirring, for 5 minutes, until a nice brown coating has developed. Add salt and rosemary; cook 3 minutes more. Add the stock and cornstarch; stir until thickened and bubbling. Remove from heat; adjust seasoning with black pepper, a few drops of lemon, and salt to taste. Spoon ½ teaspoon of mushroom ragout into each shell and serve.

**Puff Pastry**
Most supermarkets carry small frozen puff pastry shells in the freezer section. Puff pastry is also available in sheets for making your own pastry shapes. The premade shells are perfect for quick homemade bites like these.

# Steamed Asparagus and Carrots with Lemon

Serves 6

Prep time: 2 minutes
Cook time: 20 minutes
Total cost: $6.78
Calories: 74
Fat: 0g
Carbohydrates: 14g
Protein: 4g
Cholesterol: 0mg
Sodium: 194mg

½ pound baby carrots, rinsed

1 8-ounce package frozen
   asparagus spears

2 tablespoons lemon juice

1 teaspoon lemon pepper

Pinch sea salt (optional)

If you want more flavor, add a little butter or olive oil when serving!

1. Place carrots in a steamer basket above boiling water. Cover and steam about 15 minutes or until crisp-tender. Rinse the carrots in cold water; drain.
2. Meanwhile, cook the frozen asparagus spears according to package directions. Rinse the asparagus in cold water; drain. Place both carrots and asparagus in serving bowl and drizzle with lemon juice and pepper; add salt if desired. Cover and chill until ready to serve.

**Steaming Vegetables**
Steaming is a great way to cook vegetables as it brings out their color and maintains their nutrients. Plus, it's easy on cleanup, which is perhaps the best thing of all!

The $7 a Meal Healthy Cookbook

# Pan-Fried Rosemary New Potatoes

Serves 4

Prep time: 5 minutes
Cook time: 22 minutes
Total cost: $4.55
Calories: 189
Fat: 3g
Carbohydrates: 18g
Protein: 2g
Cholesterol: 0mg
Sodium: 201mg

1 pound golf-ball-size red-skinned new potatoes

2 tablespoons extra-virgin olive oil

3 sprigs fresh rosemary

Sea salt and freshly ground black pepper

These potatoes taste great baked, as well. To bake, cut into quarters and then toss with ingredients. Bake until tender, about 25 minutes.

1. Heat oven to 375°F. Slice the potatoes into ½-inch-thick rounds, and boil them in lightly salted water until crisp-tender, about 7 minutes. Drain well, and dry very well with a towel.
2. Heat the olive oil in a large, heavy, ovensafe skillet until it shimmers but does not smoke. Add the rosemary sprigs (they should sizzle), and then slip in the potatoes. Cook without disturbing for 5 minutes. Once potatoes have browned lightly on the first side, turn them over and put the pan in the oven. Cook 10 minutes. Transfer potatoes to a serving platter, season with salt and pepper, and garnish with additional rosemary sprigs.

# Garlic Mashed Potatoes

Serves 6

3 heads garlic, top chopped, peel left on

2 pounds potatoes, peeled and chopped into 2-inch pieces

8 tablespoons butter

½ cup low-fat milk

1½ teaspoons salt

White pepper (optional)

Everyone loves garlic mashed potatoes. The secret, however, is to roast the garlic first. Raw garlic flavor is very pungent and may overpower your potatoes otherwise.

1. Heat oven to 400°F. Wrap all three garlic heads into a pouch fashioned from aluminum foil, and place in the center of the oven. Roast until garlic is very soft and yields to gentle finger pressure, about 45 minutes. Turn off heat.
2. In large-quart boiler, boil potatoes in lightly salted water until tender, about 20 minutes. Using your hands, squeeze out the roasted garlic. Heat the butter and milk together in a small pan until the butter melts. Drain the potatoes well, then return them to the pot. Mash them with a potato masher or stiff wire whisk. Add the roasted garlic, season with salt and pepper, and add the milk mixture. Mix just enough to incorporate.

The $7 a Meal Healthy Cookbook

# Dominican Red Beans and Rice

 Serves 8

Prep time: 10 minutes
Cook time: 2 hours
Total cost: $6.67
Calories: 241
Fat: 2g
Carbohydrates: 31g
Protein: 9g
Cholesterol: 0mg
Sodium: 520mg

## Red Beans

1 medium onion, chopped

3 cloves garlic, sliced

3 tablespoons olive oil

1 teaspoon oregano

1 bay leaf

1 8-ounce can tomato sauce

2 teaspoons adobo con pimienta

1 16-ounce package red beans soaked overnight in 4 cups cold water, drained

½ small bunch fresh cilantro, leaves chopped

Sea salt and white pepper to taste

1. Sauté onions and garlic with olive oil over medium heat for 5 minutes in a pot large enough to hold all ingredients. Add oregano, bay leaf, tomato sauce, and adobo. Bring to a simmer and add beans and cilantro, adding enough water to cover them, about 3 cups.
2. Bring to a boil, then reduce to a low simmer, and cook 90 minutes, until beans are tender enough to mash between fingers. Season with salt and pepper.

## Yellow Rice

2 tablespoons achiote

3 tablespoons oil

1 medium onion, chopped

1 tablespoon adobo con pimienta

4 cups long-grain rice

1. Heat achiote in oil in a large pot with a tight-fitting lid over a medium-high flame until seeds sizzle and give up their color. Oil should be a dark-orange hue. Remove from heat and carefully remove seeds with a slotted spoon or skimmer.
2. Add onion and adobo to achiote oil and sauté over medium heat for 5 minutes, until translucent. Add rice and stir until it is well coated with oil. Add 6 cups water, and raise flame to high.
3. Bring to boil, and then reduce to simmer, cover tightly, and cook 20 minutes, until all water is absorbed. Remove from heat and let stand, covered, 5 minutes. Fluff with a fork. Serve together with beans.

# Sweet Peas with Fresh Mint Leaves

Serves 4

Prep time: 5 minutes
Cook time: 5 minutes
Total cost: $3.65
Calories: 102
Fat: 1g
Carbohydrates: 29g
Protein: 2g
Cholesterol: 24mg
Sodium: 35mg

2 cups shelled fresh peas
(about 2 pounds unshelled)

½ teaspoon sugar

2 tablespoons butter

Salt and pepper to taste

3 tablespoons fresh mint
leaves, chopped

Shelling peas may sound like a time-consuming task but it really is easier than you think. If you are cooking for lots of people, have a friend help you or teach your kids how to do it. They will learn about fresh vegetables and help you in the process!

Simmer the peas and sugar until bright green and tender, about 5 minutes; drain. Toss peas with butter, salt, pepper, and mint.

# Egg Fried Rice with Green Peas

Serves 4

Prep time: 5 minutes
Cook time: 13 minutes
Total cost: $4.71
Calories: 182
Fat: 3g
Carbohydrates: 19g
Protein: 4g
Cholesterol: 14mg
Sodium: 179mg

2 tablespoons peanut or olive oil

3 eggs, beaten

2 tablespoons fresh ginger, chopped

4 cloves garlic, chopped

½ cup scallions, chopped

4 cups cooked white rice

1 10-ounce package frozen green peas

1 small carrot, peeled and diced

1 tablespoon soy sauce (optional)

Sesame seeds, for garnish (optional)

Fried rice is most commonly associated with Chinese or Asian restaurants. Here, you can learn to make your own and surprise your family and friends with your own Asian night.

1. Heat a 10-inch nonstick skillet with a few drops of peanut oil over medium heat; add the eggs. Cook without stirring until completely cooked through, about 3 minutes. Slide the cooked egg onto a cutting board; let it cool for 5 minutes. Roll the egg into a cylinder, and crosscut to form long julienne slices.
2. Heat the remaining oil in large skillet or wok. Add the ginger, garlic, and scallions, and cook for 1 minute; they should sizzle. Add the rice. Over high heat, chop and stir the rice to break up any lumps; cook until very hot and some rice forms crunchy bits, about 5 minutes. Add the peas and the carrots. Cook until peas are hot, then stir in the egg julienne and soy sauce (if desired). Serve garnished with additional chopped scallions and/or sesame seeds.

# Braised Swiss Chard

Serves 4

Prep time: 8 minutes
Cook time: 15 minutes
Total cost: $5.53
Calories: 62
Fat: 1g
Carbohydrates: 2g
Protein: 2g
Cholesterol: 2mg
Sodium: 25mg

1 cup vegetable broth

1 large bunch red or green Swiss chard, stems chopped, leaves cut into bite-size pieces

Sea salt and black pepper to taste

1 tablespoon olive oil

2 medium shallots, finely chopped

1 tablespoon unsalted butter

Lemon wedges

Another culinary curveball for most people, Swiss chard can be enjoyed braised (as here) sautéed, or even grilled. Don't be afraid to experiment with it to discover how you like it best.

1. In large skillet, bring the broth to a boil; add the chard stem pieces. Season with salt and pepper; cook until tender, about 6 minutes. Transfer them to a bowl or plate, reserving their cooking liquid. Wipe out the skillet.
2. Return the skillet to medium heat. Add olive oil and shallots. Cook 1 minute until they sizzle and soften slightly. Add the chard leaves, and cook only until they wilt, about 5 minutes. Add back the stems, plus 2 tablespoons of their cooking liquid. Bring to a simmer, and swirl in the butter. Taste for seasoning. Serve with lemon wedges.

### Swiss Chard

Swiss chard is a leafy vegetable from the same species as beets. It is one of the healthiest foods you can eat as it is packed full of vitamins and minerals. It is naturally low in calories, fat, and carbs.

The $7 a Meal Healthy Cookbook

# Buttered Brussels Sprouts with Nutmeg

 Serves 4

→ Prep time: 2 minutes
→ Cook time: 15 minutes
→ Total cost: $3.12
→ Calories: 30
→ Fat: 1g
→ Carbohydrates: 9g
→ Protein: 3g
→ Cholesterol: 20mg
→ Sodium: 88mg

1 pint Brussels sprouts

½ stick unsalted butter

Salt and white pepper

Pinch nutmeg

Lemon wedges (optional)

Many people cringe when they hear you are serving Brussels sprouts. But if cooked properly, Brussels sprouts taste remarkably good and they are so good for you!

1. Remove outer leaves from sprouts, and trim the stems so that they're flush with the sprout bottoms. Halve the sprouts by cutting through the stem end. Don't worry about loose leaves, include them.
2. Boil in small batches, in 4 quarts of well-salted, rapidly boiling water for 10 minutes. Drain well.
3. In a medium saucepan over medium heat, melt the butter and add the cooked sprouts, tossing with the salt, pepper, and nutmeg to coat. Sauté for about 5 minutes. Serve with lemon wedges.

**Brussels Sprouts**
Brussels sprouts are in the cabbage family and are very nutritious, containing high amounts of the B vitamins and iron. Sauté them as here with butter or add pine nuts and a little balsamic vinegar.

# Grilled Radicchio

Serves 4

Prep time: 5 minutes
Cook time: 4 minutes
Total cost: $4.89
Calories: 9
Fat: 0g
Carbohydrates: 2g
Protein: 1g
Cholesterol: 0mg
Sodium: 9mg

4 heads radicchio

1 tablespoon extra-virgin olive oil

1 lemon, halved

Sea salt and black pepper to taste

Radicchio has brightly colored red leaves that have a natural white vein to them. Add to other grilled vegetables or enjoy fresh in salads. Grilled radicchio would also be a nice topping to burgers, which are in the next chapter.

1. Quarter the radicchio heads through the root end. In a mixing bowl, drizzle the olive oil over the pieces, squeeze on the lemon juice, and season with salt and pepper; toss to coat.
2. Heat a grill or stovetop grill pan to medium heat. Lay the radicchio, cut side down, across the grill. Cook until wilting is visible from the sides, only about 2 minutes. Turn and cook for 1 or 2 minutes more, pulling it from the grill before it goes completely limp. Serve with extra lemon wedges on the side.

**Radicchio**

Radicchio is a leafy vegetable also known as Italian chicory. It has a spicy bitter taste that mellows when grilled. As with so many other foods, balsamic vinegar pairs nicely with radicchio.

# Fresh Kale with Garlic and Thyme

 Serves 4

Prep time: 6 minutes
Cook time: 30 minutes
Total cost: $5.97
Calories: 55
Fat: 2g
Carbohydrates: 10g
Protein: 4g
Cholesterol: 2mg
Sodium: 75mg

2 pounds kale, stems and ribs removed, leaves cut into bite-size pieces

1 tablespoon olive oil

1 medium red onion, chopped

2 cloves fresh garlic, chopped

Pinch crushed red pepper

2 teaspoons fresh thyme, leaves chopped

¼ cup dry sherry or white wine

Sea salt and black pepper to taste

2 tablespoons Parmesan cheese, grated

Kale has a strong flavor which is mellowed by the other ingredients in this recipe. Add a little lemon, if you like, to mellow it even more.

1. Bring a large pot of salted water to a rolling boil. Add the kale, and cook for 10 minutes, until it has lost its waxy coating and the leaves are tender. Transfer to a colander to drain, reserving about ½ cup of the cooking liquid. Roughly chop the kale.
2. Heat the oil in a large skillet over medium heat. Add the onion, garlic, red pepper, and thyme. Cook over medium heat until the onions are tender, about 5 minutes. Add the sherry; cook for 5 minutes. Add kale; cook 10 minutes more. Season with salt and pepper. Serve sprinkled with Parmesan cheese if desired.

### Kale

Kale is a leafy green vegetable that is part of the cabbage family and is rich in iron and beta carotene.

# Cabbage Stir-Fry with Hot Peppers

● Serves 5

Prep time: 7 minutes
Cook time: 7 minutes
Total cost: $6.84
Calories: 191
Fat: 3g
Carbohydrates: 10g
Protein: 2g
Cholesterol: 2mg
Sodium: 88mg

¼ cup plus 2 tablespoons peanut oil

8 dried red chili peppers, quartered and seeded

1 (1-inch) piece fresh ginger, peeled and finely chopped

1 head napa (Chinese) cabbage, washed and chopped into 2-inch pieces

½ teaspoon cornstarch

1 tablespoon soy sauce

1 teaspoon dry sherry

1 teaspoon sugar

1 teaspoon rice wine vinegar

1 teaspoon Asian sesame oil

Cabbage is like a sponge, absorbing any flavors you give it. The combination here includes a blend of spicy, sweet, and sour for a mouthwatering accompaniment to fish or chicken, or to just enjoy by itself.

1. In large skillet over medium heat, heat ¼ cup peanut oil. Add peppers and fry, stirring gently, for 1 minute, until the peppers darken in color. Transfer the peppers and oil to a bowl and set aside.

2. Pour remaining 2 tablespoons peanut oil into the skillet; add the ginger and cook for a few seconds until fragrant. Add the cabbage all at once. Fry, stirring, for 1 minute. Combine the cornstarch, soy sauce, and sherry together in a small bowl. Add to the skillet. Stir until the cornstarch cooks and forms a thick sauce; add the sugar and vinegar. Sprinkle in the sesame oil and pour in the red peppers and their oil. Stir to combine well. Transfer to a serving bowl.

# Rapini with Garlic

 Serves 4

Prep time: 5 minutes
Cook time: 9 minutes
Total cost: $5.23
Calories: 59
Fat: 1g
Carbohydrates: 3g
Protein: 2g
Cholesterol: 0mg
Sodium: 12mg

1 pound rapini, bottoms trimmed

2 tablespoons olive oil

3 cloves garlic, finely chopped

Pinch crushed red pepper flakes

Sea salt and black pepper to
   taste

Lemon wedges

Sauté yellow onion slices and mushrooms and add to the rapini for another tasty side dish.

1. Fill large-quart boiler ¾ with water; add 1 tablespoon salt and bring to a boil. Add rapini and boil for 3 minutes. Drain and transfer to ice bath to stop the cooking process. Drain well and set aside.
2. In large saucepan over medium heat, heat olive oil. Add the garlic and red pepper flakes and sauté for 2 minutes. Add all of the rapini at once; toss to coat. Season well with salt and pepper. When the rapini is hot, serve with lemon wedges on the side.

**Rapini**
A relative of the turnip family, rapini is also known as broccoli raab (or rabe). It is commonly used in Chinese, Italian, and Portuguese cooking and is high in vitamins A and C and iron.

# Cumin-Roasted Butternut Squash

 Serves 8

Prep time: 6 minutes
Cook time: 40 minutes
Total cost: $5.69
Calories: 103
Fat: 1g
Carbohydrates: 9g
Protein: 2g
Cholesterol: 0mg
Sodium: 10mg

1 medium butternut squash
(2–3 pounds)

2 tablespoons ground cumin

2 tablespoons olive oil

Sea salt and black pepper to
taste

1 tablespoon fresh Italian
flat-leaf parsley, chopped

Butternut squash is also delicious when baked with honey, cinnamon, and butter.

1. Preheat oven to 375°F. Cut the butternut squash in two, crosswise, just above the bulbous bottom. Place the cut side of the cylindrical barrel down on a cutting board and peel it with a knife or potato peeler, removing all rind. Repeat with the bottom part, then cut bottom in half and remove seeds.
2. Dice squash into 1-inch chunks. In a large mixing bowl, toss squash with cumin, oil, salt, and pepper.
3. Spread into a single layer on a parchment-lined baking sheet. Bake (or roast) in oven for 40 minutes, turning after 25 minutes, until browned and tender. Serve sprinkled with chopped parsley.

# Fried Green Tomatoes with Lemon-Caper Rémoulade

Serves 4

Prep time: 10 minutes
Cook time: 12 minutes
Total cost: $7.00
Calories: 191
Fat: 8g
Carbohydrates: 19g
Protein: 3g
Cholesterol: 8mg
Sodium: 123mg

1 cup nonfat or light mayonnaise

Fine zest of 1 lemon

1 hard-boiled egg, finely chopped

1 tablespoon capers, chopped

1 tablespoon dill pickle, chopped

1 teaspoon fresh Italian flat-leaf parsley, chopped

Dash hot pepper sauce

6 beaten eggs mixed with ½ cup milk

1 to 2 cups plain flour for dredging

4 cups plain or seasoned bread crumbs

3 large green tomatoes, sliced ½-inch thick, about 12 to 14 slices

2 cups canola oil

Make other flavored rémoulades by substituting roasted red bell peppers, sundried tomatoes, or grilled tomatoes.

1. Make the rémoulade: Combine mayonnaise with lemon zest, boiled egg, capers, pickle, parsley, and hot sauce. Taste for seasoning and refrigerate.
2. Separately, whisk remaining eggs in a medium mixing bowl. Place flour and bread crumbs each in separate bowls. Dredge each tomato slice in flour, then eggs, then bread crumbs, pressing the bread crumbs to ensure adherence. Fry in small batches over medium heat, until they feel tender when tested with a fork. Season with salt, and serve with rémoulade.

### Rémoulade Versus Aioli

A rémoulade is a mayonnaise-based sauce that is traditionally served with fish. Mayonnaise is made using a vegetable oil such as canola. Aioli is a mayonnaise-like sauce made with olive oil and is served with practically anything!

# Oven-Roasted Vegetables

Serves 4

Prep time: 15 minutes

Cook time: 45 minutes

Total cost: $6.62

Calories: 168

Fat: 4g

Carbohydrates: 23g

Protein: 5g

Cholesterol: 2mg

Sodium: 131mg

1 small eggplant, cubed

1 red bell pepper, seeded and chopped

4 cloves garlic, chopped

1 yellow onion, chopped

1 zucchini, chopped

1 yellow squash, chopped

1 cup cremini or button mushrooms, chopped

3 tablespoons olive oil

Sea salt and lemon pepper to taste

2 tablespoons fresh mixed herbs such as rosemary and thyme, leaves chopped

2 tablespoons balsamic vinegar

If you have an outdoor grill, use it to grill vegetables. Just slice the vegetables into planks instead of chopping so they don't fall through the grill, or invest in a grill basket.

1. Heat oven to 375°F. In a large bowl, combine eggplant, peppers, garlic, onions, zucchini, yellow squash, mushrooms, olive oil, salt, pepper, and mixed herbs; toss to coat.
2. Spread into a single layer on parchment-lined baking sheet. Bake for 45 minutes or until vegetables are very tender and browned lightly. Drizzle with balsamic vinegar and serve.

**Leftover Roasted Vegetables**

Leftover vegetables like these are perfect for making roasted vegetable sandwiches (see Chapter 14) or for using in breakfast frittatas (see Chapter 3).

The $7 a Meal Healthy Cookbook

# Chinese String Beans

Serves 4

Prep time: 10 minutes
Cook time: 15 to 20 mins.
Total cost: $5.83
Calories: 110
Fat: 5g
Carbohydrates: 8g
Protein: 3g
Cholesterol: 3mg
Sodium: 191mg

Oil for deep-frying

1 pound fresh green beans, stem ends trimmed

2 tablespoons peanut oil

½ cup scallions, chopped

1 1-inch piece fresh ginger, peeled and finely chopped

3 cloves garlic, chopped

1 teaspoon sugar

1 teaspoon white vinegar

Sea salt to taste

Asian sesame oil

Frying green beans is easy. Just be sure they are completely dried before placing them in the hot oil or the oil will spatter on you while frying and you might get burned.

1. In large skillet, heat 2 inches of oil until hot but not smoking. Carefully fry the green beans in 4 small batches. They will shrivel as they cook—they take about 5 minutes per batch.
2. In a separate skillet, heat the peanut oil. Add the scallions, ginger, garlic, sugar, and vinegar. Cook 1 minute, until the garlic turns white. Add the green beans; toss to coat. Season with salt and sesame oil.

# Stuffed Onions

**Serves 4**

Prep time: 10 minutes
Cook time: 1 hr., 15 mins.
Total cost: $4.86
Calories: 49
Fat: 1g
Carbohydrates: 6g
Protein: 1g
Cholesterol: 1mg
Sodium: 8mg

4 yellow onions

3 teaspoons butter

1 shallot, chopped

1 cup cremini mushrooms, finely chopped

1 tablespoon dry white wine

1 tablespoon fresh Italian flat-leaf parsley, finely chopped

Sea salt and black pepper to taste

2 cups vegetable broth

When it comes to stuffing, onions taste great and are a fun change of pace.

1. Preheat oven to 375°F. Trim the tops from the onions and cut the roots off, but leave the root core in to hold the onion together. Peel the skins. Bring a large pot of salted water to boil; add onions and blanch (or boil) for 10 minutes. Scoop out the insides, using a melon-ball scoop or spoon, leaving ⅓-inch walls. Chop the scooped insides and sauté them in 1 teaspoon of butter.
2. Melt the remaining 2 teaspoons of butter in a skillet; add the shallots. Cook over medium heat until they are translucent, about 5 minutes; add the mushrooms. Cook until mushrooms have wilted and most liquid has evaporated; add the wine and cook to almost dry. Remove from heat; add the chopped parsley. Season well with salt and pepper. Combine the mushroom mixture with the chopped onion insides and fill into the onion shells. Place in a small buttered baking dish with the vegetable broth. Cover with foil.
3. Bake for 1 hour, basting once. Remove foil halfway through to allow the onions to brown.

# CHAPTER 14

# SANDWICHES, BURGERS, WRAPS, AND PIZZA

# Pita Tuna Melts

Serves 4

Prep time: 10 minutes
Cook time: 11 minutes
Total cost: $5.96
Calories: 334
Fat: 17g
Carbohydrates: 26g
Protein: 19g
Cholesterol: 36mg
Sodium: 813mg

4 pita breads, unsplit

4 slices Swiss cheese

1 avocado

1 6-ounce can tuna, drained

½ cup tartar sauce

¾ cup shredded Swiss
  cheese, divided

½ teaspoon dried dill weed

Pita pockets are versatile and generally lower in calories than other bread types. To serve as an appetizer, cut finished product into triangle wedges.

1. Preheat oven to 400°F. Toast pita breads in oven until crisp, about 5 minutes. Remove from oven and top each one with a slice of Swiss cheese.
2. Peel avocado and mash slightly, leaving some chunks. Spread this on top of the Swiss cheese. In small bowl, combine tuna and tartar sauce with ¼ cup shredded Swiss cheese. Spread on top of avocado.
3. Sprinkle sandwiches with remaining shredded Swiss cheese and dill. Bake for 7 to 11 minutes, until cheese melts.

---

**Sandwich Melts**

Melts are open-faced sandwiches, or sandwiches without a "lid," that are usually grilled, baked, or broiled to heat the filling and melt the cheese. Serve them with a knife and fork and with a simple fruit salad or green salad for a hearty, quick lunch or dinner.

# Salmon and Avocado on Pita

Serves 4 to 8

Prep time: 8 minutes
Cook time: none
Total cost: $6.93
Calories: 408 (two pockets)
Fat: 4g
Carbohydrates: 44g
Protein: 39g
Cholesterol: 65mg
Sodium: 630mg

1 7-ounce pouch pink salmon, drained

1 avocado, peeled and diced

½ cup mayonnaise

½ teaspoon dried basil leaves

½ cup chopped tomato

4 pita pockets, halved

Using low-fat or nonfat mayonnaise helps to cut down on the calories and fat in this recipe. Or, use soynnaise, which is a soy-based mayonnaise product that is more healthy for you and tastes great.

In small bowl, combine all ingredients except pita and mix gently but thoroughly. Divide mixture evenly between pita pockets.

# Curried Chicken Sandwich on Pita

Serves 4 to 6

Prep time: 10 minutes
Cook time: none
Total cost: $6.75
Calories: 310
Fat: 5g
Carbohydrates: 44g
Protein: 21g
Cholesterol: 50mg
Sodium: 870mg

2 cups cubed, cooked chicken

½ cup plain yogurt

⅓ cup chutney

1 teaspoon curry powder

1 cup red grapes, cut in half

3 pita breads, cut in half

Keep this delicious sandwich spread in your refrigerator and let hungry teenagers make their own sandwiches! You could substitute pitted, halved cherries for the red grapes if you'd like.

In medium bowl, combine all ingredients except pita breads and stir well to combine. Fill pita breads with chicken mixture and serve.

### Cooking Chicken

To cook chicken breasts for use in any recipe, place boneless, skinless breasts in a pot and cover with half water and half canned chicken broth. Bring to a simmer, then reduce heat and poach chicken for 8 to 12 minutes, until chicken is thoroughly cooked. Let chicken cool in refrigerator, then chop. Reserve the broth for use in other recipes.

The $7 a Meal Healthy Cookbook

# Shrimp Salad on Sourdough Loaf

Serves 8

Prep time: 10 minutes
Cook time: none
Total cost: $6.76
Calories: 312
Fat: 11g
Carbohydrates: 42g
Protein: 8g
Cholesterol: 50mg
Sodium: 342mg

2 3-ounce packages low-fat cream cheese, softened

¼ cup nonfat sour cream

½ teaspoon dried dill

3 6-ounce cans small shrimp, drained

1½ cups chopped celery hearts

4 small sourdough loaves bread

Season the shrimp mixture lightly with Crazy-Jane or other seasoned salt, if desired, for an added layer of flavor. Or, to cut down on sodium, squeeze in a little lemon juice.

1. In medium bowl, beat cream cheese with sour cream and dill until smooth and fluffy. Stir in shrimp and chopped celery hearts.
2. Using serrated knife, cut sourdough loaves in half horizontally. Spread bottom layer with cream cheese mixture and top with top layer. Cut in half and serve.

### Canned Seafood

Canned seafood can have a salty taste. Rinse before use, but be sure to drain it very well, and don't soak it. Canned salmon, crabmeat, and tuna, as well as surimi, or frozen fake crab, can all be substituted for canned shrimp in just about any recipe.

# Turkey Cheeseburger on Whole-Wheat Bun

Serves 4

Prep time: 10 minutes

Cook time: 11 minutes

Total cost: $6.99

Calories: 424

Fat: 15g

Carbohydrates: 42g

Protein: 29g

Cholesterol: 121mg

Sodium: 403mg

½ cup bread crumbs

1 egg, beaten

½ teaspoon salt

¼ teaspoon cayenne pepper

¼ teaspoon cumin

1 teaspoon chili powder

1 pound ground turkey

4 slices pepper jack cheese

4 whole-wheat hamburger buns

You can make a Tex-Mex sandwich spread to put on the hamburger buns by combining mayonnaise with some chopped chipotle peppers and adobo sauce.

1. Preheat grill or broiler. In large bowl, combine bread crumbs, egg, salt, cayenne, and chili powder and mix well. Add turkey and mix gently but thoroughly until combined. Form into 4 patties.
2. Cook patties, covered, 4 to 6 inches from medium heat for about 10 minutes, turning once, until thoroughly cooked. Top each with a slice of cheese, cover grill, and cook for 1 minute longer, until cheese melts. Meanwhile, toast the cut sides of hamburger buns on the grill; make sandwiches with turkey patties and buns.

### Make Recipes Your Own

Once you get the hang of making a recipe quickly, think about varying the ingredients to make the recipe your own. For instance, spicy turkey cheeseburgers could be made with chutney, curry powder, and Havarti or provolone cheese. Or make Greek burgers with feta cheese, chopped olives, and some dried oregano leaves.

# Pepperoni Pizza on English Muffins

Serve 6 to 8

Prep time: 5 minutes
Cook time: 5 minutes
Total cost: $6.36
Calories: 278
Fat: 11g
Carbohydrates: 33g
Protein: 13g
Cholesterol: 21mg
Sodium: 475mg

8 English muffins, split and toasted

1½ cups pizza sauce

1 6-ounce jar sliced mushrooms, drained

1 cup pepperoni, sliced

2 cups shredded mozzarella cheese

The perfect snack size, English muffins are a healthy, quick, easy way to enjoy the "feel" of a pizza without having to make or buy a whole pizza. Plus you will tend to eat less of it when there are only two "slices"!

Preheat oven to broil. Place English muffin halves on baking sheet and top each one with pizza sauce. Layer mushrooms and pepperoni over pizza sauce. Sprinkle cheese over pizzas. Broil pizzas, 4 to 6 inches from heat source, for 2 to 4 minutes or until pizzas are hot and cheese is melted, bubbly, and beginning to brown. Serve immediately.

# Mexican Pizza with Chicken

Serves 8

Prep time: 7 minutes
Cook time: 20 minutes
Total cost: $6.81
Calories: 480
Fat: 13g
Carbohydrates: 50g
Protein: 43g
Cholesterol: 27mg
Sodium: 581mg

8 flour tortillas

1 16-ounce can refried beans

½ cup taco sauce

½ teaspoon dried oregano

1 tablespoon chili powder

2 cups cooked chicken breast, diced

2 cups shredded pepper jack cheese

Fresh avocado slices are a naturally delicious addition to this already tasty meal. And remember, avocados are filled with the good fat our bodies need and have no cholesterol!

1. Preheat oven to 400°F. Place tortillas on two parchment-lined baking sheets. Bake for 5 to 8 minutes until tortillas are crisp, switching the baking sheets halfway through cooking and turning tortillas once.
2. In small bowl combine beans, taco sauce, oregano, and chili powder and mix well. Spread evenly over baked tortillas. Top with chicken and cheese. Bake for 12 to 18 minutes or until pizzas are hot and cheese is melted and beginning to brown.

The $7 a Meal Healthy Cookbook

# Open-Face Meatball Hoagies

 Serves 4

Prep time: 10 minutes
Cook time: 11 minutes
Total cost: $6.63
Calories: 280
Fat: 12g
Carbohyrdates: 31g
Protein: 13g
Cholesterol: 23mg
Sodium: 795mg

½ 16-ounce package frozen meatballs, thawed overnight in refrigerator

½ 15-ounce jar pasta sauce

½ cup frozen onion and pepper stir-fry combo, thawed and drained

2 hoagie rolls, sliced and toasted

½ 6-ounce package sliced provolone cheese

Packaged frozen meatballs are usually on the smaller side, so you may want to squeeze on a few more if you love meatballs like I do!

1. Cut thawed meatballs in half and place in heavy saucepan with pasta sauce. Cook over medium heat, stirring occasionally, until sauce bubbles and meatballs are hot.
2. Stir in onion and pepper stir-fry combo; cook and stir for 3 to 5 minutes, until vegetables are hot and tender. Preheat broiler.
3. Top each hoagie roll half with meatball mixture and place on broiler rack. Top each with a slice of cheese. Broil 6 inches from heat source for 3 to 6 minutes, until cheese is melted and bubbly. Serve immediately.

**Provolone Cheese**
Provolone cheese is a mild cheese with a slightly smoky taste that's made from cow's milk. It is usually aged for a few months so the texture is slightly firm. You can buy provolone aged for up to a year. This aged cheese has a more intense flavor and firm texture, similar to Parmesan cheese.

# Avocado and Muenster Sandwich on Hoagie Bun

Serves 2 to 4

Prep time: 10 minutes

Cook time: 5 minutes

Total cost: $6.29

Calories: 280

Fat: 13g

Carbohydrates: 30g

Protein: 6g

Cholesterol: 26mg

Sodium: 275mg

2 avocados

¼ cup creamy Italian salad dressing

2 hoagie buns, sliced and toasted

2 plum tomatoes, sliced

4 slices Muenster cheese

Hoagie buns can be a bit large for some appetites, so that's why they are perfect for slicing into smaller portions and sharing with a friend or serving as appetizers.

1. Preheat broiler. Peel and seed avocados; place in small bowl along with salad dressing. Mash, using a fork, until almost blended but with still some pieces of avocado visible.
2. Place bottom halves of buns on broiler pan and spread with half of avocado mixture. Top with tomato slices and cover with cheese slices. Broil 6 inches from heat source for 2 to 5 minutes or until cheese is melted and begins to bubble. Spread top halves of buns with remaining avocado mixture and place on top of cheese. Serve immediately.

## Tomatoes

Most tomatoes are full of seeds and water. This juiciness, while desirable in salads, is less so in sandwiches and pizzas. Choose plum tomatoes for these recipes because there is more flesh and fewer seeds.

The $7 a Meal Healthy Cookbook

# Ham and Muenster on Pita

Serves 4

Prep time: 10 minutes

Cook time: 2 minutes

Total cost: $6.85

Calories: 210

Fat: 3g

Carbohydrates: 26g

Protein: 12g

Cholesterol: 20mg

Sodium: 945mg

4 pita pocket breads

3 tablespoons olive oil, divided

2 tablespoons mustard

6 ounces sliced cooked ham

6 ounces sliced Muenster
  cheese

½ cup sliced roasted red
  peppers, drained

Roasted red peppers are sold in jars in the condiment aisle of the supermarket.

1. Preheat broiler. Using a sharp knife, split the pocket breads into 2 round pieces. In small bowl, combine 1 tablespoon olive oil and the mustard and mix well. Spread this mixture on inside halves of the pita breads.

2. Layer ham, Muenster cheese, roasted red peppers, and more Muenster cheese on one side of each pita bread. Top with remaining pita bread sides. Spread outside of sandwiches with remaining 2 tablespoons olive oil.

3. Place each sandwich on aluminum foil and place under broiler. Broil 2 minutes, or until cheese is melted and bread is golden brown and toasted. Cut sandwiches in half and serve.

# Spinach and Cheese Bagel Pizza

Prep time: 12 minutes

Cook time: 11 minutes

Total cost: $6.23

Calories: 360

Fat: 8g

Carbohydrates: 61g

Protein: 16g

Cholesterol: 5mg

Sodium: 620mg

6 bagels, split and toasted

2 tablespoons olive oil

½ yellow onion, chopped

1 8-ounce can pizza sauce

Pinch ground nutmeg

1 cup frozen chopped spinach, thawed

1 cup shredded mozzarella cheese

A healthy alternative to sometimes heavy pizza dough, bagels provide a crunchy and substantial crust and are the perfect size for an individual pizza.

1. Preheat broiler. Place bagels on a parchment-lined baking sheet. In heavy saucepan, heat olive oil over medium heat and add onion; cook and stir for 4 to 6 minutes, until onion is tender. Add pizza sauce and nutmeg; bring to a simmer.
2. Meanwhile, drain the thawed spinach in a colander or strainer, then drain again by pressing between paper towels. Spread bagel halves with pizza sauce mixture and top evenly with the spinach. Sprinkle with cheese. Broil 6 inches from heat for 4 to 7 minutes, until cheese melts and sandwiches are hot.

# Pizza with Smoked Salmon

Serves 2

Prep time: 10 minutes

Cook time: 20 minutes

Total cost: $7.00

Calories: 256

Fat: 8g

Carbohydrates: 33g

Protein: 13g

Cholesterol: 12mg

Sodium: 783mg

1 8-inch Boboli pizza crust

4 ounces garlic and herb soft cream cheese

4 ounces smoked salmon

½ red bell pepper, sliced

½ cup provolone cheese, shredded or chopped

Not traditionally thought of for pizza, this smoked salmon flavor makes this pizza one not to miss! Add some capers and freshly chopped red onion for an added treat.

1. Heat oven to 400°F. Place pizza crust on parchment-lined baking sheet. Spread with cream cheese and arrange smoked salmon and bell pepper slices on top. Sprinkle evenly with provolone cheese.
2. Bake for 18 to 22 minutes or until crust is hot and crisp and cheese is melted. Serve immediately.

# Pizza with Feta and Black Olives

Serves 2

Prep time: 10 minutes
Cook time: 20 minutes
Total cost: $6.89
Calories: 300
Fat: 10g
Carbohydrates: 37g
Protein: 13g
Cholesterol: 25mg
Sodium: 630mg

1 8-inch Boboli pizza crust

½ cup pizza sauce

Pinch dried oregano leaves

½ cup crumbled feta cheese with garlic and herbs

¼ cup sliced black olives

1 cup shredded mozzarella cheese

Sometimes pizza sauce can overwhelm the flavors of other toppings. Try brushing the pizza crust with olive oil and then adding toppings. You may find you prefer it without the usual sauce, and also prefer the savings on calories and sodium!

1. Preheat oven to 400°F. Place pizza crust on a parchment-lined baking sheet and spread evenly with pizza sauce. Sprinkle with oregano. Arrange feta cheese and olives over sauce and top with mozzarella cheese.
2. Bake for 18 to 20 minutes or until crust is hot and crisp and cheese is melted and beginning to brown. Serve immediately.

---

**Feta Cheese**

Feta cheese usually comes cut into small blocks and packed in a brine solution. You can find several different varieties of feta, including garlic and herbs, sun-dried tomato, plain, peppercorn, basil and tomato, and low fat. Don't drain the brine before you use the cheese or after opening because it helps preserve the cheese.

# Grilled Steak Sandwich

 Serves 2

Prep time: 8 minutes
Cook time: 6 minutes
Total cost: $6.13
Calories: 390
Fat: 17g
Carbohydrates: 36g
Protein: 30g
Cholesterol: 164mg
Sodium: 840mg

8 ounces Grilled Flank Steak (page 158)

½ cup roasted red peppers, drained

4 slices French bread

1 cup shredded Muenster cheese

2 tablespoons butter

Steak sandwiches are the perfect solution to leftover steak. Toss in some chopped onion with the roasted red bell peppers for extra flavor.

1. Cut steak against the grain into ¼-inch-thick pieces. Slice the red peppers into strips. Place 4 bread slices on work surface and top each with ¼ cup cheese. Arrange one-fourth of the steak strips and red peppers on top of each. Top each with another ¼ cup cheese, then top with remaining bread slices. Spread butter on the outsides of the sandwiches.
2. Grill in iron skillet or other heavy skillet for 5 to 6 minutes, turning once, until sandwiches are hot and cheese is melted.

### Slicing Bread for Sandwiches

When you're slicing French or Italian bread for sandwiches, be sure to cut the bread on the diagonal. That way there's more surface area and you get larger pieces to hold more filling ingredients. Use a serrated bread knife and grasp the bread firmly with your nondominant hand.

# The Simply Delicious Burger

Serves 4

Prep time: 12 minutes
Cook time: 12 minutes
Total cost: $5.03
Calories: 305
Fat: 20g
Carbohydrates: 0g
Protein: 29g
Cholesterol: 99mg
Sodium: 108mg

1¼ pounds ground beef

½ teaspoon seasoned salt

Black pepper, to taste

2 tablespoons oil

Use this burger as a base for any other style burger you would like to make.

Lightly mix the ground beef with salt and pepper and form into 4 equally sized patties. On stovetop, heat 2 tablespoons oil in a nonstick skillet over medium-high heat. Cook for about 5 minutes per side for medium, turning once. Transfer burgers to a plate and tent with foil to keep warm. Let rest for 1 to 2 minutes to allow the juices to reabsorb. Serve hot plain or with your favorite bun.

### Two More Easy Ways to Cook Burgers

*To grill:* Clean grill rack and lightly oil to prevent sticking. Preheat grill to medium high. Cook for about 5 minutes per side for medium, turning once. Transfer burgers to a plate and tent with foil to keep warm. Let rest for 1 to 2 minutes to allow the juices to reabsorb.
*To broil:* Clean broiler rack and lightly oil to prevent sticking. Set broiler rack 4 inches from heat source. Preheat broiler to medium high. Cook for about 5 minutes per side for medium, turning once. Transfer burgers to a plate and tent with foil to keep warm. Let rest for 1 to 2 minutes to allow the juices to reabsorb.

The $7 a Meal Healthy Cookbook

# Wrap of Roast Beef with Roasted Red Bell Peppers

Serves 4

Prep time: 10 minutes

Cook time: none

Total cost: $5.78

Calories: 305

Fat: 10g

Carbohydrates: 26g

Protein: 8g

Cholesterol: 10mg

Sodium: 732mg

2 ounce low-fat cream cheese

1 tablespoon nonfat mayonnaise

2 ounces blue cheese crumbles

Sea salt and black pepper to taste

2 8-inch flour tortillas, room temperature

⅓ pound deli roast beef, cut into ½-inch strips

¼ cup diced roasted red bell peppers

1 cup romaine lettuce, chopped

Flour or whole-wheat tortillas are the best for making wraps. Use them at room temperature for ease in folding.

1. In small mixing bowl, combine cream cheese, mayonnaise, blue cheese, salt, and pepper. Blend until smooth. Place tortilla on clean work surface. Spread half of cream cheese mixture on upper third of each tortilla, about ½ inch from edge. Place half the roast beef on the lower third of each tortilla. Top each with peppers and lettuce.
2. Roll up each wrap starting from the bottom; fold tortilla over the filling, compressing slightly to form a firm roll. Press at the top to seal the wrap closed with the cream cheese mixture. Cut the sandwich in half and wrap in plastic film. Refrigerate until ready to serve.

# Grilled Vegetables on Sourdough

Serves 6 to 12

Prep time: 5 minutes
Cook time: 5 minutes
Total cost: $6.88
Calories: 263
Fat: 9g
Carbohydrates: 19g
Protein: 4g
Cholesterol: 10mg
Sodium: 361mg

3 tablespoons olive oil

1 zucchini, cubed

1 red bell pepper, seeded and diced

1 sweet red onion, diced

Sea salt and black pepper to taste

2 mini sourdough loaves

2 ounces goat cheese, room temperature

Goat cheese is a very flavorful cheese that tastes even better when warmed.

1. Heat 1 tablespoon olive oil on grill pan over medium heat. Add all vegetables to grill, season with salt and pepper. Grill until cooked but al dente, about 5 minutes.
2. Brush rolls with remaining oil. Spread goat cheese onto rolls. Layer grilled vegetables onto roll.

**Money-Saving Tip**
This is a great recipe for using leftover grilled vegetables. Use any combination of vegetables you have. Reheat the vegetables by grilling as instructed above but for only 3 minutes.

The $7 a Meal Healthy Cookbook

# Lemon Pepper Dijon Burger

**Serves 4**

Prep time: 15 minutes
Cook time: 12 minutes
Total cost: $5.81
Calories: 307
Fat: 20g
Carbohydrates: 0g
Protein: 29g
Cholesterol: 99mg
Sodium: 128mg

1¼ pounds ground beef

¾ teaspoon seasoned salt

⅛ teaspoon lemon pepper

1 tablespoon fresh Italian flat-leaf parsley, chopped

3 tablespoons butter

1 tablespoon Dijon mustard

Juice of ½ lemon

2 teaspoons quality steak sauce

Dijon mustard enhances the flavor of the beef and blends nicely with the steak sauce. Use grainy Country Dijon if you prefer.

1. Lightly mix the ground beef with the seasoned salt, lemon pepper, and chopped parsley, and form into 4 evenly sized patties. Melt the butter in a medium-sized nonstick skillet over medium-high heat. Add the mustard and quickly blend to combine. Add the burgers to the skillet and cook for about 4 minutes per side, turning once. Transfer the burgers to a plate and tent with foil to keep warm. (Burgers will be returned to the pan for additional cooking.)
2. Add the lemon juice and steak sauce to the pan and blend to combine. Return the burgers and any accumulated juices to the pan and let simmer for 2 to 3 minutes while basting. Remove the pan from heat and allow the burgers to rest for 2 to 3 minutes. Serve with sauce ladled over the top; serve hot, plain, or with your favorite bun.

# Burger with Sauerkraut and Cheese

Serves 4

Prep time: 12 minutes
Cook time: 12 to 14 mins.
Total cost: $6.78
Calories: 354
Fat: 23g
Carbohydrates: 1g
Protein: 33g
Cholesterol: 12mg
Sodium: 250mg

1¼ pounds ground beef

½ teaspoon seasoned salt

⅛ teaspoon black pepper

¼ cup sauerkraut, rinsed and drained

8 slices low-fat Muenster cheese

If sauerkraut doesn't strike your fancy, use freshly grated cabbage or toss fresh cabbage with a little Italian dressing.

1. Lightly mix the ground beef with the seasoned salt and pepper; form into 4 evenly sized patties. Clean and oil grill rack and preheat grill to medium high. Cook the burgers for about 5 minutes on each side for medium.
2. During the last 2 minutes of cooking, top each burger with 1 tablespoon kraut and 2 slices of cheese per burger. Transfer the burgers to a plate and tent with foil to keep warm. Let rest for 1 to 2 minutes to allow the juices to reabsorb. Serve hot, plain, or with favorite bun.

# Southwestern Burger

Serves 4

Prep time: 15 minutes
Cook time: 15 minutes
Total cost: $6.97
Calories: 342
Fat: 22g
Carbohydrates: 2g
Protein: 31g
Cholesterol: 102mg
Sodium: 189mg

1¼ pounds ground beef

½ teaspoon garlic salt

¼ teaspoon red pepper flakes

¼ cup shredded pepper jack cheese

½ cup mild, medium, or hot salsa

¼ cup canned jalapeño slices

¼ cup fresh cilantro, leaves chopped

Jack cheese is common in southwestern cuisine as are spicy peppers. For a milder version, leave out the red pepper flakes and add in onion powder.

1. Lightly mix the ground beef with the garlic salt and pepper flakes; form into 4 evenly sized patties. Clean and oil grill rack and preheat grill to medium-high.
2. Cook the burgers for about 5 minutes on each side for medium. During the last 2 minutes of cooking, top each burger with cheese. Transfer the burgers to a plate and tent with foil to keep warm. Let rest for 1 to 2 minutes to allow the juices to reabsorb. Serve hot, topped with the salsa, jalapeños, and cilantro leaves, as is, or with your favorite bun.

# Chicken Wraps with Spinach, Cream Cheese, and Tomatoes

Serves 4

Prep time: 8 minutes

Cook time: none

Total cost: $5.85

Calories: 272

Fat: 19g

Carbohydrates: 12g

Protein: 11g

Cholesterol: 2mg

Sodium: 181mg

3 ounces cream cheese, room temperature

1 tablespoon mayonnaise

1 tablespoon fresh lemon juice

Pinch sea salt and black pepper

2 (8-inch) flour tortillas, room temperature

2 cups cooked chicken, cubed

½ red onion, diced

1 cup baby spinach leaves

1 tomato, sliced

For appetizer parties, make wraps ahead of time, refrigerate, and then slice into small individual servings.

1. Mix together cream cheese, mayonnaise, lemon juice, salt, and pepper in a small bowl. Mix well until smooth.
2. Place tortillas on clean work surface. Spread half the cream cheese mixture on the upper third of each tortilla, about ½ inch from edge. Place half of the chicken on the lower third of each tortilla. Top each with onions, spinach, and tomatoes. Roll up each wrap starting from the bottom; fold the tortilla over the filling and roll upward. Compress lightly to form a firm roll. Press at the top to seal the wrap closed with cream cheese mixture. Cut sandwich in half and wrap in plastic film. Refrigerate until ready to serve.

The $7 a Meal Healthy Cookbook

# Turkey Wrap with Mixed Greens

Serves 4

Prep time: 7 minutes

Cook time: none

Total cost: $4.38

Calories: 389

Fat: 9g

Carbohydrates: 24g

Protein: 8g

Cholesterol: 24mg

Sodium: 324mg

3 ounces cream cheese, room temperature

1 tablespoon mayonnaise

Sea salt and black pepper to taste

2 8-inch flour tortillas

⅓ pound deli-sliced honey-roasted turkey breast

¼ pound Cheddar cheese, shredded (about ½ cup)

1 cup mixed greens

Turkey is leaner than chicken and tastes great in a wrap. For a lighter wrap, leave out the Cheddar cheese and add tomatoes or even cucumber!

1. Mix together cream cheese, mayonnaise, salt, and pepper in small bowl. Place tortillas on clean work surface. Spread half the cream cheese mixture on upper third of each tortilla, about ½ inch from the edge. Place half the turkey on the lower third of each tortilla. Top each with cheddar cheese and greens.
2. Roll up each wrap starting from the bottom; fold the tortilla over the filling, compressing slightly to form a firm roll. Press at the top to seal wrap closed with the cream cheese mixture. Cut the sandwich in half and wrap in plastic film. Refrigerate until ready to serve.

# Italian Wrap with Salami and Pepperoncinis

**Serves 4**

Prep time: 15 minutes
Cook time: none
Total cost: $4.82
Calories: 364
Fat: 22g
Carbohydrates: 11g
Protein: 13g
Cholesterol: 11mg
Sodium: 109mg

3 ounces low-fat cream cheese, at room temperature

1 tablespoon low-fat mayonnaise

1 tablespoon oil-packed sun-dried tomatoes, chopped

2 teaspoons dried Italian seasoning

1 cup chopped arugula leaves

Sea salt and black pepper to taste

2 (8-inch) tortillas, at room temperature

⅛ pound salami

⅛ pound provolone cheese, cut into strips

¼ cup chopped pepperoncini, rinsed and drained

Pepperoncini are not overly hot peppers and appeal to most people. If you desire a spicy wrap, add your favorite hot sauce.

1. Mix together the cream cheese, mayonnaise, sun-dried tomatoes, Italian herbs, salt, and pepper in a small bowl (or use a food processor to blend until smooth).
2. Place the tortillas on work surface. Spread half of the cream cheese mixture on the upper third of each tortilla, about ½ inch from the edge. Equally divide the salami and cheese between the tortillas, placing the ingredients on the lower third of the tortillas. Top each with the pepperoncini and arugula.
3. Roll up the wraps: Starting from the bottom, fold the tortilla over the filling and roll upward, compressing slightly to form a firm roll. Press at the top to seal the wrap closed with the cream cheese mixture. Cut the sandwich in half and wrap in plastic film. Refrigerate until ready to serve.

The $7 a Meal Healthy Cookbook

# Grilled Portobello Mushroom Panini

 Serves 2

→ Prep time: 5 minutes
→ Cook time: 5 minutes
→ Total cost: $5.35
→ Calories: 95
→ Fat: 3g
→ Carbohydrates: 15g
→ Protein: 5g
→ Cholesterol: 2mg
→ Sodium: 65mg

4 portobello mushrooms

3 cloves garlic, chopped

1 tablespoon olive oil

Sea salt and black pepper to taste

½ cup mixed greens

2 slices provolone cheese

Portobello mushrooms are so meaty they can be used as a healthy substitute for bread. Because of their size and density, they are very filling as well.

1. Preheat broiler. Clean off the mushrooms with damp paper towels or a mushroom brush, and scrape out the black membrane on the underside of the cap. Mince the garlic.
2. Mix together the oil and garlic; coat each mushroom with oil mixture. Season with salt and pepper. Top two mushrooms each with ¼ cup greens and slice of cheese. Place all on aluminum foil and broil until cheese is melted. To serve, top each stuffed mushroom with the plain mushroom.

**Panini**
A panini is a grilled sandwich made from loaf bread.

# Three-Cheese Pizza with Basil

Serves 2

Prep time: 7 minutes
Cook time: 18 minutes
Total cost: $6.79
Calories: 402
Fat: 18g
Carbohydrates: 52g
Protein: 6g
Cholesterol: 94mg
Sodium: 824mg

½ cup tomato or marinara sauce

2 6-inch Boboli pizza crusts

½ cup shredded provolone cheese

½ cup shredded mozzarella cheese

½ cup pepper jack cheese

3 cloves fresh garlic, minced

2 tablespoons fresh basil, leaves finely chopped

1 tablespoon olive oil

If you get tired of cheese pizza, change up the cheeses and use blue, goat, or Gruyère for a modern twist on an old favorite.

Preheat oven to 425°F. Ladle the sauce over the crusts, spreading it out evenly over the surface. Top with the cheeses, and sprinkle with garlic and basil. Drizzle with olive oil. Place directly in oven on center rack. Bake for 15 minutes, until cheese is melted and dough is cooked through.

The $7 a Meal Healthy Cookbook

# Italian Pizza with Black Olives

Serves 2

Prep time: 5 minutes
Cook time: 15 minutes
Total cost: $6.89
Calories: 320
Fat: 14g
Carbohydrates: 26g
Protein: 10g
Cholesterol: 59mg
Sodium: 670mg

2 6-inch Boboli pizza crusts

1½ cups pasta sauce

1½ cups shredded mozzarella cheese

½ cup chopped black olives

4 sprigs fresh basil, chopped

Black pepper to taste

1 tablespoon olive oil

Boboli pizza crusts come in small and large sizes. Use the small ones for pizza parties so everyone can make their own individual pizzas! It's fun, and easy on cleanup, which is the best part of all.

Preheat oven to 425°F. Place crusts on work surface. Ladle sauce over the crusts, spreading out evenly over entire surface. Top with cheese, olives, basil, and pepper. Drizzle with remaining oil and place in center of oven directly on rack. Bake about 15 minutes or until dough is cooked through.

# BBQ Chicken Pizza

Serves 2

Prep time: 5 minutes
Cook time: 15 minutes
Total cost: $6.99
Calories: 458
Fat: 11g
Carbohydrates: 38g
Protein: 24g
Cholesterol: 85mg
Sodium: 600mg

2 6-inch Boboli pizza crusts

1 tablespoon olive oil

1 cup cooked boneless,
   skinless chicken breasts,
   chopped into 1-inch chunks

1 cup BBQ sauce

1 cup mozzarella cheese

BBQ chicken is great on so many foods. Kids will even love this pizza.

Preheat oven to 425°F. Place pizza crusts on work surface. Brush crusts with olive oil. In mixing bowl, toss chicken with BBQ sauce to coat. Spread chicken on pizza dough and top with cheese. Bake directly on rack in center of oven for 15 minutes or until crust is crispy and golden.

# Ham and Pineapple Pizza

 Serves 2

Prep time: 5 minutes

Cook time: 15 minutes

Total cost: $6.97

Calories: 375

Fat: 19g

Carbohydrates: 29g

Protein: 32g

Cholesterol: 126mg

Sodium: 563mg

2 6-inch Boboli pizza crusts

1 tablespoon olive oil

1 cup thick deli ham, chopped

1 cup canned, chopped
   pineapple, drained

1 cup mozzarella cheese

Add red onion and drizzle with honey for extra flavor and color!

Preheat oven to 425°F. Place unfinished pizza on work surface. Brush with olive oil. Top with ham, pineapple, and cheese. Bake directly on rack in oven for about 15 minutes or until crust is golden and crispy.

# Pizza of Tomato, Basil, and Mozzarella

Serves 2

Prep time: 5 minutes
Cook time: 15 minutes
Total cost: $6.69
Calories: 306
Fat: 18g
Carbohydrates: 26g
Protein: 6g
Cholesterol: 64mg
Sodium: 499mg

2 6-inch Boboli pizza crusts

1 tablespoon olive oil

½ cup shredded mozzarella

1 bunch basil, chopped

3 Roma tomatoes, sliced

Sea salt and black pepper to taste

Traditionally called a pizza Margherita, you can't go wrong with simple fresh tomatoes and basil.

Preheat oven to 425°F. Place unfinished pizza on work surface. Brush with olive oil. Top with cheese, basil, and tomatoes. Season with salt and pepper as desired. Bake in center of oven directly on rack for 15 minutes or until dough is cooked through.

# Pita Pizza with Ricotta Cheese and Chopped Tomatoes

Serves 2

Prep time: 5 minutes
Cook time: 6 to 8 mins.
Total cost: $3.58
Calories: 110
Fat: 1g
Carbohydrates: 19g
Protein: 8g
Cholesterol: 35mg
Sodium: 257mg

1 large whole-wheat or plain
  pita

2 tablespoons shredded
  mozzarella cheese

2 tablespoons ricotta cheese

1 Roma tomato, chopped

½ teaspoon fresh garlic, minced

Customize your pita pizza with red onion, fresh basil leaves, or maybe fresh asparagus tips.

Preheat oven to 350°F. Top pita with mozzarella, ricotta, tomatoes, and garlic. Place pita on parchment-lined baking sheet. Place in oven and bake for 6 to 8 minutes or until cheese has melted.

# CHAPTER 15

# DESSERTS

# Amaretto Cream Cheese Dip

 Serves 10

Prep time: 10 minutes
Cook time: none
Total cost: $4.72
Calories: 155
Fat: 15g
Carbohydrates: 6g
Protein: 3g
Cholesterol: 25mg
Sodium: 49mg

8 ounces cream cheese, at room temperature

1 cup sour cream

¼ cup brown sugar or 2 tablespoons honey

1 teaspoon vanilla extract

¼ cup finely chopped toasted almonds, plus a few for garnish

1⅓ teaspoons Amaretto or almond liqueur

For a heartier dessert, serve as a dollop on Cream Cheese Pound Cake, found on page 320.

Combine all the ingredients, leaving a few almonds for garnish, in a food processor fitted with a metal blade and process until well mixed. Transfer to a serving bowl and garnish with chopped almonds. Serve with fresh fruit such as apples, pears, and berries.

# Fresh Fruit with Orange Honey Compote

 Serves 4

Prep time: 10 minutes
Cook time: 10 minutes
Total cost: $5.86
Calories: 78
Fat: 1g
Carbohydrates: 11g
Protein: 2g
Cholesterol: 0mg
Sodium: 6mg

1 orange, segmented

¼ cup fresh-squeezed orange juice

1½ tablespoons honey

Pinch ground cinnamon

1 cup wild berries such as blackberries and raspberries

2 cups cantaloupe, diced

1 tablespoon fresh mint, leaves chopped

A compote is a dessert of whole or chopped fruit in sugared syrup. When heating, be careful not to boil the fruit in the syrup rapidly or the fruit will break down and disintegrate.

1. In small boiler over medium heat, combine the orange, orange juice, honey, and cinnamon and bring to a gentle boil. Boil for 2 minutes, remove from heat, and set aside.
2. Place fresh fruit in mixing bowl, pour orange mixture over and lightly toss to coat evenly. Serve with fresh mint.

**Segmenting Fruit**
Segmenting an orange or any similar fruit means to cut the fruit away from the pith. The pith tastes bitter and also, segmenting makes the fruit look prettier in your dish!

# Blueberries with Melon and Whipped Lemon Cream

Serves 4

Prep time: 15 minutes

Cook time: none

Total cost: $4.09

Calories: 100

Fat: 17.5

Carbohydrates: 15g

Protein: 1g

Cholesterol: 63mg

Sodium: 16mg

½ cup heavy cream

⅛ teaspoon light, sugar-free or regular lemonade drink mix

2 cups cantaloupe, peeled and cut into 1-inch cubes

2 cups fresh blueberries

Fine zest of 1 lemon

Sugar-free lemonade mix is a great way to add flavor to this dessert and keep it light on calories. As an alternative, substitute other flavored drink mixes such as cherry or strawberry.

1. Combine the cream and lemonade mix in a medium-sized bowl; whip using standing mixer or hand mixer until soft peaks form.
2. Place cantaloupe and berries in a wine glass or martini glass. Top with lemon cream. Garnish with lemon zest.

# Caramelized Pears with Brown Sugar and Almonds

Serves 4

Prep time: 10 minutes
Cook time: 6 minutes
Total cost: $2.73
Calories: 114
Fat: 12g
Carbohydrates: 25g
Protein: 2g
Cholesterol: 1mg
Sodium: 48mg

3 pears, ripe but still firm, sliced

1½ tablespoons brown sugar, plus 1 tablespoon for garnish

2 tablespoons almonds, whole or chopped

½ cup vanilla yogurt

Carmelizing sugar means to lightly brown the sugar. Pay attention when broiling, as the sugar can burn quickly.

1. Preheat broiler. Fan the pear slices in shallow ovenproof dish. Sprinkle 1½ tablespoons brown sugar over the pears. Broil until the sugar is caramelized but not burned, about 4 to 5 minutes. Sprinkle the almonds on top and broil for 1 more minute, until golden.
2. To serve, divide the pears among 4 serving plates. Top each with equal parts of the yogurt and garnish with remaining sugar.

# Chocolate Fudge Mousse with Espresso Cream

 Serves 4

1 package instant chocolate fudge pudding mix

2 cups cold skim milk

¾ cup heavy cream, chilled

3 tablespoons powdered sugar or to taste

1 tablespoon prepared espresso coffee, chilled

1 cup fresh wild berries

For a true chocolate mousse, fold the whipped cream into the pudding mixture and top with the berries. Espresso is optional.

1. Combine the pudding mix and milk in standing mixer. Mix on medium-high speed for about 1½ minutes, until smooth. Equally divide the mixture between 4 parfait glasses or wine glasses. Set aside for 5 to 7 minutes.
2. Wipe out mixer, pour in cream, and beat on high speed until cream holds its shape. Add powdered sugar and continue to beat until soft peaks form. Stir in the coffee and mix just until blended. Refrigerate until ready to serve.
3. To serve, top the pudding with equal amounts of coffee whipped cream. Served chilled with fresh berries.

### Whipping Cream

Whipping cream is better for you than processed whipped creams because it is chemical free. Plus, making your own is fun because you can add flavors to it such as vanilla, orange liqueur, or coffee as I did here. Enjoy in small portions on limited occasions.

# Grilled Pineapple with Mascarpone and Coconut

Serves 6

Prep time: 10 minutes
Cook time: 10 minutes
Total cost: $6.98
Calories: 227
Fat: 17g
Carbohydrates: 11g
Protein: 3g
Cholesterol: 38mg
Sodium: 22mg

½ ripe medium-sized pineapple

3 tablespoons dark rum

1 tablespoon brown sugar

8 ounces mascarpone cheese

¼ cup shredded coconut

I learned a similar recipe in Bourgogne, France, where I had the extreme pleasure and good fortune to learn from Master Chef Marc Meneau of L'Esperance. We arranged our dish to look like a butterfly, or *papillon* in French.

1. Preheat grill to medium. Peel the pineapple and cut cross-wise into 6 slices about ¾-inch thick. Drizzle the rum over both sides and sprinkle with brown sugar.
2. Grill the pineapple for 10 minutes total, turning once. Transfer the pineapple to serving plates. Top with dollop of mascarpone and sprinkle with shredded coconut.

**Mascarpone**

Mascarpone is a triple cream cheese made from crème fraîche (or sour cream) and sometimes buttermilk. It is particular to the Lombardy region of Italy. It's pretty high in fat and calories so enjoy in moderation.

The $7 a Meal Healthy Cookbook

# Wild Berry Parfait

Serves 4

Prep time: 12 minutes
Cook time: none
Total cost: $3.41
Calories: 227
Fat: 11g
Carbohydrates: 30g
Protein: 2g
Cholesterol: 42mg
Sodium: 48mg

1½ cups wild berries such as raspberries, blackberries, and blueberries

½ cup whipping cream

2 tablespoons powdered sugar

½ cup raspberry or blackberry jam

4 fresh mint leaves, for garnish

If you don't have enough room in your refrigerator for martini glasses, layer mixture in a decorative, deep serving bowl. Present dessert in center of table before serving so everyone can enjoy your beautiful creation.

1. Divide 1 cup of the berries equally between 4 chilled martini glasses or ramekins.
2. In standing mixer, pour in cream and whip until just combined. Add sugar and continue whipping until soft peaks form. In medium bowl, gently mix together whipped cream and jam. Dollop the mixture on top of the fruit. Top cream mixture with remaining berries and finish with fresh mint leaf.

### Substitute Granulated Sugar

If you don't have powdered sugar, you can use granulated sugar. The only difference is the powdered sugar dissolves into the cream making it perfectly smooth.

# Lime Tarts with Hazelnuts

 Serves 8

½ cup plus 1 tablespoon hazelnuts, chopped

1 tablespoon lime zest

1 cup granulated sugar, divided

2 large eggs

6 tablespoons butter, plus extra for greasing

3 tablespoons fresh-squeezed lime juice

½ cup heavy cream

Lemon or vanilla beans are also delicious in this recipe.

1. Preheat oven to 350°F.
2. Place the ½ cup hazelnuts in a food processor fitted with a metal blade and pulse until the hazelnuts are finely chopped but not puréed. Transfer nuts to a bowl and set aside.
3. Using the same food processor bowl, combine the lime zest and ½ cup sugar and process until evenly mixed, about 1 minute. Add the eggs, butter, lime juice, and the ½ cup chopped hazelnuts; pulse 2 to 3 times, then process for 8 to 10 seconds, until well mixed.
4. Lightly butter the inside of 8 4- or 6-ounce ovenproof ramekins. Equally divide hazelnut mixture between the ramekins, lightly pressing mixture into the bottoms and smoothing the surface. Place on a baking sheet and bake until lightly browned, about 15 minutes.
5. While tarts are baking, in standing mixer, pour in cream and whip until just combined. Add remaining ½ cup sugar and continue whipping until stiff peaks form.
6. Remove from oven and transfer the ramekins to a wire rack to cool. To serve, top the tarts with the whipped cream and sprinkle with the remaining hazelnuts.

# Marsala Zabaglione with Fresh Peaches

 Serves 8

Prep time: 10 minutes
Cook time: 10 minutes
Total cost: $5.65
Calories: 96
Fat: 2g
Carbohydrates: 2g
Protein: 2g
Cholesterol: 59mg
Sodium: 20mg

4 fresh ripe peaches

¼ cup granulated sugar

3 large egg yolks, at room temperature

2 tablespoons water

¼ cup Marsala wine

If you don't have fresh peaches, I don't recommend substituting canned. Instead, use fresh wild berries or plums!

1. Halve the peaches and remove the pits. Cut the peaches into ⅛-inch slices. Fan the peach slices in an attractive pattern on each serving plate.
2. Combine the sugar and yolks in the top of a double boiler over medium heat. Use a hand mixer and beat the mixture until frothy. Add the water and Marsala. Continue to cook, beating constantly with hand mixer at medium speed until the mixture becomes thickened. To test doneness, coat back of a wooden spoon with mixture. Run your finger through mixture. If you make a thick line, mixture is ready.
3. To serve, pour equal amounts of the sauce over the peach slices and serve.

# Fresh Strawberries with Grand Marnier Custard

Serves 6

Prep time: 15 minutes
Cook time: 8 minutes
Total cost: $6.38
Calories: 48
Fat: 1g
Carbohydrates: 6g
Protein: 3g
Cholesterol: 28mg
Sodium: 11mg

1¼ cups low-fat milk

1 vanilla bean, split

1 strip orange zest

1 large egg

3 tablespoons granulated sugar

1 tablespoon Grand Marnier

3⅓ cups hulled and sliced strawberries

6 fresh mint leaves, for garnish

Serve in wine or martini glasses or an other decorative dish for a refreshing and stylish presentation.

1. Combine the milk, vanilla bean, and orange zest in a saucepan over medium heat. Bring to a simmer and remove from heat.
2. Combine the egg and sugar in a small mixing bowl and beat until smooth but not fluffy. Temper the mixture by slowly mixing a little of the hot milk mixture into the egg. Add a little more of the hot milk, mix, then add the remaining milk and whisk until combined.
3. Cook over medium heat, stirring constantly with a wooden spoon. Cook until the custard is thick enough to coat the back of a wooden spoon, about 8 minutes. Do not boil or the sauce will curdle.
4. Strain the sauce into a clean bowl set on ice. Discard the orange zest. Scrape the seeds from the vanilla bean and put seeds back into the sauce; discard bean pods. Add the Grand Marnier and continue to stir the sauce until the sauce is chilled. Add more ice if needed to chill quickly.
5. To serve, divide the strawberries equally between 6 ramekins. Drizzle the custard sauce over the berries and top with fresh mint leaves. Serve chilled.

# Wild Berry Trifle

 Serves 6

Prep time: 15 minutes
Cook time: none
Total cost: $6.99
Calories: 453
Fat: 32g
Carbohydrates: 35g
Protein: 6g
Cholesterol: 58mg
Sodium: 202mg

1 cup heavy whipping cream

½ cup powdered sugar

8 vanilla cupcakes, unfrosted

3 tablespoons raspberry liqueur

½ cup raspberry jam

1 8-ounce dark chocolate bar,
  chopped

This easy dessert is delicious served immediately, but you can cover and refrigerate it for 24 hours if you'd like.

1.  In standing mixer, pour in cream and add powdered sugar; whip until stiff peaks form, about 1 minute.
2.  Unwrap the cupcakes and break into small pieces. In elegant glass serving dish, place half of the cupcakes and sprinkle with half of the raspberry liqueur. Top with half of the raspberry jam, half of the chopped chocolate bar, and half of the whipped cream. Add remaining cupcakes, sprinkle with rest of the liqueur, and top with remaining jam and the remaining whipped cream. Sprinkle top with remaining chopped chocolate bar.

### Trifle
Traditional to Britain, trifle is a dessert made with a thick custard, fruit, sponge-type cake, liqueur or fruit juice, and whipped cream. The ingredients are layered in a decorative glass bowl for presentation purposes. Trifles are similar to parfaits as both are made with custard and fruit; however, trifles always use cake, and parfaits are served in individual portions.

# Double Chocolate Parfait with Toffee Candy

● Serves 4

Prep time: 10 minutes
Cook time: none
Total cost: $5.03
Calories: 269
Fat: 8g
Carbohydrates: 18g
Protein: 3g
Cholesterol: 26mg
Sodium: 88mg

1 3-ounce package instant chocolate pudding mix

1 cup chocolate milk

1 cup whipping cream

5 oatmeal cookies, broken into pieces

¼ cup toffee candy bits

For added flavor, add 2 teaspoons of espresso coffee grounds to the pudding mixture while mixing.

1. In a medium bowl, combine pudding mix and chocolate milk. Mix well. With wire whisk, whisk until smooth and thickened. In small bowl, beat cream until stiff peaks form. Fold into pudding mixture.
2. Layer pudding mixture, cookies, and candy bits into parfait, martini, or wine glasses. Serve immediately or refrigerate.

**Parfait Glasses**
Parfait glasses and iced-tea spoons are the perfect utensils to use when making parfaits. The long and slender parfait glasses allow lots of beautiful layers to show through, and the iced-tea spoons are long enough to reach down to the bottom of the glasses.

# Petit Wild Berry Fruit Tarts

Makes 24 tarts; serves 6

Prep time: 10 minutes
Cook time: 15 minutes
Total cost: $6.99
Calories: 342
Fat: 9g
Carbohydrates: 45g
Protein: 3g
Cholesterol: 0mg
Sodium: 290

24 frozen mini phyllo tart shells

½ cup apple jelly

½ teaspoon chopped fresh thyme leaves

½ cup fresh blueberries

½ cup fresh raspberries

Your grocer's freezer section is a gold mine of prepared pie and tart shells. If it is within your budget, stock up on a few different types to make pies and tarts in minutes.

1. Preheat oven to 375°F. Place tart shells on a parchment-lined baking sheet and bake according to package directions. Remove to wire racks to cool.
2. Meanwhile, heat apple jelly and thyme in a medium saucepan over low heat until jelly melts. Remove from heat and stir in berries. Put a couple of teaspoons of berry mixture into each tart shell and serve.

**Fresh Herbs**
Fresh herbs go with everything, including desserts. Thyme is used here because of its slightly minty, lemony fragrance. Rosemary is also a natural complement to fruit desserts such as pears, and lemon, and can even be used in shortbreads.

# Blueberries with Crispy Oat Crust

Serves 6

Prep time: 6 minutes

Cook time: 25 minutes

Total cost: $6.89

Calories: 283

Fat: 14g

Carbohydrates: 40g

Protein: 2g

Cholesterol: 21g

Sodium: 38mg

1 21-ounce can blueberry pie filling

½ cup plain flour

½ cup brown sugar

½ cup oatmeal

½ cup walnuts, chopped

½ teaspoon cinnamon

¼ cup butter, melted

Because this recipe uses pie filling, you can create your own variety of flavors by substituting cherry, apple, or peach pie fillings.

1. Preheat oven to 400°F. Pour blueberry pie filling into buttered 9" square glass pan and set aside.
2. In medium bowl, combine flour, brown sugar, oatmeal, walnuts, and cinnamon and mix well. Pour butter into flour mixture and stir until mixture is crumbly. Sprinkle over blueberry pie filling. Bake for 20 to 25 minutes or until filling is bubbly and crust is light golden brown. Serve with ice cream or whipped cream.

## Crisps, Crumbles, and Cobblers

All of these old-fashioned, homey desserts are basically the same thing: fruits with some kind of topping. Crisps use oatmeal and nuts to form a crumbly topping; crumbles are the same thing. Cobblers are similar to a deep-dish pie, with a thick biscuit-type crust.

The $7 a Meal Healthy Cookbook

# Easy Cheesecake with Fresh Raspberries

 Serves 6

Prep time: 15 minutes
Cook time: none
Total cost: $6.98
Calories: 505
Fat: 24g
Carbohydrates: 62g
Protein: 10g
Cholesterol: 61mg
Sodium: 333mg

1 14-ounce can sweetened condensed milk

1 8-ounce package cream cheese, softened

¼ cup lemon juice

1 9-inch graham cracker pie crust

1 cup fresh berries, such as raspberries

**Chill**
**2–8 hours before serving**

Another way to enjoy this recipe is to place the cream cheese mixture in wine or parfait glasses and chill. To serve, top with crumbled graham cracker crust and fresh berries.

1. In standing mixer or large bowl, combine condensed milk, cream cheese, and lemon juice; beat on low speed until smooth and combined. Pour into graham cracker crust. Place in freezer for 10 minutes.
2. Place berries on cream cheese filling and serve, or cover and chill the pie in the refrigerator for up to 8 hours. Store leftovers in the refrigerator.

**Traditional Cheesecakes**
Making traditional cheesecakes from scratch takes a lot of time and can be expensive. The main ingredient to cheesecake is naturally the cream cheese. Here you can enjoy the flavor of a homemade cheesecake with a lot less effort and expense!

# Strawberries with Toasted Pecans and Balsamic Sryup

Serves 6

Prep time: 15 minutes
Cook time: 30 minutes
Total cost: $6.22
Calories: 161
Fat: 13g
Carbohydrates: 7g
Protein: 3g
Cholesterol: 13mg
Sodium: 2mg

1 cup balsamic vinegar or 1
teaspoon high-quality aged
balsamic vinegar

3 cups strawberries, stemmed
and sliced

1 cup sour cream

½ cup brown sugar

¼ cup toasted pecans

This recipe tastes so good you could actually skip the
sour cream to lower the calories and fat.

1. For balsamic syrup, in small boiler over medium-low to low
   heat, pour in 1 cup vinegar and let simmer for 30 minutes or
   until vinegar is reduced to about ¼ cup (or skip this step if
   using high-quality aged balsamic). Set aside.
2. In glass serving bowl, place one-third of the strawberries.
   Top with one-third of the sour cream, and sprinkle with one-
   third of the brown sugar. Repeat layers, ending with brown
   sugar. Top with toasted pecans, drizzle with balsamic syrup,
   and serve. Or cover and refrigerate up to 8 hours, reserving
   balsamic syrup until serving time.

### Balsamic Vinegar

It sounds a little strange to drizzle fresh fruit with vinegar, but
this is common in Italy. If using high-quality balsamic, the key is
to use an aged balsamic. Aged balsamic can be expensive, so for
lighter budgets, making your own syrup is a great little trick to
making household balsamic dessert-drizzling quality.

# Grilled Pears with Balsamic Glaze

Serves 4

Prep time: 8 minutes
Cook time: 5 minutes
Total cost: $3.97
Calories: 85
Fat: 0g
Carbohydrates: 22g
Protein: 1g
Cholesterol: 0mg
Sodium: 2mg

3 tablespoons brown sugar

3 tablespoons balsamic syrup (see Strawberries with Toasted Pecans and Balsamic Syrup, page 318), plus 1 tablespoon for drizzling

½ teaspoon cinnamon

4 pears, cut in half, seeds removed

Enjoying fruit for dessert is refreshing, healthy, and leaves you feeling satisfied but not overstuffed. Use this recipe with other fruits such as apples or pineapple.

Preheat grill. In small bowl, combine sugar, 3 tablespoons balsamic syrup, and cinnamon. Brush this mixture over both sides of pears. Place pears, cut side down, on grill. Grill, uncovered, for 2 to 3 minutes, then turn pears and top with remaining brown sugar mixture. Grill for 1 to 2 minutes longer, then remove. Drizzle with remaining balsamic and serve.

### Grilling Fruit

Grilling fruit is not something you think of everyday, but it makes for a great dessert for an afternoon barbecue. The natural sugars in the fruit caramelize and the fruit becomes tender and sweet. Just be sure not to overgrill or the fruit will become mushy.

# Cream Cheese Pound Cake

Serves 10

Prep time: 15 minutes
Cook time: 1½ hours
Total cost: $5.18
Calories: 502
Fat: 38g
Carbohydrates: 46g
Protein: 8g
Cholesterol: 173mg
Sodium: 368mg

1½ cups butter

3 cups sugar

1 8-ounce package cream
cheese

6 eggs

1 teaspoon vanilla

3 cups cake flour

Powdered sugar for serving,
about 1 tablespoon

For this recipe, don't substitute light cream cheese or Neufchatel cheese. Chances are, it will alter the consistency of the cake. If you are concerned about extra calories or fat, just enjoy a smaller portion of the real deal.

1. Preheat oven to 300°F. Grease a bundt pan with softened butter and dust with flour. Tap out the excess flour from the pan.
2. In standing mixer or with hand mixer, cream together butter, sugar, and cream cheese until light and fluffy. Add eggs one at a time, beating well after each one, then add the vanilla. Mix well. Add flour slowly until combined. Pour into bundt pan and bake for 1½ hours or until toothpick inserted comes out clean. When serving, dust with powdered sugar.

### Pound Cakes

Pound cakes are not only delicious but versatile. Use pound cake instead of angel food cake for strawberry shortcakes. For different flavors of pound cake, add cocoa powder for chocolate pound cake, and mix in ¼ to ½ cup chopped fresh strawberries for strawberry pound cake.

# Italian Bread Pudding with Frangelico

Serves 10

Prep time: 15 minutes
Cook time: 45 minutes
Total cost: $6.99
Calories: 594
Fat: 26g
Carbohydrates: 82g
Protein: 12g
Cholesterol: 190mg
Sodium: 361mg

¼ cup unsalted butter

1 large loaf day-old or toasted Italian bread

6 eggs

2 cups whole or low-fat milk

2 cups heavy cream

¼ cup Frangelico liqueur

¼ cup honey

¼ cup granulated sugar

Bread pudding is a simple dessert that can be made with raisins, berries, nuts, or any combination of the above. Just add bread pieces, milk, sugar, and eggs and you have the makings of bread pudding.

1. Preheat oven to 375°F. Lightly grease a rectangular 13" x 9" baking dish with 1 teaspoon butter. Melt remaining butter. Tear bread into large 2-inch pieces. Combine with melted butter in a bowl. Beat eggs in separate bowl. Whisk in milk, cream, liqueur, honey, and sugar. Place bread mixture in prepared pan. Pour egg mixture over top and stir to combine.
2. Bake for 30 minutes, uncovered. Stir and return to oven. Bake for about 15 to 20 minutes longer until set. Serve warm with whipped cream or ice cream.

## Recipe Substitution

If you prefer not to use the liqueur, just use a little extra cream and a tablespoon more of sugar. Or, for an orange flavor, substitute Grand Marnier.

Desserts

# Apples Poached in White Wine and Lemon with Golden Raisins

Serves 6

Prep time: 5 minutes
Cook time: 45 minutes
Total cost: $4.69
Calories: 164
Fat: 4g
Carbohydrates: 33g
Protein: 1g
Cholesterol: 1mg
Sodium: 91mg

6 Granny Smith apples, peeled

1 cup apple cider

¼ cup sweet white wine such as Reisling

Zest and juice of 1 lemon (zest first, then juice)

3 whole cloves or ¼ teaspoon ground cloves

2 cinnamon sticks or ½ teaspoon ground cinnamon

¼ cup golden raisins

When zesting fruit, only skim the top part of the fruit, stopping at the white pith. The pith has a bitter flavor that will transfer to your recipe.

1. Place apples in a large saucepan with the cider, wine, lemon zest and juice, cloves, and cinnamon. Simmer, covered, on medium heat for 30 to 45 minutes, until apples are fork-tender. Remove apples and set aside.
2. Reduce cooking liquid in half. Serve apples sprinkled with raisins and drizzled with remaining liquid.

**Apple Cider**
Apple cider is not to be confused with apple cider vinegar. If you can't find apple cider, just use apple juice.

# GLOSSARY

**achiote:** A shrub or small tree from the tropical regions of southeast Asia. It is harvested for its seeds, which are used to dye food products such as cheese, fish, and oil. It is sold as a paste or powder for cooking and can be used in place of the much more expensive saffron.

**adobo:** Spanish word for seasoning or marinade. The term *adobo* is generally used to refer to marinated dishes.

**al dente:** Italian term meaning "to the tooth," referring to the texture of pasta when cooked to optimum level with a slight firmness in center when bitten.

**antioxidants:** Molecules capable of slowing or preventing the oxidation of other molecules, thereby aiding in the prevention of damaged (cancerous) cells.

**baking powder:** A leavening agent used in baked goods, it is a mixture of baking soda, cream of tartar (acidic agent), and starch (drying agent) that produces carbon dioxide when mixed with water. The carbon dioxide fills with small bubbles in the batter or dough and expands when baked to form a characteristic crumb.

**baking soda:** Also known as bicarbonate of soda, it is used as a leavening agent in baked goods. It combines with an acidic ingredient (often buttermilk) in the dough or batter (unlike baking powder, which contains an acidic agent in its mixture) to produce carbon dioxide so the product expands while baking.

**baste:** To spoon or pour a liquid over foods during cooking to help glaze food and prevent drying.

**beat:** To rapidly stir a batter with force to incorporate dry and wet ingredients. Beating also incorporates air into the batter or dough.

**blanch:** To place foods such as vegetables into boiling water for a brief period. The blanched food is then plunged into ice water to stop the cooking process. Foods are blanched before freezing to set the color so the skin will peel off, as in tomatoes, and to stop enzyme reactions.

**blend (or mix):** To stir or gently combine several ingredients together until the separate ingredients are no longer visible.

**boil:** To raise the temperature of a liquid to 212°F (100°C) so that bubbles rise from the bottom of the liquid to the top and break on the surface.

**braise:** To cook meat in a liquid environment for long periods of time to melt connective tissue and tenderize the product. The wet-heat method of cooking is used on less tender cuts of meat.

**broil:** To cook food a few inches away from a burner or flame turned to its highest point. This dry-heat method of cooking can be done in an oven or over a grill.

**brown:** To cook over high heat so the exterior turns deep brown color while the interior remains uncooked or undercooked.

**canola oil:** An oil extracted from the seeds of the canola plant; it is low in saturated fat and high in omega-3 fatty acid.

**chop:** To cut in roughly uniform bite-size pieces with a sharp knife. Chopped food is larger in size than minced or diced food.

**condensed milk (sweetened condensed milk):** Cow's milk from which water has been removed and sugar added. Usually canned, this milk can last for months unopened.

**creole:** A style of cooking originating in Louisiana blending cuisine influences of French, Spanish, Canarian, Caribbean, Mediterranean, deep Southern American, Indian, and African tending toward classic European styles of cooking (as opposed to country French). Creole cuisine is customarily served with rice.

**crumb:** The texture of a baked good. A fine crumb means the air holes in the product are very small. A coarse crumb means the air holes in the product are large.

**cut in:** To combine shortening or fat with dry ingredients using two knives or a pastry cutter, or a pastry blender, until particles of fat coated with dry ingredients are small and blended.

**debone:** The process of removing protein from the bones in order to use the protein in a recipe.

**deglaze:** To pour liquid into a hot pan in which meat has been browned, loosening the drippings and brown particles from the bottom that form during browning.

**dice:** To cut with a sharp knife into small, even, square pieces, about ⅛ inch to ¼ inch in diameter.

**Dijon mustard:** Mustard made from ground mustard seeds typically from the region of Dijon in France. Traditionally, Dijon mustard has both white and Burgundy wines added to it during the cooking process.

**double boiler:** A stovetop apparatus used to cook delicate sauces. It is a double-decker saucepan with an upper vessel that fits into a lower pot. The lower pot is filled 1-inch deep with boiling water, which then cooks the food in the top pot by steam.

**drain:** To remove the liquid from a food, usually by pouring into a strainer or colander. Some foods, such as frozen spinach, must be thoroughly drained by pressing on them with the back of a spoon to remove as much liquid or grease as possible.

**dry rub:** A combination of herbs, salt, pepper, and spices that is rubbed into meats to help flavor and tenderize before cooking.

**evaporated milk:** Milk that has had approximately 60 percent of its water removed. Usually found canned, it can last for several months unopened.

**extra-virgin olive oil:** Oil from the first pressing of olives; it has a low acid content. Generally used in vinaigrettes, salad dressings, or for extra flavor when serving, but not the best oil for cooking or grilling.

**fold:** To combine two mixtures by an action of gently cutting a spoon or spatula down through the middle of the mixtures, scraping the bottom of the bowl, and gently turning the mixtures over until combined.

**freezer burn:** Dry, hard patches on food that is improperly wrapped and frozen, caused by moisture evaporating in the cold climate of the freezer. Freezer burn is not dangerous, but it makes the food less palatable.

**fry:** A dry-heat cooking method where the food is surrounded by hot cooking oil until it reaches a safe internal temperature.

**grate:** To shred using a kitchen utensil such as a box grater, plane grater, or food processor with different sizes of grating slots or blades to aid in the preparation of a variety of foods. Commonly used for cheese, potatoes, and citrus fruits.

**grill:** A dry-heat method of cooking, usually over charcoal or a strong heat source. Grilling cooks foods quickly and adds flavor by caramelizing the foods.

**gumbo:** A stew or soup consisting primarily of stock, meat and/or shellfish, a thickener, and usually celery, bell peppers, onions, and okra.

**julienne:** To cut food into small, thin strips, usually about ⅛-inch thick or less.

**marinade:** A combination of liquids, acids, and flavorings poured over foods, especially meats, to tenderize and flavor them before cooking.

**marinate:** To pour marinade over a food and let it stand for minutes or hours before cooking to tenderize and flavor the food.

**mince:** To cut into very small pieces with a sharp knife or food processor. Minced food is smaller than chopped or diced food.

**olive oil:** The oil from pressed olives. Olive oil, as opposed to extra-virgin olive oil, is from the third or fourth pressing, has a higher acid content than extra-virgin or virgin olive oil, and is usually used for sautéing foods.

**orzo:** Sometimes called Italian rice, *orzo* in Italian means barley. Common meaning in the United States is a rice-shaped pasta slightly smaller than a pine nut. Orzo is made out of wheat semolina.

**parboil:** To briefly cook foods in boiling water until partially cooked. Vegetables are usually parboiled before being frozen or stir-fried.

**parchment paper:** Plant-based paper used in baking.

**plain flour:** A blended wheat flour with an intermediate gluten level that is acceptable for household baking. Plain flour is not combined with any chemical leavening agents.

**poach:** To cook meats, fruits, or vegetables in a liquid that is heated to just below a simmer. The poaching liquid, whether water, broth, or wine, will simmer on the surface when the temperature is correct.

**purée:** To mash food or force it through a sieve, or to process it in a blender or food processor to make a smooth paste.

**reduce:** To cook a liquid at a rapid boil, removing much of the water by evaporation until a thick sauce forms. A *reduction* is a sauce made by reducing liquid, sometimes over lower heat.

**ricotta:** An Italian sheep's milk or cow's milk cheese, it comes from the Italian word meaning "recooked." Ricotta uses the whey, a limpid, low-fat, nutritious liquid that is a by-product of cheese production. It is a fresh cheese with about 5 percent fat.

**risotto:** An Italian term for "reboiled rice," risotto is a dish made by cooking medium- or short-grain rice, typically arborio rice, with liquid or broth, stirring to release the starch from the rice.

**roast:** A dry-heat cooking method where foods are cooked at high temperatures in an oven. Usually meats and vegetables are roasted.

**sauté:** To cook food in a small amount of oil or fat over a fairly high heat in a short amount of time.

**scald:** To place food in boiling water for a short period of time also known as blanching. Scalded fruits and vegetables are usually cooked just long enough to set color or remove peel or skin. To scald milk means to bring to a slight boil and then remove from heat so as not to burn.

**score:** To make shallow cuts on a piece of meat, vegetable, or fish to allow marinade, tenderizers, and spices to penetrate the meat and add flavor.

**sear:** To heat foods at a very high temperature in order to seal in juices and give color to the food. Searing is done with direct heat, as with a broiler, sauté pan, or grill.

**seed:** To remove the seeds from a fruit.

**self-rising flour:** Ground grain to which chemical leavening agents have been added; primarily used in household baking.

**sesame oil:** An edible vegetable oil derived from sesame seeds.

**shortening:** Solid cooking oil most often used in baking pastries.

**shred:** To cut food into thin strips with a grater or attachment on a food processor. Some foods can also be shredded with a knife or with two forks.

**sift:** To shake dry ingredients through a fine sifter or sieve to remove lumps, to combine them, and to make them lighter.

**simmer:** To cook food in liquid at a temperature just below a boil. Small bubbles rise to the surface and barely break when the liquid is at the proper temperature.

**steam:** To cook food suspended over boiling water so the steam penetrates the food. Since the water does not come in contact with the food, steamed foods retain more nutrients and flavor than poached or simmered foods.

**stir-fry:** To cook pieces of food over very high heat in a skillet or wok while moving the food constantly around the pan. Foods for stir-frying are cut into similar shapes and sizes so they cook evenly.

**strain:** To remove large pieces of foods from a liquid or a purée using a fine mesh strainer or colander lined with cheesecloth.

The $7 a Meal Healthy Cookbook

**temper:** Mixing or combining through a time- or temperature-sensitive process to achieve a desired consistency; often used when cooking with eggs or melting chocolate. When tempering, handle foods gently and slowly and combine in small amounts.

**toast:** To brown foods over or under direct heat, whether in a dry saucepan, a broiler, or a toaster.

**unsalted butter:** Butter to which no salt has been added; the preferred type of butter to use in cooking.

**water bath:** A large container filled either with ice water or very hot water that smaller containers of food can be placed into. This method is used to cool food quickly (using the ice water bath) or warm food gently and evenly (using a hot water bath).

**wax paper:** Thin paper made moisture-proof through the application of wax.

**zest:** The rind of citrus fruit, usually used to enhance flavor or to add color for plate presentation.

**zester:** Kitchen utensil used to grate (or zest) the rind of citrus fruits; can also be used to grate cheese.

# HEALTHY INGREDIENT SUBSTITUTIONS

| ORIGINAL INGREDIENT | HEALTHY SUBSTITUTION | WHAT IT REDUCES |
| --- | --- | --- |
| 1 pound ground beef | 1 pound ground turkey | Total fat, saturated fat, cholesterol |
| 1 ounce Cheddar, Swiss, or American cheese | 1 ounce low-fat cheese or 1 ounce part-skim cheese | Total fat, saturated fat, cholesterol |
| 1 egg | 2 egg whites or ¼ cup low-cholesterol egg substitute | Total fat, saturated fat, cholesterol |
| 1 cup whole milk | 1 cup skim milk | Total fat, saturated fat, cholesterol |
| 1 cup heavy cream | 1 cup evaporated milk | Total fat, saturated fat, cholesterol |
| 1 cup sour cream | 1 cup nonfat sour cream, 1 cup plain nonfat yogurt, 1 cup lowfat cottage cheese plus 1 teaspoon lemon juice, blended smooth | Total fat, saturated fat, cholesterol |
| 1 ounce cream cheese | 1 ounce nonfat cream cheese or 1 ounce Neufchâtel cheese | Total fat, saturated fat, cholesterol |
| 1 cup butter | 1 cup canola oil | Saturated fat, cholesterol |
| 1 cup shortening | 7 ounces canola oil | Saturated fat |
| 1 ounce baking chocolate | 3 tablespoons cocoa powder plus 1 tablespoon canola oil | Saturated fat |

# INDEX